THE PERILS OF "PRIVILEGE"

THE PERILS OF
"PRIVILEGE"

| WHY INJUSTICE CAN'T |
| BE SOLVED BY ACCUSING |
| OTHERS OF ADVANTAGE |

PHOEBE MALTZ BOVY

ST. MARTIN'S PRESS ⚞ NEW YORK

www.stmartins.com

Designed by Richard Oriolo

The Library of Congress Cataloging-in-Publication Data
is available upon request.

ISBN 978-1-250-09120-8 (hardcover)
ISBN 978-1-250-09122-2 (e-book)

Our books may be purchased in bulk for promotional, educational, or
business use. Please contact your local bookseller or the Macmillan
Corporate and Premium Sales Department at 1-800-221-7945, extension
5442, or by e-mail at MacmillanSpecialMarkets@macmillan.com.

First Edition: March 2017

10 9 8 7 6 5 4 3 2 1

FOR JO

AUTHOR'S NOTE

THE ONLINE PRIVILEGE conversations covered in this book occurred during or prior to spring 2016. Just as my own thoughts on the topic of privilege have evolved and continue to evolve since I began exploring the subject (around 2009) on my blog, *What Would Phoebe Do*, it's entirely possible that the writers and thinkers cited herein will have changed their own views by the time this book is published, or at some later date. I do not wish to claim that something someone published or posted in, say, 2013 defines what he or she will think for all eternity. That's not how opinions, mine or anyone else's, work.

Furthermore, I wish to remind readers that Internet Web sites and source notes referenced in this work may have changed or disappeared between when the book was written and when it will be read.

CONTENTS

INTRODUCTION: THE "PRIVILEGE" TURN   1

1   THE ONLINE YPIS WARS   31

2   LONELY AT AMHERST   77

3   THE "PROBLEMATIC FAVE"   123

4   PRIVILEGED IMPOSTORS   169

5   BIZARRO PRIVILEGE   207

CONCLUSION: AFTER PRIVILEGE   247

AFTERWORD   273

ACKNOWLEDGMENTS   275

NOTES   277

INDEX   313

"We used to live in this tiny old tumbled-down house with great big holes in the roof."

"House? You were lucky to live in a house. We used to live in one room, all twenty-six of us, no furniture, . . . we were all huddled together in one corner . . ."

"You were lucky to have a room! We used to have to live in the corridor."

—MONTY PYTHON, "FOUR YORKSHIREMEN"[1]

I'm not as ~~thin~~ privileged as I used to be.

—"SAVAGE LOVE" (DAN SAVAGE'S SEX-ADVICE COLUMN),
ONLINE COMMENTER J.R.[2]

INTRODUCTION

THE "PRIVILEGE" TURN

"[A] HORRIBLE PERSON"

In a freezing-cold flat in Berlin, I'm standing under the
shower with the water turned up as high and hot as it will
go. I'm trying to boil away the shame of having said
something stupid on the internet. The shower is the one
place it's still impossible to check Twitter. This is a
mercy. For as long as the hot water lasts I won't be able
to read the new accusations of bigotry, racism and
unchecked privilege. I didn't mean it. I don't understand
what I did wrong but I'm trying to understand.[1]

* * *

THE ABOVE RECOLLECTIONS, from a 2015 article in the *New Statesman* by the writer Laurie Penny, are where I wish to begin because they make up the most wrenching, but accurate, description that I've come across of what it can feel like to be called out online. The phenomenon she describes—the privilege call-out—is a new, if increasingly familiar, experience. Penny's reaction—"I've spent very dark days, following social media pile-ons, convinced that I was a horrible person who didn't deserve to draw breath"—may have been extreme, but such interactions aren't the high point of anyone's week. While I've never experienced quite that spiral, I know what it's like to see a new blog comment or Twitter notification, and then another . . . followed, predictably, by the heart-racing realization that the Internet (and it always feels, in the moment, like the entire Internet) has *found me out.*

The outright hateful comments are, as Penny notes, easier to handle, in a way. As unpleasant as it was the week when neo-Nazi Twitter made me its Jewess-du-jour, and as frightened as I was during the weeks when pro-gun Twitter made it known what it thought about my anti-gun stance, there's something more viscerally draining about an "unchecked privilege" accusation. What's so useful about Penny's description is that she hones in on two of the key reasons why that's the case. One is, as she spells out, that the accusation manages to tap into the accused's worst fears about her value as a person. The other, which she does not, is the lack of specificity. Unlike earlier generations of bigotry accusation, the privilege call-out is intentionally vague, while also, at times, hyperspecific. Either your privilege is showing, and you're not entirely sure which *form* of privilege (let alone how to appropriately respond), or you've suddenly learned that you're wrong because surely you've never worked in food service, something about which your interlocutor, a stranger on the Internet, is remarkably certain.

A privilege accusation prompts the accused to contemplate his or her unearned advantages, and—all too often—to publicly self-flagellate for the same. The less saintly among us, though, will soon remember (and, all too often, reply) that we haven't had it *quite* as easy as our accusers imply. And sometimes the specific privilege accusation *will* have been inaccurate. Regardless of how, exactly, all of this plays out, one thing's for sure: The conversation will have switched from one about some broader issue to the ultimately trivial question of *our privilege*.

However, I'm getting ahead of myself. What is this thing, "privilege," and why is getting accused of possessing it so fraught?

FROM PRIVILEGE TO "PRIVILEGE"

PRIVILEGE ISN'T SO much a concept as it as a worldview. It has a simple definition—unearned advantage, likely having to do with wealth—but implies *so* much more. The approach originated in academia and progressive activism, but its reach now expands to cultural commentary and mainstream (even conservative) politics. It made its cultural debut primarily through two personalities. The first is *Girls* creator Lena Dunham, noted for being the first-ever entertainment professional who grew up wealthy in New York. Or so it would seem: From 2012 on, a good chunk of the Internet has consisted of critics calling out her (often overstated) privilege.[2] Prior to Dunham-privilegegate (which, as I type, continues; Dunham had recently expressed her privilege by threatening to move to Canada should Donald Trump get elected[3]), online commenters had been accusing one another of unchecked privilege for years. Yet there weren't really opinion pieces about whether X is privileged and what it all *means*. Whereas today, that pretty much describes cultural criticism and opinion journalism.

The second is Tal Fortgang, another New York–area-reared millennial. A then-Princeton freshman, Fortgang's 2014 essay, "Checking My Privilege: Character as the Basis of Privilege,"[4] in a right-leaning student publication, was quickly reissued in *Time* magazine with the provocative headline, "Why I'll Never Apologize for My White Male Privilege."[5] Just about every publication in the English-speaking world[6] (including *The Atlantic*, with a piece by yours truly[7]) used the Fortgang episode as a starting point for a broader debate about what the "privilege" discussed on college campuses refers to, and what checking it entails.[8]

While "privilege" plays an enormous role in the online shaming culture, both of these are examples of people who've parlayed privilege accusation into celebrity. Dunham remains in the public eye, and has incorporated the image the culture has of her into her own work, effectively copyrighting the "millennial brat" persona. Fortgang, though not a celebrity of Dunham's stratosphere, is making a name for himself as a young conservative journalist on the "privilege" beat. A 2015 essay of his, "38 Ways College Students Enjoy 'Left-wing Privilege' on Campus," appeared on *The College Fix*.[9] The two faces of privilege are doing all right. The critics of privilege shaming may take some comfort in knowing that these two, at least, have not been shamed into silence.

The political conversation about "privilege," meanwhile, has its own overlapping timeline. The concept is well suited to politics. Long before privilege awareness became fashionable, candidates (often from quite privileged backgrounds) would try to portray themselves as self-made (born in, as Bill Clinton would have it, log cabins of their own creation[10]), and their opponents as out-of-touch elitists. In the 2008 presidential campaign, John Edwards offered up regular reminders of his mill-worker heritage, while Sarah Palin railed against coastal elites. Yet populism well predates the explicitly "privilege" approach. That would only come a bit later, in the years after the term had made its cultural debut: in the run-up to the 2012 elections, candidates and their supporters began framing their cases more explicitly in terms of privilege. President Barack Obama had spoken about unearned advantage and the myth of the self-made man, which led the GOP to make "We Built It" its national convention refrain.[11] The line from "We Built It" to Fortgang thinking his grandparents' struggles meant he couldn't be privileged is easy enough to trace. To be a conservative then was to reject identity politics.

It was only in 2016 that politics went full privilege turn. The Democratic contest was all about "privilege," with Bernie Sanders's and Hillary Clinton's supporters incessantly accusing the other side of supporting their candidate because of their (that is, the supporters') unearned advantages. Privilege accusation, however, is by no means limited to intra-left battles. Conservatives regularly accuse liberals of unchecked privilege, and they have been doing so for years. The old "limousine liberal" cliché became the ideological underpinning of intellectual conservatism. In 2010, political scientist (and controversial *The Bell Curve* coauthor) Charles Murray wrote in *The Washington Post* that "the New Elite spend school with people who are mostly just like them—which might not be so bad, except that so many of them have been ensconced in affluent suburbs from birth and have never been outside the bubble of privilege."[12] This insight led him, two years later, to produce a "bubble" quiz, which if anything anticipated the viral privilege-checklist phenomenon.[13] It asked (and asks; a reissue appeared in 2016[14]) well-educated white liberals to admit they had no idea what NASCAR was, and that they thus were too out of touch to know what's good for the country. The implication was that if white liberals left their bubble, they'd start voting Republican. Same year, same idea, from political commentator and journalist David Brooks:

> The problem is that today's meritocratic elites cannot admit to themselves that they are elites. Everybody thinks they are countercultural rebels, insurgents against the true establishment, which is always somewhere else. . . . If you went to Groton a century ago, you knew you were privileged. You were taught how morally precarious privilege was and how much responsibility it entailed.[15]

It isn't clear to me meritocracy would lead to a less privilege-aware elite is a convoluted argument. If anything, having parents who may have grown up less well-off (not that there's all that much social mobility in America) may make someone more plugged in to the *actually* "precarious" nature of privilege. All that much-derided upper middle-class fussing about grades and extracurriculars speaks less to privileged entitlement than to very real fears of downward mobility. Yet as a cultural critique of the hypocrisy of the left, it was spot-on. Brooks was addressing the proverbial person who grew up in a Brooklyn brownstone and pleads authentic outer-borough (as in, Queens or Bronx) scrappiness.

The notion that insufficient privilege awareness is what causes elites to lean left has only gotten more entrenched on the right. Consider journalist Irin Carmon's accurate (if tongue-in-cheek) summary of Justice Antonin Scalia's defense of capital punishment, and why his fellow judges—living, as they do, "in placid suburbia or [in] high-rise co-ops with guards at the door," wouldn't grasp its necessity: "And then it hit me that all Scalia was trying to do was to get the justices to check their privilege."[16] And he was! Conservatives and progressives alike have taken to arguing points on the basis of identity and personal experience.

"PRIVILEGE": THE BASICS

"DEAR WHITE PEOPLE: no one is saying your life can't be hard if you're white but it's not hard because you're white."[17] This perhaps overly earnest profundity comes from an August 2015 tweet, shared by thousands, by Twitter user Austin (@kvxll), that somehow made its way to my own Twitter feed. (Which is to say, someone I follow shared it.) Austin's tweets just before ("Dear straight people: no one is saying your life can't be hard if you're straight but it's not hard because you're straight") and after ("Dear cis people: no one is saying your life can't be hard if you're cis but it's not hard because you're cis") hone in on the same idea: Privilege is about all-things-being-equal advantage. It isn't personal.

The contemporary use of "privilege" emerged to address an absence in the language for discussing systemic inequality in general. In scholarship, a "privilege" focus means looking at oppression not only in terms of the oppressed, but also of the oppressor. It means studying systems of marginalization by looking not only at the marginalized, but also at the nonmarginalized. Like all new (or repurposed) buzzwords and concepts, it fills a need. Inequality *does* exist across a wide range of intersecting axes, and the "haves" in each area really *are* oblivious. We probably did need a word to convey the multifaceted nature of luck, as well as the naïveté and entitlement that so reliably accompany unearned good fortune.

THE PANACEA THAT WASN'T

IT'S WHEN YOU get into the realm of privilege theory and application that things get more dicey. The central idea behind "privilege" is that it shifts a discussion of discrimination away from the assumption that an advantaged position is the "normal" one. Rather than assuming "a person" is a forty-year-old upper-middle-class white man, unless otherwise specified, "privilege" reminds that whiteness, maleness, and so forth are *traits*, and not just the default human condition. This much makes sense. However, it also implies shifting away from the notion of rights. In a *New York Times Opinionator* interview,[18] philosophy professor Naomi Zack offers the following criticism of "privilege" as a term for discussing racism:

> The term "white privilege" is misleading. A privilege is special treatment that goes beyond a right. It's not so much that being white confers privilege but that not

> being white means being without rights in many cases.
> Not fearing that the police will kill your child for no
> reason isn't a privilege. It's a right.

This is the biggest theoretical challenge to the privilege turn: An approach that's ostensibly about achieving social justice winds up suggesting, or seeming to suggest, that everyone should be miserable.

A further flaw: "Privilege" is based on an analogy, namely that other forms of unearned advantage are similar to, and as important as, wealth. Wellesley scholar Peggy McIntosh, the thinker responsible for the current understanding of "privilege," has compared white privilege to a bottomless bank account.[19] "Privileged" used to mean "rich," and to some degree, still does. (When I've told friends and acquaintances that I'm writing a book about privilege, they've sometimes assumed I'd be researching the super rich.) At most, it would be a way of specifying that a rich person was also posh, or old money, versus self-made or otherwise *nouveau*. The word "privilege" might be used to soften a crudely financial assessment, but it might also imply wealth that was a bit more entrenched. (A lottery winner might be rich but not "privileged.")

The conflation of all forms of relative advantage with the *financial* form thereof has doubtless helped some people conceptualize racism, sexism, and more. Yet it also leads to confusion, and brings about defensiveness in people who are (say) white, and thus "white-privileged," but not necessarily both white *and*, in the old sense of the term, privileged. The bank-account metaphor makes it easier for people who are both white *and* socioeconomically privileged to have that aha moment. After all, their experience of whiteness is wrapped up with those of wealth and status. The concept is less effective at getting the point across to, say, the white working class and the white poor.

One further problem with the privilege framework (don't worry, more will come up later) is that it leads to making far too much of minor problems, and far too little of the big ones. It's about putting sensitivities ahead of on-the-ground realities. Or not even. It's about putting *theoretical* sensitivities—symbolic concerns that someone, somewhere, could find something triggering or problematic—ahead of things that demonstrably cause emotional distress in actual people. It's about prioritizing "awareness," which is essentially a kind of ever-vigilant performance.

"LIKE A PRAYER": A BRIEF BUT SINCERE CASE IN FAVOR OF USING THE TERM

THE CONCEPT OF "privilege" as we know it today comes from Peggy McIntosh's famous 1988 paper, "White Privilege and Male Privilege: A Personal Account of Coming to See Correspondences Through Work in Women's Studies."[20] In it, McIntosh explains, in accessible terms, a simple, obvious-in-retrospect parallel. Just as men often seem, to her, oblivious to their advantages as men, she has surely been unaware of her own leg up as a white person:

> I have come to see white privilege as an invisible package of unearned assets which I can count on cashing in each day, but about which I was "meant" to remain oblivious. White privilege is like an invisible weightless knapsack of special provisions, assurances, tools, maps, guides, codebooks, passports, visas, clothes, compass, emergency gear, and blank checks.[21]

The best-known part of the paper is the ur-privilege checklist.[22] McIntosh lists forty-six unearned advantages that she "think[s] in [her] case *attach somewhat more to skin-color privilege* than to class, religion, ethnic status, or geographical location, though of course all these other factors are intricately intertwined." The list is a mix of subtly brilliant insights ("I can be late to a meeting without having the lateness reflect upon my race."); prescient observations ("I do not have to educate my children to be aware of systemic racism for their own daily physical protection."); and a few entirely idiosyncratic advantages that say more about Peggy McIntosh than about life for white people generally ("If I want to, I can be pretty sure of finding a publisher for this piece on white privilege.").

In the 1988 paper, McIntosh at various points gestures toward the need for more than just privilege enumeration: "As we in Women's Studies work to reveal male privilege and ask men to give up some of their power, so one who writes about having white privilege must ask, 'Having described it, what will I do to lessen or end it?'"[23] But the ultimate outcome is, in a sense, beside the point. In a 2014 interview with *New Yorker* writer Joshua Rothman, she describes coming up with her forty-six forms of white privilege as follows: "I asked myself, On a daily basis, what do I have that I didn't earn? It was like a prayer."[24] She insists that it's *very important* to acknowledge privilege, but she admits that doing so may not lead anywhere. Nor does she rule out that listing one's privileges will make someone that much more inclined to hang onto them.

To their credit, scholarly proponents of privilege theory agree that simply acknowledging privilege isn't sufficient to accomplish anything. In his 2003 introduction to a reader in which McIntosh's essay appears, sociologist Michael Kimmel emphasizes that privilege awareness is only a first step: "Eliminating inequalities involves more than changing everyone's attitudes." As for the next step, Kimmel isn't especially precise: "Examining our privilege may be uncomfortable at first, but it can also be energizing, motivating, and engaging."[25] The only concrete aim of the privilege-awareness project might well be that it inspires more privilege workshops and for-credit privilege coursework, aimed mainly at privileged students.

Yet the project has other, more abstract goals, and those shouldn't be overlooked entirely. The expression "count your blessings" well predates the modern privilege checklist, but is a similar exercise. And as dreadful as the phrase is when used to dismiss, say, clinical depression, it's a useful response to minor unpleasantness. If you find yourself in one of those everyday slumps where it seems like the world is against you (*They're out of blueberry muffins?!*), perspective can't hurt. McIntosh included this key point in her knapsack essay: "At the very least, obliviousness of one's privileged state can make a person or group irritating to be with."[26] While the self-promoting declarations of self-awareness are annoying in their own right, it's hard to make a case against *being* self-aware.

Rebecca Solnit, the writer famed for popularizing the notion of "mansplaining," wrote in a 2015 essay that she'd "coined a term a while ago, privelobliviousness, to try to describe the way that being the advantaged one, the represented one, often means being the one who doesn't need to be aware and, often, isn't."[27] While "mansplaining" gave a name to an existing but unnamed phenomenon, "privelobliviousness" seems a bit redundant. "Privilege" implies obliviousness. Solnit adds that this sort of cluelessness "is a form of loss in its own way," which gets at another thing "privilege" contributes: it stigmatizes good luck. It doesn't just remind that others have it worse, but raises the possibility that an unfair system hurts even those at the top.

However, this—the obliviousness angle—seems key to why "privilege" caught on. It can function in a subversive way, by saying that sure, this other person *has* everything, but you *understand* things that this idiot never will. So it's not just that "privilege" is descriptive. It's also—when used internally, among have-nots in whichever area, rather than as an accusation—a way of conveying the sheer annoyance of life's systemic injustices.

There's also plenty of (legitimate) frustration, in progressive circles, with a tendency for the left to consider only economic inequality, to the exclusion of other forms of injustice. While "privilege" has *failed miserably* as a tool for discussing sexism (see chapter 4), it's shown more promise as an approach, if not necessarily to diminishing racism, then at least to explaining the phenomenon. In an excellent *New York Times Magazine* piece called "How 'Privilege' Became a Provocation,"[28] literary critic Parul Sehgal initially notes that she has qualms with the term, but then pivots to its defense. It's clear, however, from the examples she gives, that she's only talking about *white* privilege, not "privilege" in the broader, ever-expanding definition it currently holds. She mentions "a new meme on Twitter, white men have been posting photographs of themselves lying facedown on the ground, with the hashtag #takeusdown, in mock apology for their white privilege." "Privilege," she explains, is "still the most powerful shorthand we have to explain the grotesque contrast between the brutal police killings of Michael Brown, Eric Garner and Tamir Rice and the treatment extended to Dylann Roof, charged with murdering nine black people last month in a church in Charleston, S.C.— captured alive, treated to a meal by the arresting officers, assigned a judge who expressed concern for his family."

While there are problems with that approach to addressing injustice—specifically, with its implication, which is that the solution to racism is for everyone (as versus no one) to experience police brutality—on a conceptual level, she has a point.

To the extent that it does work, the use of "privilege" to discuss racism is productive because the analogy holds up: Being white in America *is* vastly easier than being black, in much the same way as being rich is easier than being poor. (The same couldn't necessarily be said about the magnitude of the benefits of being a size 4 over being a size 12, at least for those of us who are not pursuing careers as fashion models. Thus my wariness of the term "thin privilege" in many contexts.) The most persuasive use of "privilege" I've seen comes from a post about racism, by journalist Jamelle Bouie.[29] In "What Does It Mean to Be 'Privileged'?" Bouie recounts having sold his TV, and coming to the realization that simply walking down the street in

DC at night carrying it might lead to getting stopped by police, under suspicion of having stolen the set. A white man, he suspects, wouldn't have had the same concern:

> I have no idea what would have happened if I decided to walk a nice TV three blocks down the street. It's entirely possible that the police would have left me alone. But I couldn't count on that. . . . What does it mean to be privileged? It means not having to think about any of this, ever.[30]

What makes Bouie's post so effective is that we're not hearing the musings of an outside observer on what a black person might feel in a particular situation, complete with melodramatic posturing. We're hearing what he, a black man—not to mention a writer who has at times expressed skepticism about "privilege" rhetoric[31]— actually experiences. It's painful to read, because systemic racism is painful to hear about, but it doesn't *sting*, exactly, because it's not an accusation. This post remains the best example I've come across of "privilege" functioning as it should: as an empathy-promoting first step toward systemic changes. Someone who'd never quite *gotten* why racial profiling is a problem could conceivably read Bouie's post, experience some kind of realization about the burden the suspicion of criminality places on young black men, and feel moved to advocate against such policies.

Sehgal's ultimate defense of the term—"It's easier to find a word wanting, rather than ourselves"—echoes Laurie Penny's intervention from two years prior:

> New words and phrases tend to make powerful people angry not because they are new, but because what they describe is modern and threatening. Repeatedly claiming that you cannot understand simple ideas like "privilege

checking" and "intersectionality" . . . often means that
you don't want to understand. Some find it easier to
argue "we don't need this word" when what they actually
want to say is "we don't want this thing."[32]

Penny—among the term's most ardent defenders—does not restrict her discussion to white privilege ("It just means any structural
social advantage that you have by virtue of birth, or position—such
as being white, being wealthy, or being a man"), and goes to defend
privilege accusation as well:

"Check your privilege" means "consider how your
privilege affects what you have just said or done." That's
it. That's all. Being made aware of your privilege can feel
a lot like being attacked, or called a bad person, and
when that happens you sometimes get the urge to stamp
your feet and scream.

Penny then links to a piece critical of the expression, before adding,
"This is the point where it's useful to take deep breaths and remember it's not all about you."
   Of course, the expression "your privilege is showing" (YPIS) *is*
"about you." The subject at hand is, after all, "your privilege." It would
be inaccurate to dismiss that interpretation as a misunderstanding.

THE EMERGENCE OF "PRIVILEGE"
IN ITS NEW MEANING

IT'S DIFFICULT TO pin down exactly when, between
McIntosh's first theorizing and Fortgang's lament, the contemporary
idea of privilege seeped into the public consciousness. *Guardian*
writer Hadley Freeman has dated the first privilege-checking request

to "2006, on the social justice site shrub.com, when a blogger calmly wrote about how everyone to a certain extent speaks from a position of privilege and they should take into account that others are not as privileged as them."[33]

It seems to have entered the social-justice vernacular a bit earlier than that. The first online instance I've found was from a Portland-Oregon-based thread about an incident in which police had apparently pepper-sprayed protestors, including children. In August 2002, someone named Monica wrote a comment entitled, "Ken, your privilege is showing." Ken, the previous poster to the thread, had asked why the parents brought the kids in the first place. To which Monica responded, "How shall I leave my kids at home? They're not old enough to stay alone and I can't afford a babysitter. Or were you only talking to those parents able to AFFORD to protest?"[34] While it's possible that Monica was the first to use the expression, it seems unlikely. A 1997 Amazon book reviewer credited a character in a novel about seafaring, of all things, with being "aware of his privilege."[35]

My own first encounter with the social justice use of "privilege," according to the spotty personal archive that is my blog (*What Would Phoebe Do*), was in 2004, when a fellow University of Chicago undergrad wrote in the school paper that the members of the University community were "living in the warm folds of privilege."[36] I first began seeing accusations of privilege floating around online in the years that followed, only to realize, somewhere along the line, that "privilege" had become ubiquitous.

WHY NOW?

A CONFLUENCE OF factors has made "privilege" the word and concept of our age. The 2008 recession led to increased awareness of income inequality, and of the ways some young adults' families, but not others, could discreetly help them out. The Tea Party and Occupy Wall Street have both, in different ways, made it more difficult to pretend that America is a casteless society. Social media has also played a role—it's now possible to be clueless, and to call out cluelessness, on a far larger scale than ever before. The Internet has also made it more difficult both to assume everyone in a conversation shares one's own advantages, and to know much about the identities of the people with whom one is conversing. That immediate (if not always accurate) sense we have in offline life of which caste someone belongs to is absent, and the absence of all those cues opens up the possibility for abstract and often highly misleading discussions of who, according to some not-so-scientifically weighted checklist, fits where. And for all that's said about overshare, about self-pitying on-line confessions, the dominant pressure on social media is to present the best version of oneself possible. This means sharing only the positive. An atmosphere where boasting is ubiquitous, and where hardships go unstated, makes everyone look a notch more privileged than they really are. This makes the you-have-it-easy call-out that much more tempting, as well as that much less likely to be justified.

There are also more subtle reasons for its current appeal. Yes, rich-person obliviousness has been around since at least Marie Antoinette, and elites have been presenting their own ways as inherently superior since one ape was classier than another. Unfortunately, in an era of tremendous financial inequality,[37] combined with one of veneration for voluntary minimalism, has led to unprecedented insufferability in this area. The anti-stuff movement (which somehow always ends up coming down hardest on *cheap* clothes, when the high-end chains also sell factory-made goods from impoverished countries) allows the rich to feel as if their luxury consumption is really just a matter of labor or environmental concerns. There's the annual Black Friday ritual, where a certain number of Facebook friends and think-piece writers will make a point in announcing that *they're* not going bargain hunting.

This tendency of today's richer-than-ever rich to present themselves as the true bearers of humility and anti-consumerism can be more irritating than unapologetic ostentatiousness.

On the blog *Jezebel*, the writer Jia Tolentino offered a classic portrait of exactly this dynamic:

> One of my least favorite things in the world is hearing a young person whose parents pay their cell phone/buy them plane tickets home for every holiday/give them thousand-dollar gift checks say something like, "I've never gotten any help from my parents, but I've managed to save some money." Not because it's bad to get any of those things, but because it's bad not to recognize: Informal help is help.[38]

The secrecy that Tolentino (accurately) describes—"the hesitation to admit informal advantage tends to come hand-in-hand with that informal advantage"—can be infuriating. "Privilege" evokes that sense that someone just doesn't get it. The "it" isn't necessarily something all that important, in the grand scheme of things, although it can be. Part of the problem with an unjust society is that small slights add up. Without "privilege," there wasn't really a language for conveying the way that bigotry can manifest itself not just through encounters with overt racists, but also through individually minor, but repeated, slights from those who may even identify as progressive.

The privilege turn is about more than the insertion of the word "privilege" into articles and social-media posts on an ever-wider range of topics, to describe an ever-broader set of unfair advantages. It's a new conceptual framework, as well as a new way of interacting with others, of understanding society, and of critiquing arts and entertainment. Depending whom you ask, it's either an essential term that only the willfully obtuse (and excessively privileged) would object to, or a conversation stopper up there with Godwin's Law (that is, comparing your detractor in a comment thread to Hitler).

The privilege turn has been widely misunderstood. It's not a politically correct new order where white men, or the otherwise advantaged, lose out. It's not about the prize going to the greatest victim. The old order hasn't gone anywhere. It hasn't actually gotten easy (let alone too easy) to call out wrongdoing. Rather, a veneer of hypersensitivity gives the impression that times have changed, and does so just enough to stir resentment.

YPIS

SO ON THE one hand there's "privilege," a framework for understanding society, and on the other, the privilege call-out. This might be "check your privilege," although a "your privilege is showing" (from here on, YPIS) may sting that much more, with its evocation of a grooming mishap that someone has only just now told you about. Mostly, though, these accusations sting because the recipient has correctly assessed that he or she is being insulted. "Privileged" functions both as a neutral descriptor and as a synonym for "entitled and willfully oblivious." One might even go so far as to say that it's our era's number one insult. So you may be technically right in pointing out that someone is privileged, but in pointing this out, you're also telling this person off. Conversely, someone who balks at a privilege accusation *might* be denying having unearned advantage. Yet he or she could just as well be denying horrible person-ness.

For this reason, even supporters of using privilege as a framework will often draw the line at "check your privilege." McIntosh has called that phrase "a flip, get-with-it kind of statement."[39] Sehgal supports use of the term "privilege," but argued in a *New York Times Magazine* piece that "the shine has come off this hardy, once-helpful word. It looks a little worn, a bit blunted, as if it has been taken to too many fights." She attributes this shift partly to the term's online manifestations: "On the Internet, it makes for trusty kindling, and in the popular imagination, a cudgel: When people think of 'privilege' being used, it's almost always as an epithet, to shame."[40] And in a *Salon* piece otherwise favorable to the concept of privilege, Mary Elizabeth Williams referred to the privilege-checking phrase itself as "the 'Is there gluten in this?' of public discourse, an expression so promiscuously deployed it's bound to incite a few eyerolls along the way."[41]

Privilege-in-theory and YPIS-in-practice can't be so neatly disentangled. Individual accusations of privilege often go hand in hand with abstract discussions of what the term means and why it's so necessary. And at the root of probably every anti-"privilege" essay was its author's experience as the recipient of one YPIS too many.

The term "privilege" is a magic potion that turns otherwise dreary ideological debates into pile-ons. It's no coincidence that Exhibit A in author Jon Ronson's popular study of public shaming, the one that got excerpted in *The New York Times Magazine* and that stemmed from publicist Justine Sacco's Twitter joke about AIDS and Africa, was a pile-on rooted in a privilege controversy. In explaining why a tone-deaf joke—"Going to Africa. Hope I don't get AIDS. Just kidding. I'm white!"—went viral, Ronson wrote, "[I]t was her apparently gleeful flaunting of her privilege that angered people."[42] So it was.

Also not a coincidence: Sacco seems to have meant for the joke to be, as Ronson put it, "a reflexive critique of white privilege—on our tendency to naïvely imagine ourselves immune from life's horrors." Online privilege controversies frequently stem from poorly worded or otherwise naïve attempts at *challenging* privilege. The oblivious white anti-racist or male feminist—or in social-justice terms, the ally who wants a cookie—is often the person who inspires the most YPIS rage. It's not that straightforward bigots or, in more neutral terms, people outside the ally framework don't get called out at all, but when they do, it seems futile. It's clear (see chapter 2) that there was little to be gained by telling the young white woman who brought an anti-affirmative action case to the Supreme Court that she was exhibiting white privilege.[43] Not because she *wasn't* doing this—good grief, she was—but because if there's anyone in the world who isn't going to be moved by a YPIS, it's a white person making a literal federal case about "reverse racism."[44]

"Privilege," thanks to its ambiguity, is able to push all sorts of different buttons for agendas and identities of all kinds. It's not only that the phrase manages to simultaneously make one think about race, gender, sexual orientation, class, ability, and other categories that may have been added since the time of my writing this sentence. It's also that it includes built-in hyperbole. It ramps up every form of advantage to that of society's haves versus its have-nots, tsars versus serfs.

Central to the privilege turn is the question of whether people—be they celebrities, ordinary people whose gaffes have gone viral, your interlocutor in a Twitter war, or the proverbial conservative Thanksgiving uncle—*get it*. There's some further ambiguity here: Does getting it mean getting that the world is an unfair place, or does it mean getting why one must use "privilege" to convey this? Either way, the privilege-explainer social-media post is a genre in its own right, and is often designed to go viral.

A BuzzFeed video from Daysha Edewi, called "What Is Privilege?," shows an ethnically diverse group of young, good-looking men and women taking steps forward or backward according to how they answer thirty-five different privilege-related questions, and also being asked, along the way, about how the exercise is making them feel.[45] An unnamed (and perhaps mythical) high school teacher's privilege-education demonstration, which apparently involved students trying to throw crumpled-up pieces of paper into the recycling bin, went viral, receiving millions of views. It illustrated that those sitting closer to the front of the room, where the bin was located, had an easier time making the basket.[46]

Also a hit: a comic by Toby Morris that "makes privilege incredibly easy to understand." The comic traces two people's lives and disparate opportunities up to adulthood, the final image depicting the man, in a tux, saying, "No one ever handed me anything on a plate," as he obliviously takes an oyster from a plate being held up by the woman, who's working as a server at the reception that is, of course, celebrating the man.[47]

Other awareness raisers begin by acknowledging that "privilege" puts people off. Christian blogger Jeremy Dowsett, aiming to "help some white people understand privilege talk without feeling like they're having their character attacked," offers a transportation analogy: "I can imagine that for people of color life in a white-majority context feels a bit like being on a bicycle in midst of traffic. They have the right to be on the road, and laws on the books to make it equitable, but that doesn't change the fact that they are on a bike in a world made for cars. Experiencing this when I'm on my bike in traffic has helped me to understand what privilege talk is really about." These musings received over a thousand comments and over ten thousand Facebook shares.

Writer John Scalzi, meanwhile, in search "of a way to explain to straight white men how life works for them, without invoking the dreaded word 'privilege,' to which they react like vampires being fed a garlic tart at high noon," rephrases "privilege" in terms of video game difficulty settings: "All things being equal, and even when they are not, if the computer—or life—assigns you the 'Straight White Male' difficulty setting, then brother, you've caught a break." This post, too, was Facebook-shared over ten thousand times.[48] The "privilege" gospel keeps being preached, if primarily to the converted.

Yet the more interesting aspect of the privilege turn is the emphasis switch from society to individuals. Or, rather, "privilege" is about society, but its adherents insist upon defining individuals as the sum of their identifiable, systemic advantages and disadvantages. It's intensely feelings-focused—if a celebrity or someone in a comments thread has done something that offended you, or that you have every right to be offended by, or that you'd imagine a member of the marginalized group in question would find offensive, the thing to do is to call out the privilege of the person who's caused offense. And you do so by hurling a YPIS.

The interaction I'm describing is part of a broader phenomenon: call-out culture. That said, not all call-outs fall under this umbrella. Straightforwardly bigoted, hateful remarks by public figures—open ones as well as those of the didn't-know-the-mic-was-on variety—may be called out without "privilege" in this new sense entering into it. And if a politician is criticized for, say, starting a war, this criticism may take place on social media, but it's a far cry from call-out culture. What makes call-out culture in the "privilege" sense distinct isn't that it's about speech rather than action, nor that it's "politically correct" (after all, it's also politically correct to demand that politicians not spew racist obscenities), it's about alerting people to wrongs they *didn't know* they'd committed. Yet if YPIS is intended to be educational, it's education with some judgment attached. Consider this definition, retweeted and favorited hundreds of times, from the @LOLGOP Twitter account: "Privilege—n. when a whole class of people get a right they were denied and you immediately invent hypotheticals how this might hurt you."[49]

Once a YPIS has been hurled, the conversation switches from one about a broader issue to being about your interlocutor and his or her own inner life. Has this person properly reckoned with his or her privilege? Does this person *get it*? And does their exiting the thread before successfully demonstrating to you that they get it mean that they don't? Or is it possible—after all, anything's possible—that they had to get to school or work? Could it be that they were off meeting obligations to people other than their wrong-on-the-Internet[50] companions?

As things actually play out, recipients of YPIS tend not to exit quite so gracefully. Whether or not they have somewhere to be, they're more likely to get flustered and defensive, and to stick around for a while, only to dig themselves into deeper holes. While it's never fun to be reminded of your unearned advantages, there's something curious about the psychology of YPIS receipt. Even if you lack the privilege you've been accused of having, the charge stings.

PRIVILEGE AND THE CULTURE OF MANDATORY OVERSHARE

A PRIVILEGE ACCUSATION—or even just a privilege-awareness-raising exercise—is a demand for personal information. The framework leaves no space for discretion. Consider, again, that BuzzFeed "What Is Privilege?" video exercise, intended, it seems, as a model for others. (Thus the extended checklist provided in the post.) Some of the questions are just variants of asking about race and gender, which are typically visible. Others—those about religion, socioeconomic class, and sexual orientation—would require disclosing things not everyone is open about in all contexts. It's a fair bet that if you're *in a privilege-awareness workshop*, you're not about to hide the fact that you're a working-class Muslim lesbian. Yet if this information's going anywhere googleable, maybe you would?

Still other questions, though, are deeply personal: "If you have ever been diagnosed as having a physical or mental illness/disability, take one step back." Unless you are actually wheeling yourself backward (the "step" requirement seems, in the context, rather able-ist), your fellow exercise participants are bound to be curious what, exactly, you've been diagnosed with. And is everyone in this day and age really prepared to state publicly, or even just in a classroom, whether they feel as if they "came from a supportive family environment"? Isn't it starting to get a little personal about *other* people if you have to start saying whether your parents have ever been laid off? It shouldn't be taken as evidence that those who resist having a privilege conversation are doing so in order to avoid discussing their own copious privilege. It could also be that they have lacks thereof that they're not keen to talk about.

While these extra questions do help paint a more accurate portrait of the obstacles someone has faced (not a given with such checklists), the further you go from those broad, sweeping categories, the more likely you are to veer off into the realm of things people often don't wish to talk about. Indeed, feeling unable or unwilling to speak up about given obstacles can itself be a manifestation of one's lack of privilege. This limitation of the privilege approach is especially relevant when it comes to writing a college-admissions essay, or, once an undergrad, advocating for oneself in the classroom. Any system that offers points for disadvantage, but that places the burden on the disadvantaged to identify themselves, runs into these concerns.

EXAMINING THE ALREADY OVEREXAMINED

THE "PRIVILEGE" TURN encourages a focus on the privileged. This emphasis is ostensibly a feature, not a bug, of the approach. As theorized by Peggy McIntosh and others, studying oppression through not just the oppressed but also the oppressor addresses a gap in oppression scholarship, and gives a broader understanding of how society operates. This kind of makes sense, until one considers that all of such scholarship until approximately five minutes ago focused on elites. The stated reason for the focus may be diametrically opposed, but the outcome amounts to the same. In the apt words of *Jezebel* commenter ShoeFlyBunsenBurner, responding to a post about a forthcoming MTV film about whiteness: "Documentary on white privledge [*sic*] . . . Isn't that just the history channel?"[51] Through complex means it may take a sociology doctorate (or just a cynicism deficit) to grasp, getting a bunch of privileged people together to talk about their privilege is supposed to somehow reduce, and not reinforce, that privilege.

And yet, of course the privilege conversation reinforces privilege.

When people self-identify (reasonably or not) as posh and advantaged, a part of each of them is going to feel *good* about these qualities, and that much more inclined to cling to them. Tuning into one's own advantages is a route to feeling *grateful* for those advantages, not to rejecting them. There's a tweet from journalist Jamelle Bouie that sums this up nicely: "*whispers* I kind of think the excessive focus on privilege among young liberal-ish elites is a kind of political narcissism."[52] Why "whispers"? Because "privilege" has become such an unquestioned buzzword that anyone challenging it—even a left-leaning African American journalist known for his coverage of racism past and present—risks being accused of cluelessness and . . . privilege. To question its use is to invite accusations of "tone policing"—the social-justice world crime of having criticized the language or emotion level of someone's argument, and thus derailing the conversation away from their oppression.

Yet it's worth risking a tone-policing charge, because so much of the privilege conversation really *is* fancy people contemplating their own fanciness. In the past few years—thanks in no small part to the privilege turn—writing that examines privilege (as in, wealth and influence) with a critical-ish edge has gotten absorbed into the quasi-social-justice fold. In June 2015, *The New York Times* introduced "a new beat: an interdisciplinary look at . . . the richest of the rich," which would be "part of *The Times*'s deepening focus on economic inequality in America."[53] In her defense of this beat, public editor Margaret Sullivan reproduced some of the backlash tweets the announcement had inspired, and addressed the concerns head-on: "To some, it seems counterintuitive to cover the problems of economic inequality in America with a greater focus on the doings of the superrich. After all, this is not a set that's starved for media attention."[54] Sullivan discreetly alluded to the fact that the rich beat's author, Alessandra Stanley, had been under fire[55] for racial insensitivity while covering culture; from the Twitter response, it's clear that this fact entered into the skepticism the beat inspired. Sullivan then quoted Dean Baquet, the paper's executive editor, who'd given the new beat the green light: "The beat will not be 'isn't it cool to be rich,' he emphasized, but will look at the outsize role of the superrich in areas including philanthropy, art, and politics. It will be, he said, 'an anthropological approach.'"

That word—"anthropological"—brought to mind an op-ed that had recently run in the paper, a teaser by Wednesday Martin for her memoir, *Primates of Park Avenue*.[56] In it, Martin—a literature PhD (no shame in that!), but not an anthropologist—described her commentary on her fellow Upper East Side moms as if it had been a serious investigation undertaken by an outsider: "A social researcher works where she lands and resists the notion that any group is inherently more or less worthy of study than another." That she'd landed from the West Village, another posh Manhattan neighborhood, was the first clue that the project was maybe a bit less academic than it first seemed.[57] An initially positive response (largely from female professionals horrified by the idea of a "wife bonus"), turned sour. However, that's neither here nor there. The point is that rich people's upward-directed class resentments now pass for social protest.

In such contexts, "anthropological" seems to be code for, now we're going to talk about rich people in a way that seems celebratory, but that we'd prefer you to interpret as subversive. Coming full circle, here's Alessandra Stanley herself, commenting on *Primates* in a review of a TV series also about an upper-middle-class Manhattan woman who feels out of place among the very rich: "Someday there will be an anthropological study of that other exotic tribe: privileged people who devote their lives to exposing their even more fortunate neighbors." Investigating the super rich from the skeptical perspective of the merely privileged would seem to be precisely Stanley's new beat.[58]

Well, not entirely new. *The New York Times* has long covered the rich, and has long done so from an envy-snark standpoint. As writer

Jacqui Shine has pointed out in an *Awl* essay about the paper's life-style section, "Styles participates in producing and exposing public narratives about wealth and power with far more transparency and a more critical gaze than any other section of the paper does."[59] The part-critical, part-envious, but also part-self-congratulatory response that lifestyle journalism evokes has been with us since before the privilege turn, and before the 2008 recession, in stories like this gem from 2007,[60] about the plight of people who live in Manhattan townhouses that simply have too many floors: "To ameliorate the strain, they installed diaper changing stations on every floor and doubled up on kitchens, laundry rooms and espresso machines." What's new, then, is the surprisingly widely accepted belief that a focus on the privileged is a necessary first step toward *dismantling* privilege. These days, a book or article examining the habits of the rich can pass as revolutionary.

THE REACH OF "PRIVILEGE"

THE PRIVILEGE TURN, I've come to believe, isn't a radical force that upends the social order and leads those in positions of power to shake in their well-heeled boots. Rather, it manages, in a variety of ways, to reinforce the status quo. *The Perils of "Privilege"* explores exactly how the framework accomplishes the opposite of its ostensible aims.

In chapter 1, I plunge into the online privilege conversation, and I use "plunge" intentionally. I present the unwieldy mess that is the privilege-awareness online essay—not just white privilege, but all the many privileges—and the intense debates that form among journalists and Internet commenters over whose privilege, precisely, is showing. In Internet-commenter parlance, once "privilege" enters the thread, it's time for someone to post a popcorn gif; the show's about to begin. (Add "privilege" to the headline, and a story about how shoes were fastened in the Middle Ages could go viral.) I give examples of what I call "YPIS cycles"—privilege accusations leveled at articles or posts that are themselves critiques of privilege, and show how privilege (the term) is used to silence interlocutors in the threads of progressive blogs.

A sort of privilege fatigue has set in, with *Gawker* hosting a satirical privilege-checking tournament in 2013, and the expression "check your [mammalian, etc.] privilege" turning into a popular online joke. There's also an anti-YPIS reaction emerging on the left and center left, including *New York* magazine writer Jonathan Chait's 2015 article about political correctness, and the "2014: The Year of Outrage" feature in *Slate*. I explain where the backlash has ended up repeating the mistakes of that which it's critiquing. Yet YPIS's opponents have made several key points. Most crucially, privilege awareness has become a status symbol—one that, by definition, requires having privilege about which one can be aware.

Nowhere is that more dramatic than in education. As I discuss in chapter 2, American high schools and universities now regularly host privilege-awareness workshops. Privilege Studies is not a satirical invention of a conservative journalist, but a burgeoning academic field. Conversations about "privilege" dominate both student-activist rhetoric and that of their detractors. I discuss the paradox of today's college-admissions process, in which it helps as much as it ever did to come from a wealthy family, but applicants are assessed on the basis of self-awareness. The now-standard advice for college admissions essays is to avoid coming across as privileged. That "privilege" was conceived by someone who once taught at Brearley, one of the more posh of the Manhattan all-girls private schools, is, upon reflection, about what one would expect.[61]

Those wondering if perhaps YPIS is confined to seminar rooms and other spaces of ideological debate, will want to check out chapter 3, which is about the far-reaching impact privilege theory has had on the arts and on cultural criticism. Books, movies, and TV shows are now evaluated in terms of privilege, to the exclusion of all other observations or reactions. Rather than focusing on expanding opportunities for members of underrepresented groups, critics either dismiss a work because of the artist's privilege, or offer a disclaimer about how, *despite* the artist's privilege or the privileged milieu in which the work takes place, it's worth reading or watching. The privilege critique is ultimately less about opening doors than about insisting that *when* the usual suspects (rich, white, well-connected) put their work before an audience, the work in question should be privilege aware. The self-awareness requirement makes it more difficult for flawed characters to be depicted. Further contributing to this problem are two interrelated phenomena: personal essays and memoirs have largely taken the place of fiction, yet even fictional works are read as autobiographical. As the author-character distinction disappears, so, too, does the space for representing flawed (that is, privilege-oblivious) characters.

In chapter 4, I turn from culture to politics, and examine the way ostensibly progressive "privilege" rhetoric converges with reactionary ideas. The right has lapped up from-the-left critiques of feminism, readily agreeing that the white, cisgender, straight (or heteroflexible), well-educated, professional woman or (left-leaning, CSA-belonging, qualms-having) stay-at-home mom is the enemy. The far left sees this woman as the face of privilege because of her obliviousness to intersectionality, that is, to the fact that there are women who are discriminated against for more than their gender. The right, meanwhile, has never been especially fond of feminists, but now gets to call out liberal, white feminists for their racism, as a cover for calling them out for their feminism. The far left and far right agree that progressive, white women are entitled and somewhat ridiculous.

In chapter 5, I expand on the extent to which the far right has made "privilege" its own. The plight of the straight, white, middle-class male—so terribly oppressed by the new order that recognizes others as humans, too—gets cast in "privilege" terms. Meanwhile, the extreme right now also plays the "privilege" game, and has its own blog posts and think pieces about "black privilege," "female privilege," "Jewish privilege," and more. I explain why the "privilege" conceptualization so readily lends itself to causes and ideologies diametrically opposed to the ones it's purportedly there to address.

The Perils of "Privilege" is an attempt at taking a step back and asking whether the privilege-awareness project is a valuable one. And it's my sense—with some caveats—that it's been a disaster. Given the subject matter, though, I need to be very clear about what this book is *not* about. I'm definitely not arguing—as some others have been of late—that the shaming of bigotry has become as dangerous as bigotry itself. This book is not an attempt to silence or stifle activism, social-media or otherwise. I'm not interested in telling people who've experienced discrimination that their belief that they've been oppressed is surely in their heads, or in dismissing arguments simply because they've been expressed in privilege-theory terms. There are times when "privilege" is effective; those tend to be when the term is used by people whose own identities actually match up with the one they're advocating for, and who are using "privilege" to illustrate their experience. It tends to be less effective, if not all-out detrimental, when used on behalf of theoretical marginalized people, who get invented as a way of winning a point in some argument.

1

THE ONLINE YPIS WARS

MR. O'REILLY: Just remember, Mr. Fawlty, there's
always someone worse off than yourself.
BASIL FAWLTY: Is there? Well I'd like to meet him.
I could do with a laugh.

—*FAWLTY TOWERS*, "THE BUILDERS"

CHECK PLEASE!

IN THE SUMMER after graduating from high school, Noah
Phillips took a job at a Washington, DC, falafel shop. After this brief
stint in the pulverized-chickpea trade, he went to college.

A nice little story. Interesting, perhaps, if you're related to Noah
Phillips, or if you're someone interested in hiring Noah Phillips for
your own falafel stand, since you now know he has previous experience in that area. Yet why, one might wonder, was the story published,
in 2015, in *The Washington Post*? And how on earth did it wind up
with over a thousand comments?

Let's try that again:

Noah Phillips, a privileged seventeen-year-old white boy, had had enough of his privilege. Eager to shed some of that privilege, and to leave the cashmere-draped, kale-infused caviar-canapé-stuffed life he'd led thus far, he decided to expose himself to the ways of the commoners by applying to work in a DC falafel shop. ("I'm hardly the first privileged young man to go looking for grit," he wrote, while offering George Orwell as an example of what he, in applying for this job, was going for.)

Yet even there, in the sordid underworld that is life behind the falafel counter, he was unable to shed his privilege. This became evident from the mere fact that was hired in the first place, for as we all know, falafel stores only ever hire people who come from the right families. It can't have been about his qualifications: His only previous work experience was "running high school bake sales," evidence not that he was, you know, *seventeen*, but that he came from immense, almost incalculable privilege. (All your clothes were probably made by someone in Bangladesh who by seventeen would, in a just world, get to retire.) But his white privilege, his fluent-English-speaker privilege, and his socioeconomic privilege not only got him hired, but landed him the privileged position of . . . cashier.

An editorial note mentions that the *Post* contacted the falafel-shop management, presumably for fact-checking purposes, and it seems as if everyone, even the Latino colleagues Phillips found so terribly exotic, also worked the register. However, once the privileged self-flagellation has begun, its momentum is too great for it to stop over such trivialities. Everything about the falafel-salesman experience must be viewed through the lens of privilege. The fact that this would be a *privilege* essay was announced in what was, let's admit, a pretty great headline: "I Tried to Escape My Privilege with Low-Wage Work. Instead I Came Face to Face with It." But what really brought out the commenters may have been the inadvertently hilarious subhead: "The Advantages of Race and Class Are Not Easily Shed, Even in a Falafel Shop."[1]

If what Phillips was looking for was further confirmation that he is, in fact, an oblivious soft, rich kid, he was in luck. Sample comment: "Writing a story about your summer job, and then getting to have it published in the *Washington Post*. That's an example of white privilege. I have a suspicion that it's the product of other types of privilege."[2] Others pointed out that hipster falafel shops are not the scrappiest work environments around, and reminisced about their own, far scrappier youthful employment. Others pointed out—redundantly, it might seem, since this was Phillips's very point—that most people work because they need to, and not because they're trying to learn about "blue-collar" life.

The issue for readers wasn't Phillips's privilege, exactly. It was that he presented his falafel-store experience not as a summer job, but as a play at being working class. Had the angle been different, the response might have gone otherwise. After all, here's a rich kid who opted out of unpaid internships or voluntourism (that is, the trips well-off Westerners take to developing countries, ostensibly to help, but also to have some fun in the sun), and who avoided that classic rich-person fate of being one of those people who's never worked in food service and who treats servers atrociously. Instead, he wove the experience into a "privilege" narrative. In one sense, he didn't have to do this. Yet a bait-free, "privilege"-free version of the tale wouldn't have been published.

It's a truism, at this point, that where there is privilege, it ought to be checked. Thus the discussions that take place in comment threads, where participants order one another to check their privilege, or announce that someone's privilege is visible (as in, YPIS). The route to being a decent person—and, maybe, to making the world a better place—begins with a frank and candid assessment of one's own unearned advantages.

And yet. In his essay, Phillips is copiously, cringe-inducingly privilege aware, just not *self*-aware. But that's it's own quality, one disconnected from social-justice commitment. It's more about having a sense of humor, I suppose, which would explain why Louis C.K.'s self-deprecating privilege riffs are so often held up as the epitome of awareness.[3] What Phillips suffers from isn't underexamined privilege, but *overexamined* privilege, which ends up amounting to the same thing.

THE "BEHOLD, MY PRIVILEGE" CONFESSIONAL ESSAY: A SAMPLING

PHILLIPS WAS BY no means the first young adult to beat himself up over privilege in front of an online audience, and to wind up flaunting his privilege in the process. By the time his appeared, the confessional privilege essay had already become a well-established form. Online publications regularly publish reflections from people examining their own unearned advantages.[4] *Thought Catalog,* a site that falls somewhere between social media and a publication, is more or less a privilege-confession generator: "Confronting My Privilege,"[5] "With Great Privilege Comes Great Responsibility,"[6] "The Uncomfortable Privilege of Being Catcalled."[7] A site-wide search for "privilege" brings up over a thousand items, many but not all of them introspective.[8]

The earnest self-privilege check might seem a painful read, but more squirms still come from another branch of this subgenre: essays and blog posts by people sick of being faulted for their privilege. Months before Tal Fortgang's privilege-denial essay went viral, Kate Menendez, the woman behind "Being Privileged Is Not a Choice, So Stop Hating Me for It"[9] got the *Gawker* treatment: "Brave Privileged Person Speaks Out Against Anti-Privilege Privilege."[10] And way back in 2011, *Jezebel* reposted a hand-wringing *Advocate* essay by

Zack Rosen, "a white, cisgender gay man," who couldn't help but wonder: "Can a nontrans, white gay man ever truly leave the comforts of his own identity without having to make frequent and loud apologies for the crimes of his ilk?"[11] Oddly enough, writing a defensive essay about one's own privilege never seems to have the intended effect.

If Rosen had had enough of being alerted to his privilege, perhaps offering up his navel-gazing to *Jezebel* wasn't the best idea: "Thank you, sir, for that perfect demonstration of exactly WHY privileged people get called out for their privilege," wrote one commenter. Another: "Oh my God, a white dude made other people's identity issues ALL ABOUT HIM? Alert the media, I'm shocked. Snark over, here's the deal; this article REEKS of privilege." There were plenty more along those lines. Anyone looking for concrete examples of the phenomenon Rosen was describing could simply go to the comments and take their pick.

Yet the tone-deaf privilege-confession essay probably hit its peak with a massively viral *xoJane* one, whose title went as follows: "There Are No Black People in My Yoga Classes and I'm Suddenly Feeling Uncomfortable with It: I Was Completely Unable to Focus on My Practice, Instead Feeling Hyper-aware of My Skinny White Girl Body."[12] Actually, that wasn't quite the whole thing. Technically the headline began with the series name, "It Happened to Me," one that, in context, made it seem as if the arrival of "a young, fairly heavy black woman" in the author's yoga class was something the author felt had *happened* to her. After all, merely seeing a fat black woman do yoga apparently caused the author to cry.

In all fairness, the point of the essay, as best as I can tell, was that seeing a heavyset black woman doing yoga (and, in the author's opinion, struggling) set forth, in the author, a stream of consciousness about yoga as cultural appropriation; the unfair advantages of being thin and flexible; and the systemic injustices revealed by the fact that her particular yoga studio doesn't have a lot of black customers. It was this moment of self-righteous awakening that her black classmate inspired—and not the fact of having a black classmate—that caused the tears to flow: "I got home from that class and promptly broke down crying. Yoga, a beloved safe space that has helped me through many dark moments in over six years of practice, suddenly felt deeply suspect." The tears were for a lost innocence. Whichever seal had thus far sheltered the author to life's unfairness had been broken.

Apart from the striking absence of the word "privilege,"[13] the essay had all the elements of a privilege confession, most notably, an attempt at demonstrating awareness gone massively awry. The *entire Internet* weighed in on the author's obliviousness. (Over three thousand comments to the post itself, and enough outraged and mocking responses from other sites to merit a "5 best responses" roundup.[14])

If the yoga and falafel examples teach us one thing, it's this: Examination of one's own privilege, unless done *really* deftly, reads as conceited—conceited, and presumptuous. When, exactly, had the black student in the author's yoga class asked for her sympathy? Privilege awareness asks that a white, skinny woman enumerate the unearned advantages that these qualities provide her with (i.e., white privilege, thin privilege, able-bodied privilege, etc.). This articulation of one's own advantages is, at its very essence, the point of the privilege project—that where there is privilege, it should be owned. Yet when that articulation actually takes place, it ends up reading as an unsolicited pity-fest directed at someone whose life probably isn't as tragic as all that. Writer Teju Cole points out the "false" and "condescending" aspects of that self-deprecating reflex in a takedown of the "first world problems" meme, noting that Nigerians, too, fuss about cellphones, and adding, "All the silly stuff of life doesn't disappear just because you're black and live in a poorer country."[15] The line between admirable self-awareness of advantage and oblivious exaggeration of others' disadvantage is thinner than a self-flagellating white girl in a yoga class. Even if in theory, or in private, it's good to contemplate your privilege, in practice, in public, it's not.

If, however, these essays get to teach us *two* things, the second would be that "privilege" sells. It can't be terribly expensive—even by personal-essay standards—to publish navel-gazing musings of young people who, by their own admission, aren't hard up for cash. (Since universities ask for such essays in their applications, every privileged young person has one hanging around.) And the payback is huge. The more tone-deaf a piece is, the more viral (and virulent) the response. Yet because "privilege awareness" is this supposedly noble goal, publications get to churn these out in good conscience, and to pretend surprise when, time and again, an author of one of these essays attracts a pile-on.

Granted, not all privilege introspection is quite so painful to read. However, even the *professional* version of this genre gets called out in much the same terms. In a 2015 *New York Times Magazine* piece, "White Debt: Reckoning with What Is Owed—And What Can Never Be Repaid—For Racial Privilege," the writer Eula Biss explored her own white privilege with sentences such as, "Our police, like Nietzsche's creditors, act out their power on black bodies." Reflecting on a time when, as a college student, she'd failed to get in more serious trouble for illicit poster distribution, she writes:

> The word "privilege," composed of the Latin words for private and law, describes a legal system in which not everyone is equally bound, a system in which the law that makes graffiti a felony does not apply to a white college student. Even as the police spread photos of my handiwork in front of me, I could tell by the way they pronounced "tagging" that it wasn't a crime invented for me.[16]

Writing in *The Daily Beast* months prior to Biss's essay, the linguist and commentator John McWhorter expressed doubts about this sort of exercise: "Nominally, this acknowledgment of White

Privilege is couched as a prelude to activism, but in practice, the ac-knowledgment itself is treated as the main meal."[17] More recently, in *The Washington Post*'s "Post Everything" section, writer Freddie de-Boer offered similar disillusionment with the model: "[I]t's unclear what asking people to identify their racism or white privilege actu-ally accomplishes. Presumably, acknowledging white privilege comes before some substantively anti-racist action, but specific definitions of such action remain elusive."[18]

Indeed, as with the other, more obviously silly privilege essays, it's never spelled out what Biss has done, or will do, thanks to her awareness of her own privilege. She acknowledges that giving up white privilege is functionally impossible, sharing multiple anec-dotes demonstrating just that notion. One *Times* commenter re-sponded, not unfairly, "As a black guy, this ain't doing anything for me. Her existential hand-wringing is her own, it doesn't uplift anyone else really."[19] Another commenter calls out Biss's privilege, if indirectly: "This obsession with 'white privilege' seems to be confined to elite universities and tiny wealthy portions of major cities. In the real world, none of us are privileged enough to feel guilty about it."[20]

Biss's essay reads like an eloquent version of the "criming while white" hashtag, which involved white people flagging instances of po-lice giving them a pass. The idea was for white people to demon-strate their awareness of racial bias in policing, and in doing so, to model that awareness for others. In practice, as the feminist writer Jessica Valenti explained in *The Guardian*, it didn't sit right:

> White people acknowledging white privilege is important, but in the midst of national tragedies, tweeting about how you got away with criminal acts feel[s] like a performance of awareness that you are privileged rather than what we really need—a dismantling of the power obtained through that privilege.[21]

Given the steady stream of news about horrific deaths of black Americans at the hands of police, there isn't all that much lag between "national tragedies" of this sort. There's no particularly good moment to weigh in along these lines.

To her credit, Biss lays out—perhaps a bit too persuasively—the problems with the introspective approach to anti-racism:

> Guilty white people try to save other people who don't want or need to be saved, they make grandiose, empty gestures, they sling blame, they police the speech of other white people and they dedicate themselves to the fruitless project of their own exoneration.

True. Then she goes on: "But I'm not sure any of that is worse than what white people do in denial. Especially when that denial depends on a constant erasure of both the past and the present." Her case for white guilt—and for the privilege framework—isn't a promise that self-flagellation will lead to activism, but rather a claim that it might: "[W]hy not imagine guilt as a prod, a goad, an impetus to action? Isn't guilt an essential cog in the machinery of the conscience?" The "essential" bit is key. Across contemporary progressive rhetoric—in Biss's analysis, and even in Valenti's takedown of "criming while white"—there's a pervasive sense that personal enlightenment *must* precede efforts to improve the world. There's also a dangerous ignorance of the ways the ritual can make things worse.

THE HUMBLEBRAG OF THE
PRIVILEGE NONCONFESSION

PRIVILEGE CONFESSION HAS now become, paradoxically, the default way to speak about one's own *disadvantage*. That sort of essay is the self-awareness sweet spot. It's a way of discreetly announcing the obstacles you've endured, while not seeming self-pitying or like you're trying to win at Oppression Olympics. Or, to put it more generously, it's the natural self-expression of the sensitive. In a *Slate* piece called "I'm a Butch Woman. Do I Have Cis Privilege?" writer Vanessa Vitiello Urquhart lays out why she'd resisted the idea that she did—"Heck, I'm a butch lesbian living in Tennessee, for goodness' sake"—only to conclude that yes, as someone who can readily correct those who call her "young man," she is in fact cis-privileged.[22] Along the same lines, in a massively viral piece, "Explaining White Privilege to a Broke White Person," *Huffington Post* contributor Gina Crosley-Corcoran explains that as someone who "came from the kind of poor that people don't want to believe still exists in this country," the sort that involves "making ramen noodles in a coffee maker with water you fetched from a public bathroom," she'd initially balked when called "privileged" online, only to learn about intersectionality and see the light: "I know now that I *am* privileged in many ways. I am privileged as a natural-born white citizen. I am privileged as a cisgender woman. I am privileged as an able-bodied person."[23] This pops up in the political realm as well. There was that time when Marco Rubio explained that he came "from extraordinary privilege" because he had a loving childhood, albeit, you know, not a wealthy one.[24] If you're going to confess to privilege, his is the way to do it.

Yet even these privilege nonconfessions don't always hit the right note for all audiences. Once you use the word "privilege" in reference to yourself, you've introduced the *meme* of your privilege. You've planted the idea, and thus invited the accusation. Urquhart's willingness to admit that she, a gender-nonconforming gay woman in a red state, doesn't have it the absolute worst was still an insufficient admission of privilege as far as Claire-Renee Kohner, at the Web site *Planet Transgender*, was concerned: "Does Vanessa Vitiello Urquhart have cis privilege? Yeah, I'm just not sure she knows how much privilege she actually has."[25] Kohner interprets the following sentence from Urquhart's piece—"Occasionally, to my shame, I've even argued on the Internet about whether it makes any sense to say a butch like me has cis privilege"—to mean that Urquhart "feels she doesn't have cis-privilege," which would seem to be the very opposite of what it means when someone expresses "shame" for past behavior.

"PRIVILEGE" AS CONTENT

THE PRIVILEGE SELF-ASSESSMENT essay only makes sense in the context of the massive online conversation about privilege, one that overlaps with, but is ultimately distinct from (and detrimental to), online conversations about wealth inequality, racism, sexism, and other specific forms of injustice. These privilege-themed personal essays are all, in one way or another, attempts at deflecting or preempting accusations of unexamined privilege. The privilege turn is intricately tied up with social media and online journalism, with anonymous interactions and with posts that can't exceed 140 characters. "Privilege"-themed content of all kinds—essays, quizzes, cartoons—is a central part of the viral-content marketplace. Where the initial privilege checklists, from Peggy McIntosh onward, encouraged quiet self-reflection,[26] the newer ones are part of that whole online-identity-curating apparatus. Your every facet of privilege must be shared, without privacy settings, on social media. Thus the interactive checklists, like the "What Is Privilege?" *BuzzFeed* video exercise, which is currently at close to three million views,[27] and all those this-is-what-"privilege"-means videos, the ones that high school classmates keep posting to Facebook. On social media, you can share not just which forms of privilege you possess, but also— more importantly—the fact that you're privilege sensitive, privilege aware. The way that politicians must always say the right thing, and must avoid not just outright gaffes but also subtle comments that could potentially alienate some constituency, everyone with any kind of public presence, however slight, must take now care along these lines.

YPIS IN ACTION

Y P I S , I N I T S classic form, is about educating the inadvertently insensitive. If you, a progressive, say something that reveals your personal lack of familiarity with a particular form of oppression, you've let your ignorance slip. Such slipups matter, according to the rules of YPIS, regardless of whether anyone was actually offended. There's a clever and accurate description of the dynamic in a column by British journalist Hugo Rifkind, involving a self-declared feminist being asked by online left-wing detractors, "'But have you canvassed the views of Somalian refugees who are weekending female impersonators in Anglesea?'"[28] Rifkind got taken to task in the comments for having gone with a fictitious example. If this sort of thing really happened, why did he have to invent?[29] A fair point; the below list are an array of the sort of real-life examples he might have chosen:

> A Chow.com post referred to a $20 "Thanksgiving feast" from Walmart as "a disturbingly long list of edible features for a disturbingly low price." The first commenter, which set the tone for some subsequent commenters wrote: "I'm guessing that for some, this is a far cry from disturbing and simply a godsend right now. Your privilege is showing, and it might indeed be disturbing."[30]
>
> From a *Bitch* magazine comment thread on punk, one commenter starts off, "Ideally, white women should just realize their privilege and step in a[nd] do something that actually matters. However, our ignorance into what it is like being POC

[people of color] prevents a lot of us from even realizing our privilege. Without people in the scene pointing out my privilege and opening up discussion on this topic, I would not, and I still do not fully, realize my privilege." This same commenter then refers to the original post as "bitter" and not feminist. Another responds: "Hey, you said you wanted people to point out your privilege. Your privilege is showing with this comment." And another: "You're right about one thing: you haven't fully checked your privilege. It's not the responsibility of POC to attempt to force themselves into spaces they feel are hostile to them. It's our responsibility as white people to try to eradicate that hostility." Further discussion switches to whether the term "sisterhood" is offensive to trans women.[31]

A *Book Riot* blog post takes a *Huffington Post* writer to task for saying there's no point in having libraries in New York now that everything's online: "Watch out, Mr. Rosenblum, your privilege is showing! Might want to cover that up. Look, I understand that people have access to wonderful things these days in terms of technology . . . but these things are NOT easily accessible to EVERYONE. It's not as simple as clicking a button for many, many people in NYC."[32]

The above list are but three examples of YPIS (approximately 3,640 results in a Google search of the spelled-out expression), and that's not even starting on "check your privilege" (363,000), although many of these are discussions of the phenomenon. Searches on either expression on Twitter, however, tend to bring up examples of the phenomenon in action.

YPIS tends to crop up when someone with a history of making call-outs writes something worthy of one. When the self-righteous slip up, they can be accused of hypocrisy. Plus, it's more likely that someone versed in call-out culture will *care* that he or she has been

YPISed; someone who isn't (or who's simply unapologetically privileged) may not.

Peak sinkhole YPIS involves what I call YPIS cycles: One person will accuse another of unchecked privilege, only to end up accused of obliviousness for having even made the accusation. Take, for example, what happened when writer Jessica Coen wrote a post for *Jezebel* calling out an unnamed job applicant for putting in a cover letter that past experience working with crime victims made her a good fit for a job at a bridal salon.[33] The gist of Coen's post was that the job applicant couldn't see the difference between bridal stress and the crime-victim variety, and was therefore, in some convoluted way, part of the wedding-industrial-complex problem. Commenters, however, weren't convinced. Coen, who had failed to grasp that someone applying for a job, even in retail, has to put *something* in the cover letter that connects past experience to current qualifications, was the real oblivious one.

While the commenters were, I think, correct, everyone involved was participating full throttle in the YPIS process. That cover letter couldn't just *sit* there, but had to be turned into content. And "content" is found by combing something, anything—if no sitcom or romcom is available, some random cover letter will do—for unexamined privilege. Absent the YPIS context, it would read as straightforward bullying to mock a retail cover letter. Yet once the letter has been found to contain insensitivity to a caste of marginalizeds, it becomes fair game, a "punch up."

THE INADVERTENT HUMOR
OF "PRIVILEGE"

IF YOU'RE READING this and thinking these interactions all sound ridiculous, you'd be correct, but far from the first to point this out. YPIS's absurdity has turned "privilege" into a kind of running joke, and not just on the right, where anything that liberal academic sorts are into has been fodder for years. *The Guardian* accompanied a spate of privilege articles with a "handy, and not-entirely-serious, questionnaire," allowing readers to select from grievances such as "Although born in this country, I still face constant prejudice for daring to produce unpasteurised boutique cheeses" and "My African-sounding name is invariably spelled wrong on my latte."[34] *Jezebel*, a site whose comments section often turns into a YPIS-fest, nevertheless called a post about cuttlefish "Check Your Vertebrate Privilege."[35] ClickHole ran a parody explainer: "This Cartoon Does a Bad Job of Explaining What Privilege Is."[36] The cartoon captioned "White Privilege in One Simple Image" depicts a white man with enormous feet, thinking about the Empire State Building but talking about the Eiffel Tower, face-to-face with a black woman with enormous hands, whose own speech bubble, in turn, contains an image of an anthropomorphized lit cigarette, sporting a top hat. (It would have been maybe a little bit more spot-on had an accompanying text not spelled out that the image was "gibberish.")

However, *Gawker*'s "Privilege Tournament," a sports-inspired, multiround extravaganza that pitted zoophiles against asexuals, gluten allergies against latex ones, and so forth, is probably the best known, and was certainly the most involved.[37] While the categories themselves weren't satirical, the project itself was a far cry from the sincere checklists it was riffing on. (From *Gawker* writer Hamilton Nolan's introduction: "Privilege has its benefits, but the *lack* of privilege confers that sweet, sweet moral superiority.") In the end, *Gawker* readers voted the homeless the least privileged group, a result that could be read as a subtle dig at the new understandings of "privilege," all of which in one way or another amount to dismissals of the importance of material wealth.[38]

Those skeptical of the privilege turn are reliably (and sometimes fairly) accused of having proved their accusers' point. After all, privilege is, by definition, the sort of invisible advantage that people deny and get defensive about. However, while some rejection of "privilege" could be attributed to defensiveness, other criticisms would be more difficult to dismiss along those lines. Even apart from the flaws of call-out culture, the privilege framework has certain important drawbacks as a progressive strategy. And while the right has its own qualms with privilege checking, some of which stem from a rejection of the very notion of systemic inequality (see chapter 5), much of the criticism of YPIS call-outs has come from the left. And while it's possible—anything's possible—that every single liberal critic of "privilege" is either a secret conservative or exhibiting unexamined privilege, once you look at what the criticisms are, it becomes clear that there's substance to at least some of those criticisms.

THE FAR-LEFT REJECTION OF PRIVILEGE

Here's an experiment for the interns, service workers, graduate students, freelancers, and temps: Think deeply about your privilege, your advantages, your family history, that some may have it better or worse off than you do. Then, forget all of it.

So wrote April Wolfe, in a 2012 *Good* essay called "We're the Privileged Poor. Why Aren't We Talking About It?"[39] Wolfe was—by her own account—a well-educated but penniless creative, a genuine-article starving artist. Yet she came to see "privilege," with its emphasis on cultural capital, as a distraction from postrecession facts on the ground:

The fact is, we can no longer tell someone's financial reality by what they eat, how they dress, and where they grew up. While I've technically surpassed my parents in terms of education and advantage, I am still dependent on a restaurant job, and my peers are now considered the first generation of youths to do worse than their parents.

In the piece, Wolfe explains that she had, at one time, focused on the trappings—her knowledge of tofu, her MFA—and held off from calling herself poor. Part of what changed, it sounds like, was that this cultural capital never managed to transfer—as the privilege framework theorizes it will—into capital-capital. Yet that wasn't all:

> My first instinct: There's no way anyone can compare the harshness of the life of an undocumented migrant worker to that of a former graduate student. But this implies both that I should pity migrant workers and that I'm too good to be associated with their class.

Two things about Wolfe's remarks are worth noting. The first is that, as Wolfe suggests, there's something snobbish about the choice to identify, long-term, as broke rather than poor. The "privilege" framework asks broke, young (and youngish; Wolfe mentions being "on the cusp of [her] 30th birthday") people not to dare conflate their situation with that of more authentic poor people. Taking the penniless to task for failing to properly *categorize* their penury is an odd mix of well meaning (that is, sensitive to the feelings of the poor who lack even cultural capital) and condescending. Is the "broke" person holding off from identifying as poor so as not to unfairly claim a marginalized identity, or so as to avoid admitting that past a certain point, "broke" stops being a temporary situation? Is all that painstaking analysis of whether your parents took you to plays or museums about saving "poor" for those who truly merit the title, or is it a way of clinging to whichever (dubious, and financially useless) capital you do have?[40]

The other, more important one is that word, "class," which Wolfe—radically—uses in reference to status within the broader economy. Rather than working through a privilege checklist to demonstrate how her situation differs from that of her food-service colleagues, who might not be as knowledgeable about soy products or creative writing as she is, she concludes that poor is poor, gesturing toward labor activism as the answer.

Given that "privilege" is about asking progressives to set aside questions of wealth inequality, it shouldn't come as much of a surprise that some socialists have been dubious of the framework. Back in 2012, on the news site *Socialist Worker*, writer David Judd argued that a "Checking Your Privilege 101" document making the Occupy Wall Street rounds was actually a "barrier" to the movement's goals.[41] Judd considered the privilege approach sound when it came to race, but unhelpful in describing class interests, and in drawing connections between different forms of oppression. Perhaps most importantly, Judd objected to the document's "focus on self-education to the exclusion of everything else": "There's a nod to 'the root systems that give you privilege,'" he writes, "but we are called on to 'understand' them, not to do away with them." The earliest version of this from-the-left critique I've come across in any mainstream US publication was progressive writer Courtney Martin's 2011 piece in *The American Prospect*, "Moving Past Acknowledging Privilege." Martin wrote, "The impulse to do some of the intellectual and emotional labor of calling out unchecked privilege, as a person benefiting from some version of it, is a valuable one, but it can't end there." Martin presented privilege awareness as a necessary first step toward activism, but found that college students especially "get sort of stuck in a muck of guilt" and don't use their newfound awareness for anything good, or really, anything: "The question is not just about what unearned privileges we have been walking around with but also about what it would take to change the systems that gave us these privileges in the first place." While Martin was overall quite sympathetic to these young people, she allowed that for some, "testifying to their own lack of ignorance in public spaces" is a way of sending the message, "'I'm one of the good ones.'"[42]

This criticism was echoed in a 2014 post by writer Mia McKenzie on the Web site *Black Girl Dangerous*:

> What I find is that most of the time when people acknowledge their privilege, they feel really special about it, really important, really glad that something so significant just happened, and then they just go ahead and do whatever they wanted to do anyway, privilege firmly in place. The truth is that acknowledging your privilege means a whole lot of nothing much if you don't do anything to actively push back against it.[43]

Like Martin, McKenzie presents privilege acknowledgment as a well-meaning first step: "I understand, of course, that the vast majority of people don't even acknowledge their privilege in the first place. I'm not talking to them."

Others on the left, such as journalist Tom Midlane, have gone further, arguing that the "privilege" framework—however well-intended—ends up aiding the right. Wrote Midlane:

> The kind of semantic nit-picking that "privilege" encourages is aloof thought, un-coupled from questioning or attempting to change the hegemonic order. It's a kind of identity politics which assumes the post-ideological position as fact and embraces the idea that nothing will change beyond small shifts. Within this assumed safety net you're given your own playspace to act out divisive and willifully [sic] obscurantist verbal games. Corporate lobbyists couldn't invent a better system for neutralising collective action if they tried.[44]

However, for socialists especially, the problem with "privilege" is its focus on cultural capital, to the exclusion of capital-capital. This—and not the emphasis on racial or gender identity—is where the disagreement seems to lie, at least some of the time. (There are also the occasional racist and sexist socialists. I hear they're active on Twitter . . .) In a persuasive 2016 *Jacobin* essay,[45] contributor Kate Robinson describes how her disillusionment with privilege-centric pop-culture criticism as a means of social change wound up leading her to socialism: "While it's undeniable that all kinds of people are capable of enacting oppression, the idea that everyone is automatically complicit in oppressive systems by virtue of living within them can have ugly implications." This realization, she explains, left her believing that "the best way to change people's behavior is to attack the systems that force them into competition, and that the material self-interest of the working class is a better motivating principle than concepts of sin and redemption." While she admits the allure of a cultural approach ("I loved to analyze the ideological currents of fiction and saw pop culture as a useful source for illustrating broader issues"), she couldn't ultimately get behind entertainment criticism as a path to actual change.

And as Connor Kilpatrick argues, also in *Jacobin*, in a piece with the excellent headline, "Let Them Eat Privilege," [46] the cultural trappings that make up privilege checklists distract people from their true class interests: "[T]he one-percent concept isn't about a lifestyle or individual consumption habits—a graduate degree and a kale smoothie do not a one-percenter make. It's based on concrete socio-economic relations . . ." Kilpatrick also makes the useful point (similar to one I'd made a few years prior, in reference to Charles Murray's "bubble" quiz[47]) that the supposed giveaways that someone is upper class are often nothing of the kind. Some cues may very well announce that someone is middle class rather than poor, while others don't much indicate anything. (If your pumpkin spice latte comes from McDonald's, are you privileged because you are drinking a "latte" or marginalized because you purchased it from "McDonald's"? What if you were just thirsty?)

Kilpatrick wraps up his essay with a plea: "'Check your privilege?' Sure. But for once, let's try checking it against the average hedge fund manager instead of a random Whole Foods shopper."

Now, the generous, or even just reasonable, interpretation of this would be that it's a suggestion that activists focus on economic inequality. That's how I read it, in any case. Yet one could always argue that we're merely witnessing the defensiveness of a Whole Foods regular. Maybe all Kilpatrick's efforts—the graph showing just how stark income inequality really is, the references to French economist Thomas Piketty and other experts in inequality—are nothing more than an attempt by a male writer to keep attention on the one form of injustice that affects him personally, namely that of not being among the nation's wealthiest few. I mean, it *could* be that Kilpatrick has examined the evidence and found "privilege" lacking. It would certainly seem that way from the piece. Yet wouldn't it be so much more fun to speculate about all of his privileges, real or imagined?

"[A] STANCE BASED ON PRIVILEGE": THE CLINTON-SANDERS PRIVILEGE WARS

INITIALLY, IT APPEARED that the Hillary Clinton side had the "privilege" argument sorted out: She was the candidate of choice among many black voters,[48] not to mention the first serious female contender for the presidency. However, the Bernie Sanders side fought back, countering—not entirely unfairly—that Clinton supporters are too rich to want socialism. After all, Clinton swept the posh Upper East Side in the New York primary,[49] and could therefore be cast as the preferred (Democrat) candidate of those with the least to gain, and most to fear, from economic redistribution.

The "privilege" criticism of Clinton was, to some degree, a takedown of her own use of the phrase and framework. A tweet from the candidate's official account, "We need to recognize our privilege and practice humility, rather than assume that our experiences are everyone's experiences.—Hillary," came in for some not-entirely-unjustified YPIS of its own.[50] *Salon* writer Ben Norton responded, "The Clintons made $140 million in the past 8 years, but @HillaryClinton is telling people to check their privilege."[51] In one sense, Norton was changing the subject; Clinton had been talking about *white* privilege. In another, however, he was spot-on.

Critics from the left presented Clinton as the candidate of the new, fashionable, symbolism-driven liberalism, with Sanders representing a true progressivism rooted in the fight for socioeconomic justice. On the *Medium* Web site, in a piece called "Please Recognize Your Privilege If You Can Afford Eight Years of Hillary Clinton and the Status Quo," Tony Brasunas wrote, "Some people say Bernie Sanders and Hillary Clinton are approximately the same on the issues. These people likely have a lifestyle and a level of income that is comfortable and that they're not too worried about losing."[52] Kilpatrick, also a Sanders supporter, tweeted, "If a liberal says 'mere *economic*' issues, close your eyes and you can probably see the upper middle class household he or she grew up in."[53] Later, calling out a specific, older female journalist, he tweeted, "If a journalist shrugs off free college & $15 min wage, I'm sure they wouldn't mind stating their income/assets/Manhattan zip in the DEK."[54] His fellow progressive, Freddie deBoer tweeted his criticism of Clinton's supporters as follows: "It takes a position of incredible privilege to think you should vote based on meaningless social signaling rather than on actual policy."[55] While rejecting the frivolity of privilege rhetoric, these Sanders supporters went with another standby: the privilege critique of YPIS. Which is to say, they called out the privilege of those who'd think to make privilege arguments in the first place.

The Clinton side couldn't exactly rebut the accusation that rhetorical progressivism was a cover for center-left policies with an insistence that their candidate was, in fact, the better socialist choice. Instead, what emerged was an argument that insistence on Sanders being the nominee was itself a sign of privilege, because it meant being able to "afford" a Republican president. Once more, from Clinton's official Twitter account: "Some folks may have the luxury to hold out for 'the perfect.' But a lot of Americans are hurting right now and they can't wait for that."[56] Quartz ran a piece called "Privilege Is What Allows Sanders Supporters to Say They'll 'Never' Vote for Clinton," by Melissa Hillman. "How privileged do you need to be," wrote Hillman, "to imagine that it's a good idea to risk the actual lives of vulnerable Americans because you 'hate' Clinton so much that you vow to stay home if Sanders doesn't get the nomination?"[57] Another headline, from *The Guardian*: "Bernie Sanders or Bust? That's a Stance Based on Privilege."[58] In that piece, writer Michael Arceneaux spells out exactly whom he believed this "stance" would harm: "People who refuse to vote for a less-favored Democrat on principle are just punishing a second constituency unlikely to vote: those who know very little about the power they yield because they are so marginalized they feel their say doesn't matter."

Yet the prime target of pro-Clinton YPIS was one particularly enthusiastic (and unusually glamorous) Sanders supporter, the actress Susan Sarandon, who told MSNBC's Chris Hayes that she wouldn't necessarily support Clinton over Trump, seeing as the latter might inspire a "revolution."[59] A *Daily Kos* headline—"Susan Sarandon: A Privileged Fool"—neatly sums up the response.[60] Dan Savage, who also appeared on Hayes's program that day, later explained on his *The Stranger* blog why, in his view, Sarandon's views stemmed from her demographics:

> It's easy for white people with a lot of money to fantasize about what might happen if Donald Trump gets elected . . . because if Trump's election doesn't bring the revolution,

if his election only visits misery on Mexicans, Muslims, African Americans, LGBT Americans, women who get abortions, etc., the wealthy and white can jet off to their homes in France and wait it out.[61]

New York Times columnist Charles Blow went with a more direct privilege accusation: "The comments smacked of petulance and privilege. No member of an American minority group—whether ethnic, racial, queer-identified, immigrant, refugee or poor—would (or should) assume the luxury of uttering such a imbecilic phrase, filled with lust for doom."[62]

That Sarandon is a woman is, apparently, canceled out by her place on other axes of privilege. Meanwhile at *Slate*, writer Michelle Goldberg honed in on Sarandon as an individual: "Inasmuch as #NeverHillary is a phenomenon . . . Sarandon, a rich white celebrity with nothing on the line, is a perfect spokeswoman for it." Goldberg concluded the piece with a most YPIS of parting lines: "No matter what happens, Susan Sarandon will be just fine."[63]

While I must admit I kind of agreed with the Sarandon takedown (we all have our hypocrisies), I found this back-and-forth YPIS-fest alternately hilarious and exhausting. Permit me to quote a tweet of mine from that March: "Amused by/collecting the various 'if you prefer Hillary/Bernie, that demonstrates your enormous privilege' arguments."[64] I wasn't alone in finding that line of argument frustrating: In April 2016, Hayes tweeted the following complaint: "Worst part of D primary: Privileged white ppl telling other privileged white ppl they only hold their views bc they're privileged & white."[65]

The problem with the "privilege" election analyses wasn't that they were wrong. On the contrary, it's that all of them were right. Privilege surely *does* inform political decisions, but in too many directions for it to be possible to label anyone the true *candidate of the privileged*. There were, I suspect, voters who went with Sanders out of misogyny or limousine-liberal obliviousness, as well as others who picked Clinton out of greed. And while the "working-class" status of Trump's supporter base was in dispute,[66] it would be tough to claim that *no* legitimate underdog-type grievances motivated his appeal. In a democracy, any candidate relying solely on the votes of a privileged few is screwed, so politicians do tend to make cases for themselves that appeal to a broader audience. And this doesn't consider the phenomenon of not-rich people voting aspirationally for candidates who promise to help the rich. For all these reasons, it's never possible to claim that support for a particular candidate, on its own, *demonstrates* privilege.

However, the most frustrating aspect of the political "privilege" take is its ability to derail otherwise worthwhile conversations. Rather than hearing about facts, or even opinions, about the issue at hand, one ends up neck-deep in speculation about an individual. Case in point: In *Jacobin*,[67] political scientist and progressive activist Corey Robin tore into a *New Yorker* article by staff writer Alexandra Schwartz, a Clinton supporter who'd claimed that young voters were misguided for supporting Sanders.[68] The missing piece in Schwartz's article had been *free college*, and therefore an end to student debt—something Robin rightly pointed out.

Schwartz's central observation—that young people are idealistic, older ones pragmatic—wasn't especially out there, but wasn't helped by her openness about being "a voter north of twenty-five, south of thirty," which is to say, *not old*. While this made sense to note in the context of the piece—she was pointing out an intragenerational divide—this sort of assertion sets off the reader's alarm bells: This person is under thirty and works at *The New Yorker*. Is life fair? Why no, it's not.

So it's maybe not so surprising that she met with a YPIS. Which is where Robin, after making a more substantive defense of Sanders, turns:

What really strikes the reader is just how removed
Schwartz is from the experiences of her generation, how
utterly clueless she is about the economic hardships so
many young men and women face today.

So far, fair enough. Schwartz wrote from a first-person perspective, mentioning her age. If you dismiss economic inequality
concerns as *so last season,* you have an "utterly clueless" coming to
you.

However, Robin didn't leave it at that. Instead, we get treated to
a mini biography of Schwartz, who is, it would seem, kind of posh:

It's true that Schwartz graduated from the tony Brearley
School in Manhattan (annual tuition: $43,000) in 2005 and
Yale (annual tuition, fees, and costs: $65,000) in 2009,
whereupon, after a few detours, she landed a spot at
The New Yorker, from which she reports on Paris (cost:
priceless).

After establishing Schwartz's fanciness (well, presumed fanciness; for all we know, she had scholarships throughout her education),
he moves on to painting a broader portrait of her and her life, as he
imagines it:

But does she have no friends or relatives who are
struggling with student debt, low-paying or nonexistent
jobs? Has she not read an American newspaper or
magazine in the last twelve months? Is the cognitive
divide between the haves and the have-nots that stark,
that extreme?

And it's there that he lost me. Since when is reporting on Paris
for *The New Yorker* a luxury good? (Which is, after all, what the

context—and MasterCard ad reference[69]—suggests.) It's an enviable situation, but why assume it wasn't earned?

Left unstated: Who, exactly, is Corey Robin in all of this? In the piece in question, he never says. Its voice is that of an omniscient, disembodied progressive, who forms opinions merely based on what would be the best for society's most downtrodden. We might assume, from his remarks about Brearley and so forth, that he grew up deprived, and is nursing understandable resentments at Schwartz's presumed trajectory.

Having once written a profile on Robin,[70] I did not have to google his bio, but his publicly known, readily searchable demographic categories in this area would put him at the same scrappiness level as that of the journalist whose background he'd just gotcha'd. He grew up in Chappaqua, a posh suburb of New York (and home of the Clintons), and went to Princeton for college, Yale for graduate school. Chappaqua-Princeton-Yale is effectively the same thing as Brearley-Yale-*The New Yorker*.

Is Robin privileged? Yes. Is Schwartz? Yes. I say this not to YPIS them—I share their demographics—but to point out the absurdity of one YPISing the other. It doesn't make sense to dismiss someone else's argument on the basis of his or her identity if you, the person who thinks otherwise, *share that identity.*

The only YPIS here that could possibly make sense is if Schwartz had responded to Robin by noting (and forgive me for noting this) that it's typically only *female* accomplishment that gets dismissed as privilege. Could it be—and here I only speculate—that the gendered dynamics of who receives privilege call-outs may have helped sway Schwartz in favor of Clinton in the first place? The Twitter shaming of journalist Jill Filipovic, who tweeted about getting accused of privilege for . . . reporting from abroad, provides another example.[71] If referring to a man, *foreign correspondent* evokes swagger and a sense of adventure. Meanwhile, a woman reporting from abroad stands accused of being, in effect, on vacation.

Here's what I, a Clinton supporter who agreed with parts of Sanders's platform, his stance on college tuition in particular, found so frustrating: Robin could have just defended the goal of free college, the part of Sanders's plan most relevant to his point. He could have cited the flaws in Schwartz's argument, and noted that her claims about the "staleness" of economic-inequality rhetoric were way off. Why the need to paint the author as a brat? What does that add? Even if we had hard figures on Schwartz's family wealth—which we don't—who cares?

Free college is a plausible goal, at least compared with a society free of individual cluelessness. Yet Robin—elsewhere a critic of the "privilege" approach (see chapter 5)—winds up going with the cluelessness-fighting strategy, because *that's what's done*. It's no longer enough to point out that someone is wrong, and to be—as Robin is, in this case—correct. That wrongness needs to be attributed to "privilege."

WHEN GOOD LIBERALS GET YPISED

IN HER OTHERWISE spot-on analysis of "check your privilege," Hadley Freeman described a trajectory according to which the accusation "stopped being a calm, thoughtful and still faintly academic phrase, and became the subject of ferocious debate." She concluded, "Ultimately, a well-meaning reminder to listen to other people occasionally has been turned into an angry cliche through misunderstanding, mockery and overuse."[72] When, I wondered when reading Freeman's piece, was the golden age of respectful YPIS? As I understand it, *privilege* once had that nuanced, reasoned use, but once *checking* started to enter into it—certainly once the "your" got involved—the problems with it began.

With the exception of far-left, from-the-left quibblers, liberals often embrace the privilege framework as a way to understand society, and as a tool for self-reflection. What the mainstream left is less sure about is the privilege call-out. In principle, it's a way of telling someone to reflect on how their identity may have impacted their worldview, and to give the proverbial subaltern a chance to get a word in. In principle, YPIS increases empathy. But in practice?

According to those who support its use, YPIS is only received as an insult because people find it upsetting to confront their privilege. People don't like hearing about their unearned advantages. That's because everyone likes to feel self-made, so learning that you're not can be a letdown. That, and it stings to hear that you're benefiting from an unjust system. Yes, YPIS is criticism, and no one wants to be told they've said something ignorant or insensitive. Yet maybe people who've been ignorant and insensitive deserve to have their feathers ruffled! Why be so sensitive to the feelings of the privileged, while letting them trample on those of the marginalized? As Midlane put it, in an anti-YPIS piece in the *New Statesman*, "Privilege becomes an inescapable feedback loop: any attempt to critique privilege-checking is met with the retort: 'You're privileged enough to have the luxury not to think about privilege.'"[73] The assumption, then, is that the person getting YPISed is in fact privileged, and that their resistance to YPIS is simply a matter of resistance to hearing about it.

Wounded feelings and #whitetears do, without a doubt, enter into it. Yet there are also other, more sympathetic reasons YPIS often angers its reasonably-good-person recipients. Separate even from the question of call-outs (that is, of whether there's value in telling someone they've said something inadvertently bigoted), there's the way that "privilege" obscures what, exactly, has caused offense, and to whom. There's a specific frustration in being accused of something ambiguous. Telling someone that they've been sexist or racist actually points that person to the issue at hand. Activist phrases like "Black Lives Matter" inspire their share of defensiveness, but it's tough to argue that the backlash they inspire is a result of genuine confusion over what the phrase means. (Nowhere does the expression state that other lives *don't* matter.) YPIS, on the contrary, puts the burden on the person being criticized to figure out *why*. And even if you can guess from the context which sort of privilege is being referenced, that the accusation is "privilege" obscures what might possibly be done in response. It starts to look as if what's being demanded isn't something doable (switching to up-to-date identity terminology, say), but some kind of single-handed overhaul of how society operates. The framework dooms the "privileged" to fail, to say the wrong thing, and to go on doing so indefinitely. The hand-wringing, defensive, awkward response is inevitable given the nature of the accusation.

The dynamic I've just described assumes that the recipient of a YPIS is in fact privileged in the manner accused. Which is, alas, not always the case. In her entry to *Slate's* "outrage" series, Amanda Hess told the story of a fellow journalist who went moderately viral for her alleged white privilege. Alleged, that is, because this journalist happens to be black: "With a few assumptions and a quick Photoshop job, even a black woman complaining about a white dude on the bongos can be framed as an emblem of white entitlement."[74] As Hess explains, the bongos complaint had been interpreted—willfully misinterpreted, it seems—as being from a white gentrifier who wanted black existing residents to keep the noise level down. That made for a better story, so some YPISers went with it, unmoved by this pertinent new information about the identity of the accused.

The YPIS call-out is shorthand for another: the surely-you've-never. The classic of these would be a "surely you've never worked in food service," to someone who thinks tipping isn't necessary.[75] And one flaw of the surely-you've-never is that often enough, the accused actually *has*. Plenty of rich people have, at one point in their lives, worked as servers (or falafel cashiers). Once you get into the business of announcing, with confidence, what strangers on the Internet have and haven't experienced, you risk being wrong. Take the case of late-April 2016's YPISed villain, Brandon Friedman. Friedman, a CEO, tweeted the following: "Looking at intern resumes. Having college kids describe their work experience is such a waste of time. The restaurant job isn't helping."[76] While there are more charitable interpretations possible (maybe), it seemed as if he was saying that students who need to pay their own ways through school aren't worthy of a professional internship. The tweet got called out—and not unreasonably so—by many, including Soledad O'Brien, a journalist with hundreds of thousands of Twitter followers.[77] Much of the response was a painstaking attempt at getting Friedman to understand why his remark was so off the mark. However, at least one Twitter user made it personal: "Sounds like you never worked a job in college."[78] To which Friedman responded, "I worked in a scrap yard cutting copper ends off AC cooler cores with a blowtorch in 100+ degree heat in Louisiana."[79] In doing so, Friedman won a battle, but an altogether irrelevant one. The conversation should never have been about his background to begin with. It's a problem if employers reject entry-level applicants for service-industry experience, no matter the socioeconomic origins (or selectively chosen biographical details) of those employers. YPIS allows the accused to dismiss other, more constructive criticism of his or her ideas. Rather than convincing a bad tipper to be more generous, if you reach for the surely-you've-never, you're asking to lose the argument on a technicality.

Yet the surely-you've-never can be even more counterproductive. Offering up an accusatory guess that someone has never been seriously ill or obese, or that they've never had financial troubles, is a way of putting someone on the spot to reveal things they might not have wanted to. Technically, this point hasn't been entirely absent in discussions of YPIS—online writer Flavia Dzodan made a version of it in a 2011 blog comment—but it's not one that generally comes up.[80] YPIS makes it so that all reticence reads as *privilege*. Silence reads as a YPIS doing its good work of making a privileged person uncomfortable. Given how often the reticence comes from the exact opposite situation, the equation of reticence with privilege is a pretty big flaw of YPIS as an activist strategy.

THE ORIGINS OF THE ANTI-YPIS
CRITIQUE

TO THE BEST of my knowledge—that is, going by my blog's archives—I first encountered (and complained about) the YPIS meme in 2008, which may have been in the prememe era, now that I think of it. I wasn't an activist, just a left-leaning French literature grad student with a blog and maybe a bit too much time on my hands. The inspiration for my first YPIS post appears to have come from the response an earlier post I'd written, arguing that interns should be paid. An anonymous commenter had offered the following: "Poor little rich girl."[81] While there were other, more substantive comments (some from known offline quantities), that anonymous comment was the one that stuck. It may have been off-topic, but tapped into *something*—and that something was deeply neurotic. I wasn't even quite sure why I was being called a poor little rich girl. The situation I was discussing was that of unpaid interns at fashion magazines. I'd never been an unpaid intern, at a fashion magazine or anywhere else. (Was *I* even the poor little rich girl, or was the comment a reference to the photo of a crying Lauren Conrad of *The Hills* that illustrated the post I'd linked to?)

Even though I owed "Anonymous" nothing, even though there exists an expression for what not to do in this situation ("Don't feed the trolls"), I was still relatively new at these online exchanges, and was in the throes of the emotions a privilege check can elicit. So I followed up with another post, in which I not only referred to the "poor little rich girl" remark, but confessed my own privilege, specifically the privilege of having taken jobs as an undergrad not out of roof-over-head necessity (that would come after college graduation), but because I wanted pocket money. I did not—and I'm thanking my younger self as I type—go full Falafel Guy and describe my college jobs as an ethnographic exploration of "blue-collar" life (the motivation, for me, was the desire to pay for my own mochas and H&M outfits, and I was never under the impression that shelving books at the University of Chicago library made a person working class). Yet I did nevertheless a) discuss nonhardship motivations for working in one's late teens or early twenties, and b) implicate myself. Had my post made it to a major publication, I, too, might have gone viral for navel-gazing obliviousness.

As for why "poor little rich girl" read to me at that time as a variant of "your privilege is showing," who can say? The meme must have already been floating around. Regrettably, I did not record my first encounter with privilege as a charge, and have no reason to believe the first time I heard it, it was as a recipient.

In any case, my initial impression of YPIS was that it was a way for rich kids to hide that fact about themselves, by highlighting it in others. It seemed like an online version of how, in real life, rich people play up the scrappiness of their backgrounds, while those actually from poorer families than their peers tend not to announce this fact.[82] While adolescents are almost uniformly embarrassed by their families, only poor kids will do things like not have friends over to their apartment. Rich ones, meanwhile, will happily host, but will let you know that when their parents bought the brownstone, prices in that area weren't what they are today.

By 2011, I had a slightly different interpretation, viewing YPIS less as scrappy one-upmanship than as what I called sanctibullying— online pile-ons where the competition was over who could be the most sensitive (as demonstrated by insensitivity to the target of the moment).[83] The YPIS I was talking about wasn't a kind of activism. It wasn't about black women alerting white feminists to intersectionality. It was about posturing and privilege *denial* through privilege accusation.

At that point, apart from some blog commenters who seemed to agree with me, I had little sense that there was any wider objection to

this phenomenon. Then along came a post called "Online Bullying—
A New and Ugly Sport for Liberal Commenters," revised and reis-
sued as a *Guardian* op-ed.[84] Its author, Ariel Meadow Stallings, was
the woman behind "Offbeat Bride" and other "Offbeat" lifestyle
Web sites geared at the alternative-bourgeois demographic. (As in:
"Two tattooed brides and an adorable California spring wedding."[85])
Stallings—to my delight—lamented the phenomenon of "privilege-
checking as a form of internet sport":

> Over the past couple of years, I've watched the rise of
> a new form of online performance art, where liberal
> internet commenters make public sport of flagging
> potentially problematic language as insensitive, and
> gleefully calling out authors as needing to "check their
> privilege" (admit their privileged position within society
> and its associated benefits).

In the piece, Stallings refers to this manifestation of privilege
checking as "a kind of trolling," one that aligns, in principle, with her
politics, but that amounts to "bullying." Some similar objections had,
I've since found, appeared earlier still, in a 2011 Tiger Beatdown post
by Flavia Dzodan.[86] Dzodan had a slightly different take on this than
Stallings: "Call out culture might, at times, dangerously resemble
bullying. However, it is not exactly the same. It certainly shares its
outcome, however, unlike bullying, call out culture is part of the per-
formative aspect of blogging. Unlike bullying, *a call out is intended
for an audience*." So, in essence, the same point—plenty of bullying
(the self-hating homophobic variety comes to mind) is aimed at a
larger public.

More interestingly, for our purposes, Dzodan described a "privilege
checklist game . . . wherein the blogger needs to qualify every opinion
by opening up with disclaimers to constantly prove her situational lived
experience to the point that they can sometimes acquire parody

proportions: 'As a White, cis gender, right handed, myopic only from my left eye, gluten intolerant, middle class double income home owner, left leaning but politically independent woman, I believe Mercedes' performance in Glee was vastly superior to Rachel's'." Dzodan went on to argue—and this was in 2011!—what so many think pieces have more recently critiqued: "Call out culture, a phenomenon that casual readers might not even notice, is to me, the most toxic aspect of blogging."

The most surprisingly viral anti-YPIS essay, "A Note on Call-Out Culture," appeared in 2015 in *Briarpatch* magazine. Surprising, that is, because essays in obscure Canadian journals don't generally get tens of thousands of Facebook shares. In the piece, Asam Ahmad made what was by then a familiar point, about how call-outs are often "a public performance where people can demonstrate their wit or how pure their politics are," adding, "[W]hen people are reduced to their identities of privilege (as white, cisgender, male, etc.) and mocked as such, it means we're treating each other as if our individual social locations *stand in* for the total systems those parts of our identities represent." Hear! Hear! Yet why did this incarnation of the argument hit such a nerve?

While the piece made a number of fine points, the content may gave mattered less than the source. It can't have hurt that Ahmad was identified in the piece's bio as a coordinator of "the It Gets Fatter Project, a body positivity group started by fat queer people of colour," and that an author photo confirmed that Asam met at least two of the three marginalized categories in question.[87] That someone from the deepest reaches of the social-justice movement, an activist who was himself marginalized and not some naïve ally, saw "a mild totalitarian undercurrent not just in call-out culture but also in how progressive communities police and define the bounds of who's *in* and who's *out*" was pretty damning. While Ahmad wasn't the first self-identified social-justice activist to publicly condemn YPIS—Melissa Fong had done so in the previous year—there was just something about this essay that had people thinking, "If even *this dude* thinks this has gotten out of hand . . ."[88]

In his remarks about "a language and terminology that are forever shifting and almost impossible to keep up with," Ahmad hinted at one of the biggest problems with YPIS, namely its exclusivity along precisely the lines it ostensibly opposes. Do you need privilege to talk privilege?

THE PRIVILEGE CRITIQUE OF "PRIVILEGE"

SINCE THE EARLY days of YPIS, critics of the phenomenon have been pointing out that you need spare time and Internet access to even have arguments on the Internet in the first place. However, not long after, more sophisticated arguments along these lines began to emerge. *Atlantic* writer Conor Friedersdorf offered one of the first privilege critiques of "privilege": "[I]f you're among those for whom every matter must be reduced to privilege, consider what happens when your preferred mode of conversation is so complex in its jargon and etiquette that it disadvantages everyone who wasn't socialized into it at liberal arts school."[89] While Friedersdorf leans libertarian, similar criticisms pop up on progressive blogs as well.[90] And Sharon Smith, whose anti-"privilege"-framework arguments have appeared in the *Socialist Worker*, has made a similar, if gentler, point: inaccessible jargon turns away would-be activists.[91] While Smith doesn't say anything about the relative *class* of those who might be confused and thus put off (perhaps trying, as a socialist, not to further divide labor), it's difficult not to jump to Friedersdorf's conclusion.

The "jargon" case against privilege is somewhat persuasive, but misses a key reason why even poor-to-middle-class people initiated in the terminology may resist it. Privileged used to mean "rich," and to a certain extent still does. And if you aren't the commonsense definition of privileged, the accusation is simply *confusing* in a way it's not going to be if you are. As Urquhart notes in her piece about cis privilege, "The word *privilege* just seems to set people off, myself included. I've often thought that the connotation of luxury and ease, of waltzing obliviously through life while others struggle, makes it a word more likely to divide people than improve their empathy for one another."[92] I'd add that "white privilege," far from immediately evoking the advantages held by white people regardless of socio-economic circumstance, suggests the state of being white *and* privileged, that is, of a country-club milieu. Conversations about inequality that are only allowed to conclude once someone admits that they're "privileged" have a way of getting stalled, and it's not necessarily because people don't like admitting to having benefited from injustice. Sometimes the word simply doesn't seem to fit.

However, there are other, even simpler reasons why a "privilege" framework favors the already advantaged. Anyone prepared to own and reject unearned advantage probably has some to spare, and here's a framework that asks people to cop to being haves and to give it all up. If you're already of the mind-set that you have too much—a mind-set shared by approximately five people, and they're all well-off nineteen-year-olds—then you're going to be receptive to the idea that you should give up what you've got.[93] Otherwise, you may need more convincing. "Privilege" encourages a zero-sum approach to bigotry, defining all basic rights and any bare-minimum standard of living as luxurious advantages. In doing so, it ends up appealing most to those whose money and standing in the world are already secure. A better approach would be along the lines that Jamelle Bouie has suggested: "Better to discuss the ways in which racism *hurts them [whites] too*. How their lives are made worse by racial hierarchies."[94] In 2008, President Obama acknowledged a weakness of the privilege approach, noting, "Most working- and middle-class white Americans don't feel that they have been particularly privileged by their race."

From there, he went on to advocate for "all Americans to realize that your dreams do not have to come at the expense of my dreams; that investing in the health, welfare, and education of black and brown and white children will ultimately help all of America prosper."[95] It's truly difficult to see how any approach to fighting injustice whose only reward is the promise of assuaged liberal guilt will be of use in convincing anyone other than those who start out as guilt-drenched liberals.

And on an even more basic level, there's the fact that a prerequisite of being "privilege aware"—that thing that's now come to define the pinnacle of sensitivity—is possessing privilege in the first place. This is why the word "narcissism" comes up in criticisms of privilege checking.[96] Privilege awareness is just one more way of showing off, a kind of abstract version of noting that your green juice is organic.

Writer Maureen O'Connor elaborated on one aspect of this phenomenon in a *New York* magazine piece called "The New Privilege: Loudly Denouncing Your Privilege."[97] O'Connor discussed the "elite populism" of Ivy League graduates who publish books and articles denouncing the Ivy League (while surreptitiously reminding everyone that they went to these schools themselves). While the piece is mainly about elite college graduates specifically, and not "privilege" in a general sense, her point is more broadly applicable:

> [W]aving away your own privilege—and looking with
> disdain upon those who aspire to it—is the most
> old-fashioned form of snobbery. It's Edith Wharton
> characters with austere taste and Dutch last names
> sniffing with disgust at the vulgarity of new money. It's
> the owners of decrepit New England family summer
> homes shaking their heads at encroaching McMansions.

Those at the top have long opposed the flaunting of privilege, as a way of distinguishing themselves from those on society's slightly lower rungs. What's new is that discretion has become the ultimate progressive ideal. It's not just, as O'Connor (correctly) writes, that "an age of anti-elitism" has forced elites to humblebrag. It's also that this curated stance with respect to one's own privilege has become the highest purpose on the left. Thus "your privilege is showing." By all means, be privileged! Just don't let your privilege *show*. It's unclear whether YPIS results in an elite broadly defined more sensitive to the feelings of all of society or whether—and this is what I suspect—it has incorporated a kind of new-media training *into* privilege itself. That is, a new divide is emerging between the people in whom it's ingrained how to avoid saying something YPIS-worthy, and those who are always a few keystrokes away from putting their foot in it.

EVERYTHING IN MODERATION

IT WOULD BE a mistake to dismiss all backlash against YPIS as defensiveness. While much of it probably was, on some level, inspired by personal encounters with the accusation, there are too many substantive problems with YPIS—and "privilege"—to ignore criticism on that basis alone. Some people, however, including some prominent liberals, have conflated the excesses of YPIS with the phenomenon of peons not revering them sufficiently. Some have also arrived at what are essentially right-wing conclusions, rejecting jargon and identity politics offhand.[98]

A spate of books and articles (Jon Ronson's *So You've Been Publicly Shamed*; Jonathan Chait's hit *New York* magazine essay, "Not A Very P.C. Thing To Say";[99] *Slate*'s "2014: The Year of Outrage"[100]; Northwestern professor Laura Kipnis's *Chronicle of Higher Education* quasi manifestos[101]) have offered up a third way of sorts for those who identify as liberal and agree that systemic injustices should be remedied, but find much of what passes for progressive rhetoric these days off-putting and counterproductive. My own sensibilities lie with this cohort, and whenever I read one of these things, I do feel some sense of relief at having found *my people*. A part of me wants to host a dinner party that writers Emily Yoffe and Judith Shulevitz (both skeptics of the new sensitivity) would attend, and to just leave it there. Yet there's something about the way these criticisms end up playing out that makes me wonder whether it's YPIS they're objecting to, or something else entirely.

For example, one big issue with YPIS is that it doesn't differentiate between people who actually have some kind of significant influence—and thus whose unpleasant remarks could actually impact a lot of people—and those who don't. When Nobel-winning biologist Tim Hunt made a public statement to rooms full of journalists widely interpreted as not thinking women should be in the workplace, this was an actual problem. Yes, the word "privilege" came up in the discussion about how he came to hold those views, and in how other men came to support him.[102] But the fundamental issue wasn't Hunt's inner life. It was his worldly impact. Whereas with a Justine Sacco–type situation, what were the stakes of *her* having unchecked privilege? What matters, for the YPIS set, is identifying and calling out errors. What matters is that someone, somewhere, has unchecked privilege; if a million people learn about an incident, however minor, then a million people should by all means flag it on social media.

Unfortunately, many liberal but from-the-right critics of YPIS are imprecise in just the same way. They see outrage, they see the word "privilege," and they immediately know that as members of Team Political Correctness Has Gone Too Far, it's their role to defend the culture of hypersensitivity's latest victim.[103] This imprecision was especially apparent in Chait's article, which dwelled a bit too much on examples of prominent people having their work criticized (but keeping their jobs, status, etc.), a scenario that it would be a stretch to refer to as politically correct silencing:

Two and a half years ago, Hanna Rosin, a liberal journalist and longtime friend, wrote a book called *The End of Men,* which argued that a confluence of social and economic changes left women in a better position going forward than men, who were struggling to adapt to a new postindustrial order. Rosin, a self-identified feminist, has found herself unexpectedly assailed by feminist critics, who found her message of long-term female empowerment complacent and insufficiently concerned with the continuing reality of sexism. One Twitter hashtag, "#RIPpatriarchy," became a label for critics to lampoon her thesis.

He then quotes Rosin on why she now avoids being too controversial on social media: "'The price is too high; you feel like there might be banishment waiting for you.'"

Where's the "banishment"? Even setting aside that hashtag activism *against* a book may help sell copies—a benefit with no real parallel for more typical victims of social-media pile-ons—it seems a mistake to conflate criticism of ideas with criticism of an individual, to conflate criticism (which, even if you're a famous writer and the critic is a pseudonym on Twitter with zero followers, surely always stings) with real influence. Rosin herself would later, in *The Atlantic,* come out against privilege checking, but also, it would seem, against Chait's approach:

Want to avoid a debate? Just tell your opponent to check his privilege. Or tell him he's slut-shaming or victim-blaming, or racist, or sexist, or homophobic, or transphobic, or Islamophobic, or cisphobic, or some other creative term conveying that you are simply too outraged by the argument to actually engage it. Or, on the other side of the coin, accuse him of being the PC thought police and then snap your laptop smugly.[104]

That symmetry is key. It's not as if the left consists of, on the one hand, YPIS-hurling "social-justice warriors" (abbreviated by their detractors as SJW), and on the other, calm and thoughtful free thinkers. If Team YPIS performs outrage and claims to be offended by everything, Team Anti-PC makes equally hyperbolic assertions about witch hunts and pitchforks. One portion of the left finds everything "problematic," while the other finds it problematic that established liberal journalists and academics aren't universally revered by their younger, less-ensconced counterparts.

There was a time when only conservatives would look at jargon on the fringes of academia and the far-left blogosphere and start making apocalyptic predictions. That center-left writers are now throwing fits about university "safe spaces" and "trigger warnings" and other by all accounts silly but marginal phenomena may point to gains being made by the YPIS-ish extreme left. It may also, however, point to the time-honored phenomenon of people moving to the right as they get older. It's hard to avoid thinking that the latter may enter into it when one reads about whichever latest *stalwart* of the left has now had his or her progressive credentials challenged.

Otherwise reasonable liberal (in one sense or another) critiques of YPIS will often segue into takedowns of the few decent things privilege politics have to offer. A *Daily Kos* post that starts off with several helpful points about why the term "white privilege" excludes rather than educates ends up segueing into one suggesting that white men are the real victims.[105] In one follow-up to his big essay, Chait writes, "The most simplistic misunderstanding of p.c. is to imagine it as a form of victimization of white males."[106] In another, he insists that—contrary to view of many critics—he does not feel victimized as a white male, and that wasn't the point.[107] (Just the sort of protest-too-much likely to invite further such accusations.) Yet there's one line—one argument—in the initial essay that gives credence not so much to the idea that *he personally* feels himself to be victimized, but that his definition of YPIS is very much about the victimization of white men: "Under p.c. culture, the same idea can be expressed identically by two people but received differently depending on the race and sex of the individuals doing the expressing." I'm not sure how to interpret this except as an argument that white men are being silenced. There's a branch of anti-YPIS backlash that's really just a complaint about identity politics, and about a new order in which previously marginalized groups have, in some very limited ways, gained more ground.[108]

That said, whether a particular objection to YPIS comes from the left or the right isn't always so straightforward. It's long been a conservative trope to complain that liberals (feminists especially) concern themselves with the relatively minor setbacks experienced by marginalized groups in the West, when the women of Afghanistan, say, have it so much worse and what about *them*, hmm? This has long been recognized on the left as a derailing tactic, one that's basically about trouncing on rights at home (and justifying military interventions abroad). It has also long been a tactic, on the right, to sniff out limousine liberals. Thus a 2011 *Daily Mail* story about "privileged" Occupy Wall Street protestors. ("While they dress down to blend in, the youngsters' privileged backgrounds are revealed by glimpses of expensive gadgetry or the absent minded mention of their private schools during heated political debates."[109])

Yet the privilege turn has led to a dramatic shift away from not just materialist analysis, but even commonsense discussions of injustice. "Privilege" has been broadened to encompass an ever-growing list of ever-more-subtle (or fleeting, or dubious) advantages: Average intelligence is a form of privilege with respect to "genius," a plight a Tumblr user claims to suffer from.[110] There is "monogamous privilege," as though the voluntarily polygamous were an oppressed caste akin to, say, the poor.[111] Do you really have to be a conservative to call this absurd?

I suppose what I'm getting at is that I'm not sure where, politically, I'd put a *New York Observer* op-ed by novelist Sandra Newman, called "Hysterical Activism," which includes the following criticism of today's activists: "If the outsider expresses a dissenting idea, he's invited to 'check your privilege,' which has the weakness of not being an argument."[112] The subhead, "There's Something Pathetic About the Way Social Justice Warriors Would Rather Repel Potential Supporters," could go either way—SJW is a dog whistle, and is generally used only by activists' right-leaning detractors. Yet in the piece, Newman complains as well that activists' techniques are setting back causes she herself cares about. And then there's this privilege critique of privilege, which seems fairly progressive to me:

> The final, and most significant, failure of the social justice movement is in the issues they prioritize. These tend to be the concerns of highly educated people living in affluent liberal enclaves; people, that is, who have never experienced what most people think of as oppression. . . . Even campaigns against racism often foreground microaggressions—to such an extent that it's understandable that a writer at Time magazine, among many others, would take it as a sign that macro racism is a thing of the past. Of course it isn't. These are just the first world problems of the world of inequality. A million incarcerated African-Americans would love to have these problems.

It's perhaps not the best sign about the efficacy of the "privilege" framework that it inspires otherwise progressive sorts to write quasi-reactionary think pieces. Ideologically, "privilege" has built up a kind of conservative-to-center-left coalition, united in the view that activists are Stalinist, and their jargon hilarious.

The backlash to the online "privilege" movement has, on the one hand, pointed out real problems in the discourse. The dynamics that critics of YPIS have described, where everything anyone says has the

potential (however distant) of going viral for perceived obliviousness, is real. Resistance to "privilege" on the far left does not, upon
examination, mirror the conservative rhetoric of focusing on the
socioeconomic as a way of avoiding a discussion of racism (and, by
extension, affirmative action). Rather, a group of people who agree
with the overall goals and diagnoses the privilege framework purportedly addresses have found that conceptualization lacking.

On the other, YPIS's opponents have too often objected for the
wrong reasons, mistakenly conflating YPIS with identity politics or
Oppression Olympics, as though YPIS were about (as in the *Gawker*
parody version) declaring the most marginalized the winners of
arguments. Are the powerful protestors against "privilege" actually
bothered by the silencing of the relatively powerless (that is, fellow
classmates, or strangers online), or are they just annoyed that nobod-
ies on the Internet—or students in their classrooms—are now challenging them? It can, at times, seem as if the backlash is primarily
about defending the right of important people to say the sorts of
things that would get anyone else fired, without even the slight-
est repercussions. A chorus of tremendously loud voices, from high-
up platforms, announcing that they've been silenced by the call-out
culture is maybe not so convincing. The far stronger case against the
privilege turn is the extent to which it has wound up solidifying and
exacerbating existing inequalities. It's that it has, if anything, given
the powerful—the privileged, if you will—even more of a voice.

2

LONELY AT AMHERST

DIVERSITY IN BLOOM

LIFE AT YALE sounds pretty great, at least according to the *Life at Yale*[1] Web site, surely an authority on the matter: "Yale is more than an institution of higher learning; it is a community where people of diverse cultures and nationalities live, work, and play—connected by their similarities and enriched by their differences." Swoon!

Yale, that . . . that *thing* in our culture, that member of the triumvirate that haunts every high-achieving high school student (and every unrealistically ambitious parent of an apathetic one), isn't just a university. It is—going by the Web site—far warmer and far fuzzier than that. A link to the "Arts & Culture" subsection reads, "Discover the countless ways that creativity and diversity bloom on the Yale campus." What does it mean for diversity to "bloom," outside of any botanical context? Whatever it is, it sounds vaguely progressive and upbeat; let's go with it. The "Service" section, meanwhile, is introduced as follows: "Yale community members are dedicated to transforming the world for the better." Translation: These aren't just a bunch of former go-getter high school students who pretended to care about the poor for a few weeks, to check a box on their applications. Alternate translation: Anyone who made the cut is a *good person*; if you don't get in, you may want to consider the possibility that it's because you are not.

Let's skip on over to the "Health & Wellness" section, which is cozier still: "We strive to keep our students, staff, and faculty healthy in every respect." No paltry health insurance, this. We are in the realm of *wellness*, which is, in the context of an elite university Web site, a buzzword evoking Gwyneth Paltrow, green juice, and gratuitous gluten free. Appropriately, the accompanying photo is of a woman, from the back, doing yoga, in a shirt that says—what else?— "Yale" on the back.

My reason for close-reading this Yale online brochure is not that I'm thinking of applying there for college; I think that ship has sailed. It's because it seems as if there might be some sort of relationship between the 2015 student protest movement—the one exemplified by the episode at Yale, where students objected to an administrator's letter in defense of the right to wear offensive Halloween costumes— and life on campus, the real or idealized version.

CAMPUS PROTESTS: FANTASIES AND REALITIES

STUDENT PROTESTS HAVE been going on since forever, but have, in recent years, merged in the popular imagination with preexisting complaints about student hypersensitivity. Versions of that think piece kept appearing; the most notable is probably Greg Lukianoff and Jonathan Haidt's big *Atlantic* story, "The Coddling of the American Mind," which offered a psychological explanation for students' purported belief in "a right not to be offended."[2] Lukianoff, head of the Foundation for Individual Rights in Education (FIRE), an academic free-speech nonprofit, and Haidt, a social psychologist, conferred an air of authority to a question that had already been answered as far as public opinion was concerned. Ask someone with no personal connection to today's college students what they're like, and you're bound to hear something about their outrage-prone ways.

Anyone trying to sum up, in a sentence, what the student protests of the last several years have *actually* been about will come up against a problem: They've been kind of all over the place, location-wise and thematically. Does a Columbia student hauling around a mattress[3] to protest her alleged sexual assault have much in common with Princeton students wishing to rename the Woodrow Wilson School?[4] How much overlap do either of these have with students at the University of Missouri protesting racist incidents on that campus and in the state more generally (that is, in Ferguson)?[5] There have been so many protests that *The Atlantic*—the publication most dedicated to covering the students-these-days beat[6]—published a "cheat sheet" for keeping track of them.[7] A *New York Times* roundup of letters in response to several op-eds about campus protests covers so much ground ("safe spaces"! "use of the N-word"! "the ossification of old norms"!) that it's unclear what, exactly, is being debated, except in the broad sense of, "So, students today, huh?"[8]

The most that can be said is that they fall into three overlapping categories: sexual assault, racial sensitivity, and free speech. The "speech" in question will generally be that of professors, or of prominent invited speakers known for controversial views on topics relating to those first two items. What draws the student protests together, and perhaps separates them from earlier varieties, is the intense focus on improving the schools themselves, and on what the schools can do to fix any problem, big or small, that may arise.

As the brochures suggest, college in the United States today isn't something so banal, so pedestrian, as *school*. Yes, there are classes, professors, and so forth, but it's *so much more*. It's an all-encompassing, *24/7 experience*. And no, I don't mean the continuous landscaping, and the dining halls whose offerings are no longer limited to grayish slop. I'm not talking about the student as consumer, or not only. What these schools are promising is sort of . . . everything. And not "everything" in the sense of what would be provided at a spa. Everything in the sense of, every minute of the day will be spent with people who were, like yourself, handpicked for all-around perfection, as well as for serving some kind of preordained role in the impeccably balanced community. Your peers were not just accepted to college, but *holistically* admitted, their every trait (current and projected) having met the approval of gatekeepers who no doubt went through some sort of rigorous selection process of their own. Your professors are the result of a winnowing system that excludes the vast majority of ostensibly qualified, doctorate-granted candidates. Yet most importantly, an administrative apparatus exists, or seems from brochures as if it would, to make it so that nothing goes wrong. Ever. Every moment will be inspirational. Every facet of your being—mental, physical, spiritual, cultural—will be looked after, and looked after *by your college*. Who needs police, hospitals, or, for that matter, supermarkets? Everything ordinary people avail themselves of—all public and private services—is, for those four-ish years, superfluous. The point is to live in a bubble where everything is taken care of, to an extent that exceeds what would have been the case for just about every high school kid still living at home.

A word about the fact that not all schools are Yale, or, for that matter, its competitors: Nope, they're not. What these schools do, however, is offer a portrait of how everything *should* go, according to the ideals of our age. As in, if money is no object, and if a school can get anyone it wants, what's valued? Another way to put it is that elite schools set the tone. Whether one looks at it as entitlement or empowerment (or simply as misdirected grievances, some more reasonable than others), the fact remains that today's student protests are narrowly tailored requests for their schools to get it, whatever *it* is, right.

While brochure hypocrisy has long been a pet peeve of mine,[9] the notion that the phenomenon might somehow relate to campus unrest is reasonably widespread, if never quite front and center, where it belongs. In a December 2015 *New Yorker* essay,[10] Vassar English professor Hua Hsu speculated that a discrepancy between what schools claim they're offering and what actually happens on campus might be behind the student protests that so dominated the news in that year: "Maybe the efforts of students pushing to fulfill a brochure's promise of community and belonging feel purely symbolic or naïve." Sure enough, in a *Medium* post from the previous month,[11] Yale senior Aaron Z. Lewis offered exactly that assessment:

> [T]he protests are not really about Halloween costumes or a frat party. They're about a mismatch between the Yale we find in admissions brochures and the Yale we experience every day. They're about real experiences with racism on this campus that have gone unacknowledged for far too long. The university sells itself as a welcoming and inclusive place for people of all backgrounds. Unfortunately, it often isn't.

Brochures, though, aren't the whole picture. Universities continue to sell themselves, as it were, to matriculated students as well. Meghan O'Rourke pointed out, also in *The New Yorker*, that the Yale Halloween costume protests were really more about protestors asking for what they were told they'd receive: "When one of those students insisted . . . that 'in [Nicholas Christakis's] position as master' it was his 'job' to create not just an intellectual space but 'a place of comfort and home,' she was simply insisting on the story that Yale itself spun her."[12] O'Rourke presents this as specific to Yale, and to its residential college system. Could be, but I doubt it; one only needs to hop over to yet another *New Yorker* piece, this one by Harvard law professor Jeannie Suk, for examples of home-and-coziness rhetoric elsewhere.[13]

Student entitlement, or hypersensitivity, or whatever one wishes to call it, may be excessive, but it's an excess that universities have invited. It's not only that college costs so much, although that's part of the picture. It's not that the brochures are glossy, or that the gyms are state of the art, although these may enter into it. It's more that what's promised is a progressive utopia, while what's delivered is a system that perpetuates inequality. The "perpetuates inequality" bit wouldn't cause such concern—and wouldn't inspire such seeming overreactions— if students hadn't been told that college would be perfect. The "safe space" fuss is, at its root, about the fact that a safe space was *promised*. Sexual assault—tragic under any circumstances—becomes that much more shocking when students have been told that they and their classmates were hand-selected for character.[14] How can someone who made the holistic cut be a rapist? The campus sexual-assault *crisis* is in the fact that it happens at all; that rape is less common on campus than off is irrelevant. So, too, with racism. Are there more dire questions in American racism today than comments three young black women at Harvard have received about their hair?[15] I should think so. Yet small-scale racism is still racism, and, in principle, a school like Harvard couldn't possibly have any.

"PRIVILEGE" ON CAMPUS

WHAT'S RILING TO today's progressive college students is hypocrisy. Privilege awareness so often serves as a cover for a system that actually perpetuates inequality. The scholarly examination of inequality coexists with, and obscures, the fact that it costs $70,000 a year to be sitting in the seminar room contemplating life's unfairness in the first place. Academia remains as hierarchy obsessed as ever, and with white men still at the helm. Yet seminar classes pore over theories of power imbalance and symbolic "violence." Having been in such classes, it seems to me at the very least *possible* that this is where a lot of the campus radicalism one hears about is coming from. That is, it's not that campuses are the most racist and tragic places in America. Far from it. However, they're the only places claiming to be havens from life's ills.

The possibility that these schools are overpromising—and that the solution is simply that they need to promise *less*—never seems to come up. Or maybe it does, but in a very roundabout way, through objections to the student-as-consumer setup, like when Freddie deBoer writes:

> If students have adopted a litigious approach to regulating campus life, they are only working within the culture that colleges have built for them. When your environment so deeply resembles a Fortune 500 company, it makes sense to take every complaint straight to H.R.[16]

However, the answer is always, somehow, that the university must do *more*. Not necessarily *spend* more, but offer a finer product. DeBoer frames his *New York Times* piece about the university's "corporate" turn around Purdue University's decision to replace a garden with an expanded "research park" (hardly a luxurious amenity, but apparently a problem because it wouldn't interest undergrads), which is sad, in his view, because he finds the garden charming. This romantic notion of the university amounts to almost the same thing. David Brooks, in a column musing on the flaws of the modern university, suggests that schools need to "foster transcendent experiences."[17]

All too often, though, as deBoer and others point out, attempts to address college inequality—on campus, and at the level of admissions—are quite pricey. I'm thinking of Brown's controversial[18] decision to answer student unrest by spending $100 million on increased privilege-awareness efforts.[19] Moves like Brown's not only serve to alert marginalized students to their marginalization, but also add (indirectly but still) to the cost of college. If the aim is increasing accessibility, adding a Center for Niceness, or whatever, may not be the best way.

And while I think they overestimated student fragility (and more on why in a moment), Lukianoff and Haidt were correct in placing the blame on the schools themselves. Yet they, too, fall into the trap of assuming this is a problem that could be solved via further administrative intervention:

> Teaching students to avoid giving unintentional offense
> is a worthy goal, especially when the students come
> from many different cultural backgrounds. But students
> should also be taught how to live in a world full of
> potential offenses. Why not teach incoming students
> how to practice cognitive behavioral therapy?

Or: Why not teach incoming students? (Period. The end.) What if all the angst (and I'm including the adult angst over purported student angst) stems from the college as an impossibly ideal experience?

THE IVORY DILDO

IN A YEAR-END roundup, Karin Agness of *Forbes* asks readers to "consider the ten most ridiculous student protests of 2015."[20] The examples she lists tilt toward the titillating, or visual. What they are not—not uniformly, at least—is "ridiculous." A "free-the-nipple" gender-equality protest does sound silly. But is a protest for "tuition-free public college" all that hilarious? Idealistic, sure, but by that standard, what *is* an acceptable student protest? She brings up the Oberlin cafeteria food "cultural appropriation" episode, wherein uninspired Asian-fusion dining hall dishes got recast as a microaggression against Asian students. One can debate whether students who make such demands deserve a public shaming, but it's clear enough that this would fit the "ridiculous" bill. Yet how about "UT Austin Students Protest[ing] Concealed Carry with Dildos"? The university allows guns in classrooms, but not sex toys, which suggests that the school itself needs the reality check. Unfortunately for Agness's argument, the protestors make a good point. Yes, yes, dildos, *hilarious*, but the absurdity would seem to be allowing guns in classrooms in the first place. ("Trigger warnings," indeed.) If the height of student entitlement is that time when students wanted to go to class without getting shot, it would seem that the panic over student hypersensitivity isn't entirely justified.

Despite its timely framing, Agness's top ten reads as a throwback to a simpler time on the campus-criticism landscape: the conservative critique of education.[21] In *my* day—which is to say, when I was just out of college, so 2007-ish—the big thing was for right-wing writers to churn out fountain-penned screeds against the pool of decadence that higher ed had, in their view, become. These concerns were rooted in wider political debates, and had only a tenuous connection to actual college students. Those discussing student crises tended not to have any particular stake in the topic (that is, academia), beyond a vague gesture at the importance of Great Books (or, conversely, of learning something practical), and a desire not to see the youth corrupted.

In 2011—after the arrival of "privilege," but before the latest round of student protests—Joseph Epstein, the conservative cultural critic and emeritus Northwestern English lecturer, wrote a *Weekly Standard* essay riffing on *that* moment's college dildo scandal.[22] Much of what's changed in the past few years—not on campus, but in media discussions of college life—comes through if we lay these two dildo-gates side by side.

The episode in question seemed tailor-made to fit with what right-wing commentators on academia had long feared, or excitedly imagined: Northwestern professor J. Michael Bailey had hosted a live sex-toy demonstration for his undergraduate class. Not *in* class, but as an optional after-class activity, perhaps not the best idea. While not entirely unprecedented—remember the sex-demo-as-lecture scene from *Monty Python's The Meaning of Life?*—it was certainly *odd*, and noted in the media as such.[23] The demonstration seems to have involved a naked woman, a (clothed?) man, and something called a fucksaw, which—contrary to what the name would suggest—can apparently bring a woman to orgasm. Outrage wasn't universal; Joseph Bernstein defended the dildo prof, and class, in *The Awl*.[24] But—lest this need stating—you don't have to be all apocalyptic about the state of academia to think that maybe a "fucksaw" demonstration for undergrads is not why you sent your kids to college. It also wasn't representative of anything. Not of college courses, nor of "studies" or otherwise newfangled disciplinary areas. Not even of this professor's human sexuality class. Yet that didn't stop Epstein from using the episode as a starting point for a wholesale condemnation of modern campus life.

At the time,[25] I read Epstein's essay as a greatest hits of the conservative critique of education, touching upon all the key tropes. (Sample sentence: "Who is to say that the films of Steven Spielberg are less important than the plays of Shakespeare, or for that matter that Shakespeare himself wasn't gay and a running dog of capitalism into the bargain?") Which is why I think it's useful to look at where his grievances differ from today's. And oh do they ever!

Epstein's article amounts to a case for limiting campus speech. His first non-dildo-related grievance is with Northwestern's president, over the school's pick for commencement speaker. (Stephen Colbert. Not serious enough.) Yes, that's right—a conservative protesting a commencement speaker! Next, Epstein moseys on over to the topic of student-professor romance, which he is unequivocally against: "Does sleeping with one's undergraduate students come under the shield of academic freedom, or was it instead an academic perk, or ought it, again, to be admonished, if not punished by dismissal?" Approving of such relationships is, he seems to be saying, something *liberal* professors do. How far, indeed, from the conservative rush in 2015 to defend Laura Kipnis, another Northwestern professor, when an article she wrote in *The Chronicle of Higher Education*, defending professors who sleep with their students, inspired student protests.[26]

In the heyday of the conservative critique of education, the students were the sacred innocents, and the professors, the villains. Two clichés dominated this period: the maligned (probably male) conservative student, bringing underappreciated ideological diversity to campus; and the naïve coed (think *I Am Charlotte Simmons*), dreaming of a boyfriend-turned-husband but stuck coming of age in the era of hook-up culture. Today, students themselves are the shared enemy of conservative critics of academia (who are very much still around, giddily declaring the campus *worse than ever*[27]) and a fairly wide coalition of moderates, liberals, center-left, and contrarian-left sorts. (Defenses of Kipnis spanned the *National Review* all the way over to *The Nation*.[28]) A range of at times contradictory, complaints about college students have emerged, creating a portrait of student as consumer, student as victim. The radical, 1960s-relic professor is no longer this menacing brainwasher, but is instead the *true* victim. Yes, quite possibly of his or her own ideology, but there's surprisingly little I-told-you-so to go around. Something has shifted, because today's puritanical students (that is, the subset of students who are vocally puritanical) often identify as progressives, while from-the-left critics of liberalism, as well as conservatives, wind up siding with the profs.

If I've been suspicious of this latest campus-crisis narrative (and, spoiler alert, I have been[29]), it's partly because I've taught hundreds of undergraduates (at New York University and the University of

Toronto) on and off throughout the era of supposed disaster, and apart from the usual unhappiness over not everyone being able to get an A, I haven't found the students all that sensitive or entitled. (I know, *NYU!*) I kept waiting for the spoiled-and-pampered brigade to appear, but it didn't happen. I move in academic circles as much as the next PhD with an academic spouse, which means my friends and acquaintances span plenty of universities and disciplines, and even so, my knowledge of mandatory "trigger warnings" and so forth comes from op-eds, not anecdotes.

My skepticism derives from the campus pseudocrises of the early 2000s, my own college years. Specifically, I remember the near-complete lack of overlap between what I'd read was happening on campus, and what either my friends at other schools or I experienced. Canonical texts were still assigned, and the much-hyped "hook-up culture" hadn't supplanted dating or monogamous pairing off. (Or, for that matter, chastity, voluntary or otherwise. It was not unheard-of for college students to remain virgins at graduation.[30]) A "crisis" served political ends once; why not once more? The conservative critics of academia (I've gone with CCOAs, an acronym to convey the seriousness of their endeavor) built the student-crisis story; today, a far broader coalition lends its support.

Evidence also, initially at least, looked scant. The quantitative information available on the topic—principally a 2015 National Coalition Against Censorship (NCAC) survey, suggests that the prevalence of the trigger warning, while implicating more than one student, isn't terribly extensive:

> Although fewer than 1% of survey participants reported that their institution had adopted a policy on trigger warnings, 7.5% reported that students had initiated efforts to *require* trigger warnings on campus, twice as many (15%) reported that students had *requested* warnings

in their courses, and 12% reported that students had complained about the absence of trigger warnings.[31]

I'd pause on that "fewer than 1%" bit, and keep it front and center when trying to sort out whether free speech on campus is kaput.

THE GLIMMER OF TRUTH BENEATH THE SEA OF PANIC

IF YOU WERE hoping to read about campus PC run amok, you will be disappointed. But the culture does, indeed, shift over time, and at least some of today's students have bought into a "privilege" worldview, if not necessarily full-on anti-"privilege" activism. A 2015 Pew survey showing that far more millennials than students of earlier generations, want the government to ban speech offensive to minorities suggests that speech concerns are grounded in *something*.[32] Another survey, released in 2016, found today's college freshmen "more likely to participate in a student-led protest than each of the nearly five decades of classes that preceded them," as *The Chronicle of Higher Education* put it.[33]

And then there was the mess at Wesleyan,[34] where, as the *Jezebel* headline bluntly put it, the "Student Government Retaliate[d] for Dumb Op-Ed By Dramatically Slashing Newspaper Funding."[35] The episode—which involved one student writing an op-ed critical of Black Lives Matter, and more than a hundred petition signers boycotting the publication—was plainly awful.

Regardless, whether or not the amount of "awful" is as great as some imagine, it matters that universities themselves are taking these complaints seriously, which they are (and which they have to be, given the media attention), both by restating commitments to free speech[36] and by ramping up sensitivity efforts.[37] There's also a self-fulfilling prophecy. The NCAC survey informs that "[w]hile there were widespread expressions of concern and respect for students, nearly half of respondents (45%) think trigger warnings have or will have a negative effect on classroom dynamics and 62% think they have or will have a negative effect on academic freedom." Maybe there's an epidemic of *professorial* hypersensitivity, but that, too, seems important.

WHERE THE PRIVILEGED STUDY "PRIVILEGE"

THE "PRIVILEGE" WARS all seem to stem, in one way or another, from the campus: from Peggy McIntosh, privilege awakening Wellesley women and Brearley girls, to Tal Fortgang, the Princeton undergrad whose privilege was checked one too many times. The concept comes out of academia and—as the prevalence of campus "privilege" education suggests—continues to be popular among students as well.[38] And the juxtaposition of so much *have-ishness* with so much talk of deprivation makes elite-campus privilege controversies easy targets for hypocrisy call-outs[39] as well as more lighthearted mockery; for a mix of both, check out the *South Park* episode about a (white) frat obsessed with privilege checking.[40] What was so great about that bit was that it didn't simply showcase campus PC, but slyly emphasized the extent to which self-righteous bullies share demographic categories with their less noble-minded equivalents.

And now, a disclaimer. Not a privilege disclaimer, but a can't-cover-everything one.

There are approximately a trillion things to say about the place of privilege and "privilege" in academia, and I have, by necessity, not addressed all of them. There are "privilege" controversies within scholarship, such as the question of whether sociologist Alice Goffman is fully aware of hers, but in a discipline-specific sense that only somewhat overlaps with popular understandings of "privilege." (As writer Gideon Lewis-Kraus explained in a *New York Times Magazine* feature, "Above all, what frustrated her critics was the fact that she was a well-off, expensively educated white woman who wrote about the lives of poor black men without expending a lot of time or energy on what the field refers to as 'positionality'—in this case, on an accounting of her own privilege."[41])

Debates about the academic profession are also sometimes YPIS-fests. In a (public) Facebook post sharing a *Chronicle of Higher Education* piece[42] he'd cowritten with a fellow prof, Penn State literature professor Michael Bérubé wrote, "Jennifer Ruth and I have a new essay up, and I am glad to see that it took only half an hour for someone to complain that we are 'privileged.' (True! But apparently we forgot to check.)"[43] In that context, "privileged" is less (directly) about unearned advantage, and more a criticism of the academic hierarchy itself, where tenured professors enjoy vastly higher pay and better job security than other college instructors. A mini-controversy also erupted surrounding a Princeton professor who nobly publicized his "CV of failures," a document[44] confessing to such shameful moments as the times when *Harvard* turned him down. Did this professor get called out for privilege? Why yes he did.[45]

As for the place of privilege in higher ed—that is, the extent to which colleges just replicate the existing social structure—there's a ton out there already, plenty more that should be further researched and explored, but it's a bit late in the game for another piece of writing whose purpose is to announce that "college educated" functions as a proxy for middle class, "Ivy League educated" for upper middle or upper class. What's more relevant for our purposes is the way that the idea of "privilege" guides the student experience from even before students arrive on campus. When I was neck-deep in what sure felt like every facet of this topic, I kept getting drawn to the college-admissions angle. Everything's sort of set up to be *about* "privilege." It's built into the way the schools are, at this point, designed.

THE SEMINAR-TUMBLR CONNECTION

MY OWN OVERT introduction to the concept of privilege—although it beats me if the word itself was used—was almost certainly during my freshman year at the University of Chicago, where I took a course called "Power, Identity, and Resistance"—one of the options in the famed core curriculum—and read what Foucault, Bourdieu, and other gentlemen of a Caucasian persuasion had to say about life's systemic and microscopic unfairnesses . . . as interpreted by professors and instructors who were themselves, as I recall, of those same demographics. There's little reason to believe that either of these details—the "oppression" course, or the faculty's identity categories[46]—have much changed since I graduated from college in 2005, or French literature grad school in 2013. Concepts like "cultural capital"—or the idea that anything mildly unpleasant ought to be labeled a "violence"—were and are set forth within a deeply hierarchical and dare I say *conservative* structure.

What is new, however, is social media, with its porous link to college life. The result is continuous YPIS in all directions, among college students and at them from the outside, and at their critics. If you don't learn about "privilege" in a seminar room, maybe you will on Tumblr from someone who did. Although the learning goes both ways. In a blog post with the fabulous title, "When Your Curriculum Has Been Tumblrized,"[47] sociologist Tressie McMillan Cottom discusses the impact Tumblr and social-media activism have had on classroom discussions: "[S]tudents are very comfortable talking about 'oppressions', 'intersections', and the macks of them all, 'privilege and microaggressions'." This familiarity with sociological terminology, she explains, has some advantages (students arrive interested in the material), but can lead to confusion when the scholarly definition of these terms doesn't match up with the Tumblr one. (McMillan Cottom compares the two varieties to "scalpels" and "hammers," respectively.) And so, even in courses *about privilege,* a kind of privilege overload sets in: "I have taken to sending some terms on vacation in my class (e.g. privilege) and pulling others out of retirement to play first string for a bit (e.g. power)." Think, for a moment, about what it means that a leading public intellectual and academic who's *involved in social-media activism*—and, not to mention, who happens to be an African American woman—is telling students, gently, to lay off the "privilege" talk.

NO, YOU'RE *PRIVILEGED!*

LIKE ALL CONTEMPORARY culture wars, the question of whether student activists are to be admired or reviled somehow ends up revolving around divergent notions (and exchanged accusations) of privilege. In one interpretation, the students are leaders in the fight against various forms of systemic injustice. They've become aware of privilege,[48] and are damn well going to do something about it! Anyone who doesn't get why students today are worked up—about sexual assault, about debt, about racism from fellow classmates and unfortunately named buildings—is out of touch, and operating on some version of liberalism that may have seemed progressive a zillion years ago, but that is now sort of . . . privileged.

In the other, it's the student protestors and sympathizers who exemplify privilege. After all, there are worse plights in the world than being young and American and in higher education. That, and the fact that the specific concerns raised are sometimes comically minute. Agness concludes her 2015 protest roundup with a privilege critique: "What all of these campus protests have in common is that they demonstrate just how out-of-touch college students are with how the world works beyond the college bubble," adding, "Here's hoping that these protesting college students become more self-aware in 2016." Finally, the schools whose crises make the news tend to be elite liberal arts colleges or Ivy League universities. The more privileged the student body, and the more micro the aggression, the more likely we are, it seems, to hear about it.

Critics of the recent student activism have flipped the "privilege" script, pointing out that anything Ivy League students are complaining about is pretty much by definition first-world problems. Writer Meghan Daum, for example, took to the *Los Angeles Times* to YPIS Columbia's sexual-assault protests:

> Why is Mattress Girl generating more headlines and
> postings than the victims of Boko Haram? Why (other
> than the usual vagaries of the class divide) are so many
> young women ignorant of the big picture captured by the
> FBI's Uniform Crime Reporting stats—that if you lived
> in, say, Gallup, N.M., in 2013 you were 47 times more likely
> to get raped than if you were enrolled at Harvard?[49]

While she also found space in the very same piece to mock privilege rhetoric ("just as we are told not to 'privilege' one kind of trauma over another, any suggestion that young American activists might want to also focus on traumas other than their own probably will be dismissed as schoolmarmish finger-wagging"), the point about Boko Haram is about as YPIS as it gets.

In an *Atlantic* piece, Conor Friedersdorf, meanwhile, offers the following, in reference to the Yale-Halloween situation:

> These are young people who live in safe, heated buildings
> with two Steinway grand pianos, an indoor basketball
> court, a courtyard with hammocks and picnic tables, a
> computer lab, a dance studio, a gym, a movie theater,
> a film-editing lab, billiard tables, an art gallery, and four
> music practice rooms. But they can't bear this setting that
> millions of people would risk their lives to inhabit because
> one woman wrote an email that hurt their feelings?[50]

The essay that passage comes from, "The New Intolerance of Student Activism," built upon an argument he'd been making (and that I've been discussing with him[51]) for some time. In 2014, he spoke out against some privilege-awareness training provided to Harvard public policy grad students. Specifically, Friedersdorf pointed out that as nice as it is to sort out who stands where *among Harvard students*, these are people who are all, by definition, vastly ahead of the general population.[52] The gulf between Harvard students and everyone else, he suggests in that piece, is the big picture.

So which is it? Whose privilege is most in need of a righteous takedown, the students' or society's?

As is so often the case with such matters, both interpretations are correct. Yes, there's something absurd about having "privilege" wars on elite college campuses, which are places where "class conflict" gets defined as the troubles of upper-middle-class kids who are made to feel poor. (As an example, see conservative columnist Ross Douthat's presciently titled 2005 memoir, *Privilege: Harvard and the Education of the Ruling Class*, which explores the obstacles faced by a somewhat-privileged kid among hyperrich classmates.) Indeed, one of the main problems with "privilege" is that it's a framework often geared toward the sensitivities of people who are, as things go, doing just fine. A caption to a *New York Times* photograph of an Amherst student apparently critical of campus life (but not otherwise mentioned in the article itself) reads, "A Latina sophomore . . . said she could feel lonely."[53] Could the same not be said of every college sophomore, or, for that matter, every human being? That Amherst has failed to successfully eliminate *loneliness* is somehow more out-there as a complaint than the already objectionable student-activist concerns mentioned in the article itself. (Such as: "They wanted students who had posted 'Free Speech' and 'All Lives Matter' posters to go through 'extensive training for racial and cultural competency' and possibly discipline.") There's reluctance even on the part of some of the protestors' supporters to put too much weight on their concerns.

In a *Harper's Magazine* piece that's ultimately sympathetic to student protestors,[54] the writer Wesley Yang admits, "The theory of microaggression can't help but seem to me mostly an indicator of how radically devoid of other threats our lives in America have become—at least in the fortunate part of the country where people go to college." The privilege lens, which guides many of today's student complaints, is worth condemning, and is, in some intrinsic way, associated with higher ed, and with elite schools especially.

However, I don't think it's helpful to dismiss the student protestors themselves as "privileged." That meme, which mainly took off on the right, with less nuance than Daum or Friedersdorf brought to the topic, has all the same flaws as YPIS on the left. Why, I asked at the time, [55] are we talking about the students' identities, and not their arguments? In a *New York Times Magazine* essay about the concept of "resilience,"[56] Parul Sehgal brought up Friedersdorf's "pianos" remark and criticized him for "assuming that an atmosphere of wealth should inoculate you from experiencing racism." Aaron Z. Lewis, a Yale senior, took the entirely sensible point further: "I've heard a lot of people dismiss this situation out of hand because Yale is a 'place of privilege.' But if racial discrimination of any kind can happen at a place like this, then it's certainly happening elsewhere in this country."[57] Those protesting a lack of one form of "privilege" are likely to have more than their share of another. That's who has a platform.

It also seems worth mentioning that some students at Yale and the like *don't* come from privilege. Many "inclusivity"-type concerns are coming from the (handful of) students at these schools who are first generation in college or working class. While there are, as I've argued, some major problems with thinking *increased privilege awareness* is what will help the students in question,[58] it's important for schools to remember that these students exist, and not to fall into the trap of classifying those rare instances of upward mobility as "privilege."

In a sense, the "privilege" critique was tailor-made for intergenerational conflicts. When were the young *not* chastised for being spoiled ingrates? And when were the old *not* taken to task for having drifted to the right, to the establishment?

ON THE RIGHT TO BE YOUNG AND FOOLISH IN PRIVATE

IF THERE'S ANY consensus, it would seem to be over the necessity of commenting on campus trivia. Which is unfortunate. As Daum herself notes, it's entirely possible that "when these women aren't protesting the overrepresentation of white male authors in their classics curricula, they're volunteering at inner-city domestic violence shelters or developing global strategies to empower women in the developing world." So shouldn't the issue be *media coverage*, and not the priorities of campus feminists?

On that note, a third way has emerged in response to the outrage on all sides. Some have argued—and they have a point—that we shouldn't be putting students in the spotlight in the first place. In a *New Inquiry* piece, "Against Student Stories," writer and academic Aaron Bady discussed an article in the Duke student paper that wound up going viral in the way that articles now do: via a sea of hot-take-infused aggregation, which Bady helpfully illustrates with snapshots of those near-interchangeable headlines.[59] A Duke University *Chronicle* article about one Christian student's reluctance to read a lesbian-themed graphic novel became a national news story about how Duke students, or just "students," were hypersensitive religious freaks. No, but it made for good content. In a *New Yorker* essay I mentioned above, writer and Vassar professor Hua Hsu's "The Year of the Imaginary College Student,"[60] a similar picture emerges. Hsu writes about the "archetype" that the media keeps bashing: "The imaginary college student is a character born of someone else's pessimism."

Bady and Hsu have different ideas about why the student-controversy story fascinates. Bady mostly attributes it to "the collective hunger of the online, for-profit media for tasty content," elaborating:

> The collective news consciousness is vaguely aware that college students are Anti-Speech Social Justice Warriors not to mention generally bad news, because we keep seeing op-eds declaring that it's a real problem. It's an easy story, especially when there's a Man-Bites-Dog twist, such as the students in question being Christians.

Precisely.

Hsu, meanwhile, projects a kind of world-weary pessimism onto the student-crisis-article audience. Maybe, he writes, "the reason that college stories have garnered so much attention this year is our general suspicion, within the real world, that the system no longer works. Their cries for justice sound out of step to those who can no longer imagine it. Maybe we're troubled by these students' attempts to imagine change on so microscopic a level."

The "microscopic" bit seems right. As for the rest, I don't think it's quite so complicated. Student controversies make the news because eighteen- to twenty-year-olds—middle class and wealthy ones, at any rate—are a sexy-but-wholesome topic. As for why *Yale* makes the news if a student there has a hangnail, while something actually has to happen at Mizzou for anyone to learn of its goings-on . . . Well, look at who reads and writes for middle- and highbrow publications.

Campus speech controversies—that is, the ones involving middle-aged speakers getting turned away by self-righteous student activists—aren't as obviously exciting, so it's not as clear how *they've* become so hot right now. However, they do appeal to broader audiences, in part because "young people today" complaints are a timeless winner, but also because of our cultural fascination with jobs where you could say outrageous things (and insult your clients and employer) without getting fired. Point being, student life is put under the microscope, which has the inevitable impact of making it look like students think their internal, campus-based complaints are the most important thing happening in the world.

As for whether it's an ethical violation of some kind to "put" student controversies in the news, there's no easy answer that covers all cases. I've drawn a firm line against professors writing about what goes on in their own classrooms (as in, discussing specific students' assignments or behaviors[61]), and would extend that to professors who comment on controversies involving named or readily identifiable students at their own universities.[62] Students' learning processes shouldn't be treated as real-time fodder for culture-wars observations. There are many ways a professor who wishes to speak out on issues relating to academia may do so without specifically calling out students in his or her class. Oh, and if you're a college president, maybe don't use an anecdote mocking a student at your school as an opener to an open letter to be shared in *The Washington Post*.[63]

Yet what if—as is generally the case—the criticism comes from outside the academy? It's certainly wrong for journalists (and I'd include student journalists, such as the one in the case Bady describes) to go onto ostensibly private online forums in search of pointless clickbait. In 2013, a glitch allowed gossip Web sites access to application essays written by Columbia's incoming freshmen. *Gawker* published excerpts of a bunch, but reprinted two in full, even offering a download option.[64] A commenter (who won a nod in the following comment from a *Gawker* staffer) rationalized the mockery:

> I kind of want to chastise you for having a laugh at the expense of . . . what a bunch of 17- and 18-year-olds wrote to try and sound interesting to a college admissions office, but then I read what these

> 17- and 18-year-olds thought would sound interesting,
> and holy shit. Could these be anymore vapid and
> self-aggrandizing?[65]

A low point, I think, even for a site with plenty of low points.

Meanwhile, when cringe-inducing student-paper op-eds serve as content for mainstream publications, perhaps a measure of forgiveness is in order. Yet those papers are now public and online, put online by students themselves. There are some student writers who'd have been well served by the old model, where student writing practically never left campus. Others, though, are more than pleased to use a widely denounced student essay as a launching pad for a media career; an essay that infuriated one side will have generally delighted the other.[66] This is true not just of student writers, but of student activists as well. As Hsu notes, "The logic of virality that governs life on the Internet has given student activists a sense of common struggle, as well as the means to escalate their grievances with relative ease." College students, with few exceptions, are adults. To treat their publicly accessible writing as sacred is to fall into the "coddling" trap; why is the college paper private, but, say, the Tumblr of a nobody who may not have gone to college (and may not be an adult!) fair game? It seems best to place student publications in the same treat-gently pile as other public writing by people without real platforms, and who aren't quite public figures.[67] The students themselves, at any rate, are far less outrageous than the system they've landed in.

PAY FOR THE PRIVILEGE: ADMISSIONS AND HYPOCRISY

THE JUICIEST "PRIVILEGE" controversies seem, at first, to be the ones on campus. However, the really egregious stuff is, as I've alluded to, happening at the level of admissions. The entire apparatus for selecting each entering class—that is, at the schools where selection is possible—is infused with "privilege" rhetoric. I'll get at what this means, but first, a note about what it *doesn't*. It's often thought—and, less often, announced—that having privilege makes it harder to get into college these days. In a (very funny) post connecting Ben Carson's life story with the college admissions process, *Washington Post* writer Alexandra Petri wrote, of college and politics, "Privilege is an anti-credential." While she notes that a *very* scrappy background poses problems of its own, she presents the issue as, it's now harder to get into college if you're rich: "For personal narrative purposes, humble origins in adversity are priceless beyond rubies. (Rubies, after all, are something a privileged person would have.)" Privileged applicants are, she explains, in a bind: "There is no good way to overcome" the preference for a "rags-to-riches" narrative, she explains.[68]

Petri's right about rich parents trying to find ways to present their kids as poor. Yet it isn't actually harder to get into college if you're privileged. Privilege is, was, and probably always will be *the* credential, in college and politics alike. It's not as if there's a dearth of serious politicians and candidates who bear the same last name as their predecessors. Privilege is great! It's "privilege" that's frowned upon.

"TRUFFLE DOGS"

THE QUESTION OF elite college admissions in the United States is always framed as one of how to select the right students, as though if only a proper sorting mechanism were arrived at, justice would be achieved. While opinions differ over who those students are and how they're best discovered, what rarely gets questioned is whether fine-tuning the sieve is even a task that makes sense in the first place. Alternate possibilities—a flawed-but-simple system (say, a GPA cutoff, plus SAT, then a lottery) or a system where everyone just goes to the nearest large public university—aren't as exciting as seeking out new ways of finessing the admissions process. Cheaper, but less compelling.

And so goes the end-in-itself quest to find the high school seniors who officially and objectively *belong* at elite schools. In an *Atlantic* book excerpt, Columbia professor Jonathan Cole argued that admitting students to college "is too important to leave to well-meaning young administrators." Rather than recognizing that admissions committees are fallible, in part because *there is no "right" group of applicants*, Cole endorses a more involved sort of sifting: "There could be a standing committee of experienced and judicious faculty members who work on shaping the class—the 'truffle dogs,' with the ability to sniff out talented individuals who may have gone against the grain but who have exceptional potential."[69] I'll start by questioning the comparison of seventeen-year-olds with prized fungus. Yet in all seriousness: Why are we assuming it's possible for anyone to "sniff out" which seventeen-year-olds will wind up where? And—more to the point—why is it tragic if the kids who wind up at the top of their fields don't spend four years at, say, Harvard? I get why *Harvard* would want the most illustrious alumni possible. But is creativity squashed when creative types wind up elsewhere?

And should we really be comparing the desired college applicants to something so upscale? Why truffles? Why not, say, some hearty root vegetable, inexpensive but roastable all winter long, with a video of food critic Melissa Clark advising on the best preparation?

It's by now a college-admissions tenet that one must not come across as privileged. "Privileged," in the college-admissions context like all others, isn't a fixed category, so much as a euphemism for that which is, in whichever setting, undesirable. Privileged applicants, as in rich ones with connections and opportunities flowing their way, *do just fine.*

Truffle admissions is simply a hyped-up version of "holistic," the process currently in place. "Holistic" means that rather than simply evaluating applicants on the basis of materials submitted, admissions committees are—we're to believe—using them to arrive at assessments greater than the sum of their parts, with the goal of figuring out who each applicant is as a person. Assessing strangers as *whole human beings* is, of course, impossible. In practice, "holistic" is simply the way colleges justify their choice to admit the pool they wish to admit, without external critics (legal or otherwise) second-guessing their decisions. It's a means to quietly correct for biases within a purportedly meritocratic system, but it's also a cover for introducing a host of new ones. If you're a brilliant inner-city kid whose high school doesn't offer APs, or—at the other end of the spectrum—a dim-witted heir, "holistic" is for you. "Holistic" makes an enemy of members of the so-called overrepresented minority groups. (For more on the place of such groups under a privilege framework, see chapter 5.) If you're from a group that's not super privileged, but that tends to do well in school, "holistic" is one way of making sure you *don't* get in.

Yet "holistic" also appeals to academically mediocre wealthy and middle-class (white) students and their families, because it suggests that the usual metrics for assessing academic performance aren't the true tests of a student's college-worthiness. What really counts is how special your child is, and whose child isn't special? Denouncing quantitative assessment is, as I've argued in *The Atlantic*, a way for a certain well-off, left-leaning demographic to both advocate for the underprivileged and receive unearned advantages for its own.[70]

And so, in this climate, where the worst thing in the world is to be reduced to a number, college admissions become geared toward the assertion of individuality. This emphasis encourages and is even partially responsible for the ubiquity of the "privilege" framework. Students are being socialized into a culture of curated personal confession, one where the greatest good is to express oneself in the proper tone. What matters isn't what you do, but how you come across when describing it.

The privilege framework is thus at the core of the holistic assessment. Privilege awareness has become an essential competence. An otherwise qualified applicant who demonstrates unchecked privilege is suddenly out of the running. And so, while privilege itself can be sussed out from other parts of an application (where a student lives, which high school, etc.), "privilege" needs to slip out inadvertently. And the slip-out-inadvertently part of every college application is, of course, the essay.

ON A SOCIETY THAT ASKS SEVENTEEN-YEAR-OLDS TO WRITE MEMOIRS

THE COLLEGE ESSAY isn't a cover letter but, as parenting writer Caren Osten Gerszberg put it, in a post on *The New York Times*'s college admissions blog, "a short form—or a portion—of their memoir."[71] American high school students are told that getting into college is achieved by presenting one's most authentic self. Yet not too authentic, or *New York Times* columnist Frank Bruni might write a column about how you wrote about being poorly endowed on your application to Yale and then, insult to injury, didn't get admitted.[72] No one likes a sob story, but colleges do want to know if you've had to contend with any "special circumstances." A broad, broad category that can, according to a 2012 handout on the National Association for College Admission Counseling Web site, include having "[r]idden public transportation (buses) on a regular basis."[73] Fantastic—I grew up riding, among others, the M4, down Fifth and up Madison. I guess that counts!

The college essay isn't autobiographical in manner of, say, a cover letter. It's not just that college essays are written in the first person, and are (targeted) descriptions of the self. It's that their purpose—like that of literary memoir—is to get at the person within. The goal isn't, as with other application letters, to demonstrate that you know how to come across as reasonable for a sustained period of time. (Which is, after all, what's needed to hold down a job.) What's sought is something far more extensive. You're applying not merely for the hours each week you'll spend in seminar, but for the chance to have late-night dorm conversations about Hegel (something that could well have once been how a college evening was spent) with a hand-selected cohort. You're applying not just to be a student, but a friend, a spouse. Given the all-encompassing nature of what's on offer, it seems almost natural that colleges would demand a level of openness above and beyond what, in any other case, a perfect stranger might ask.

Less recognized, but no less important, is the way that the privilege turn in education constitutes an invasion of young people's privacy. The road to meritocracy that's been settled on these days involves asking students to confront their privilege or lack thereof. It's not sufficient to level the playing field through broad demographic factors—that is, by giving a boost to poor students and those from underrepresented minorities. Every student's unique mix of advantages and disadvantages must be assessed; for this to happen, the student must self-report. Somehow, all of this navel-gazing is meant to inspire the haves to give up their unearned edge, and to inspire confidence in the have-nots. How exactly self-examination is meant to bring about justice isn't really explored—the idea is that it just *will*, and that you'll look insensitive if you question the benefits of this approach.

To get into college, students must offer up confessional essays, while somehow avoid oversharing. That balance eludes many professional essay writers, yet random seventeen-year-olds are meant to have figured it out. In their admissions essays and, once on campus, in activities like the "privilege walk," in which students are asked to take a step forward or backward according to, say, whether their parents went to college, students are asked to dwell on and, more troublingly, make public statements about the most sensitive aspects of their backgrounds. (There's also a T-shirt checklist version.[74]) Part of being well educated is having achieved this higher plane of self-awareness.

In this grand quest to eliminate obliviousness, there's actually quite a great deal of it. Everyone seems to miss that the most vulnerable students are precisely the ones who won't come forward about their disadvantages. Meanwhile, the students socialized to view themselves as deserving of special help tend to be . . . privileged. The edge provided to students who know how to, and are prepared to, speak out about their disadvantages is a built-in flaw with a system that classifies everyone who fails to cop to disadvantage as advantaged. As with other incarnations of the privilege approach, privilege gets reinforced.

Yet even apart from the further hypocrisy concerns, there's a broader ethical question: Do students owe university administrators or professors their life stories, and by extension, those of their relatives? Is it right that students get penalized for reticence, or rewarded for candor? Right or wrong, it's viewed as acceptable, unquestionable. Consider the New York Times College Scholarship Program, an academic grant announced on the paper's Web site alongside the strictly charitable Neediest Cases Fund.[75] The program is, on the one hand, to be praised for mitigating (if only for a handful) the racial and socioeconomic disparities in college accessibility. And yet there's something unsettling about the accompanying article, where (named) students' family tragedies (stories of extreme poverty, but also of parents' physical and mental illnesses) are made public.[76] These students *are* more impressive than most, and it's indisputably right that they'd be recognized, but this apparently must involve publicizing their misfortune. At the very least, this way of assessing merit demands that students disclose personal histories on their applications. And it's not especially difficult to picture why many would be wary of doing so.

THE "DELICATE DANCE"

MEANWHILE, ON THE other end of the advantaged-ness spectrum, students who haven't faced *Times* scholarship-worthy obstacles scramble to portray themselves as something other than privileged. And there are so very many ways an applicant might come across as privileged in an essay. The first is straightforward boasting. It's not wise, say the experts (and anyone with common sense), to use the limited space offered by the personal statement to share how delighted you are with your new Audi. That sort of materialist bragging is, however, easily avoided, compared with some of the *other* privilege pitfalls.

In a wonderful blog post called "Checking Whose Privilege," writer and former independent admissions counselor Lacy Crawford presents the "delicate dance of self-effacement [that] plays out across America every fall, when high school seniors whose families can afford college contort themselves to obscure this fact."[77] It is indeed striking, given the cost of college—not to mention the persistence of legacy policies, legs-up for donors' kids, and the myriad more subtle but entrenched ways rich kids benefit in college admissions—how central the warning against coming across as privileged is to application advice. *Be* privileged, by all means! Just don't seem it. "Unfortunately, many applicants submit essays that show their privilege a bit too much," advises one admissions site.[78] "Hard-earned accomplishments speak louder than privileged opportunities," offers another.[79] A third includes, in a list of the top five ways an essay can go wrong, "You Sound Like a Privileged Snob." (Materialism gets its own separate entry.)[80]

THE HUMANITARIANS OF HIGH SCHOOL

ON HER BLOG, *The Neurotic Parent,* J. D. Rothman offers reasons "brilliant" applicants get rejected. (Granted, the post title—"Why Your Brilliant Child Didn't Get into the Ivies"—reads as sarcastic.) Coming in at number three:

> **Your child's application stinks of privilege.** You had the best of intentions when you sent your son or daughter to Oxford last July to read the classics. But guess what? The colleges, who eventually are happy to accept your $200,000, aren't thrilled about $11,000 summer programs, even the life-changing ones.[81]

The nonproblem anecdote (the sports injury is, it seems, a standby[82]) announces that an applicant has no idea what true suffering is. But the absolute worst, as *all the Web sites* and *all the articles* insist,[83] is the voluntourism essay:

> During the summer before my junior year of high school, I spent a weekend volunteering with the poor in post-Katrina Louisiana and realized that I am privileged. Most of what these people had had been ripped out from under them and life was very different there from my life in suburban Massachusetts. Amazingly, though, these people still seemed happy. I learned from this experience that money isn't everything.

So goes a sample college-admissions essay introduction, offered on a *New York Times* education blog, as part of a post aimed at high school teachers seeking what-not-to-do examples to hand out to their students.[84] Given all the many ways a college essay might go wrong, why this one? Surely there's worse than a grammatically written, if banal, reflection on volunteer work. Surely thoughts far worse than "money isn't everything" have been expressed. Worse, perhaps. But not more boring. In the post, called "Going Beyond Cliché: How to Write a Great College Essay," Amanda Christy Brown and Holly Epstein Ojalvo suggest teachers read that paragraph aloud, and then ask students to role-play as admissions officers deciding the fate of the poor (and, one hopes, fictional) sap behind that intro. "Does this paragraph grab you?" (No, you'll say if you're one of those students, to your teacher's delight.) "Are you interested in reading more of this essay?" Judging by your teacher's tone and body language while asking you this question, the answer had better be no.

Then it gets personal: "What do you think this paragraph says about this student?" Tellingly, the exercise asks students to judge this theoretical classmate not as a college applicant, or even as a writer, but as a person. The implicitly correct answer is that this isn't merely a bad essay, but a bad person. But bad how? And here's the implicit answer: Never in as few words has anyone come across as quite so privileged. Or quite so dull. It's almost as if the paragraph were composed *by professional writers* as an example of what "privilege" minus personality would sound like. Can this (theoretical) applicant hear himself? (For some reason, the passage reads male, and since there's no such thing as misgendering a straw applicant, that's what I'm going with.) Two *days* this kid spent volunteering? No wonder he thought Katrina victims were "happy." And "suburban Massachusetts?" Ack. Why not just open with, "I am demographically over-represented, criminally unoriginal, and will contribute nothing unique to the incoming freshman class"? The privilege-acknowledgment portion of the paragraph—as is so often the case with such confessions—reveals the opposite. The worst things a college applicant can be are sheltered and suburban, and literally all we know about this applicant is that he's both of those things.

The voluntourism choice is the educational equivalent of the

"Humanitarians of Tinder"[85] phenomenon, where white, Western hook-up app users pose with beaming, impoverished African children as a method of impressing would-be sex partners. Here, the would-be seduced are admissions committees. And they are not impressed.

In case the point hadn't been hammered home quite enough, there's the fact that humor writer Paul Rudnick parodied one of these essays in a *New Yorker* "Shouts and Murmurs":

> When I was twelve, I first became aware of the world's suffering, and I used the dividends from my trust fund to fly to Berlin to help the victims of the recent tsunami. Upon my arrival, I discovered that, while the tsunami hadn't affected Berlin, I could still express my empathy for the victims by joining an activist performance troupe and mounting a piece entitled "Younami: The Superstorm Inside Us All."[86]

It would be one thing if colleges frowned on these essays because if narcissistic musings on expensive trips to far-off locales are the best a student can come up with, the kid may not be that bright. Yet phrasing it as "privilege" suggests there's a social-justice component to rejecting these applicants. And there's a further hypocrisy: Families pay tutors to show their kids how to seem less privileged in these essays, thus creating a system where the students who seem the most privileged in their applications are, by definition, not the ones getting the most help. A tutor might, for a healthy fee, tell you to mention the job flipping burgers, but gently urge you away from spelling out that you did this for two weeks in the Hamptons, at an upscale restaurant owned by a family friend. In a post on admissions site Essay Hell, called "Is Your Privilege Showing?," college admissions coach Janine Anderson Robinson offers up a list of nine sample phrases that would lead to a yes to that question, helpfully placing the offending terms in bold.[87] "During a **shopping trip** to **Paris** with my mom..." should apparently be avoided, because—as must be painstakingly spelled out to naïve high schoolers fresh from a Petit Bateau restock—not everyone does this. There's a gendered-male version as well: "While flying to Boise in **my dad's plane**..." (Why Boise? I'm too New Yorker–privileged to get its significance as a marker of status.) Robinson insists that there's "nothing wrong with being privileged," but that "you just want to show that you have a realistic sense of the world and your place in it." As she notes, "Many of the students I work with are from privileged backgrounds. (Hey, it's expensive to hire a tutor!)" True enough. I'm thinking of that Dolly Parton quote, "It costs a lot to look this cheap."[88]

WEISS PRIVILEGE

IN THE LIKABILITY sweepstakes, few fare as badly as an academically unimpressive white kid who thinks he deserved to get into Harvard. When—as it inevitably does—Harvard sends a many-qualified-applicants letter to the unremarkable B student from Scarsdale, who really had no business applying to the Ivies in the first place, any disappointment that kid voices will get classified as "privilege." In this understanding, "privilege" isn't the discreetly Kennedy-affiliated legacy who gets in, but the suburban nobody who does not.

That said, the nobody contingent does little to help its own case, focusing its resentment on affirmative action and other diversity efforts, and not on the myriad ways the system benefits the super rich. The cry of the aggrieved, entitled elite-college reject is that the admissions process benefits the underprivileged, leading sensible people everywhere to remind that no, it does not. It's a behind-closed-doors sort of sentiment, but one that makes the occasional public appearance, as in a *New York Times* letter to the editor from an Oxford student named Jaimie Arona Krems, responding to a piece that had detailed the tremendous overrepresentation of the highest-income families at selective colleges. Krems acknowledged that her parents had paid for her entire education, private school through grad school, and that this had, you know, made her life a bit easier. Yet she objected to the idea of colleges giving a boost to applicants without those advantages: "In theory, hardworking, low-income kids deserve help; in practice, their 1,250 SAT scores' counting for more than my 1,300 doesn't reflect meritocracy."[89] The letter reads less as a thought-through rejection of income-based affirmative action, and more as an average student who faced no particular obstacles (or none worth mentioning) asking for a medal for having managed not to massively screw things up. The most public face of this sort of resentment, however, is Abigail Fisher, who took up her altogether reasonable-sounding rejection from the University of Texas with the Supreme Court. She didn't fall into the top 10 percent of her high school class—the way most of that school's admits get selected—but she really wanted to go to that school, and shouldn't wanting something be enough? The expression "white privilege" comes up time and again regarding Fisher,[90] as it will if one volunteers to be the textbook example of a phenomenon.

Not that Fisher doesn't have competition. Then-high school senior Suzy Lee Weiss's 2013 humor op-ed for *The Wall Street Journal*, "To (All) the Colleges That Rejected Me," went viral in the brash, sorry-not-sorry, budding-conservative way that Tal Fortgang's privilege essay would the following year.[91] It is, at first glance, almost a point-by-point guide to what not to put in a college essay in order to avoid coming across as privileged. Along with some sensible observations about voluntourism and holistic admissions, there were these sentiments: Weiss suggested she'd have gotten into her dream school if only she had "two moms," and complained, "I offer about as much diversity as a saltine cracker." Her cutesy way of lamenting colleges' emphasis on ethnic diversity—"had I known two years ago what I know now, I would have gladly worn a headdress to school"—was casually racist on enough levels to fill an entire master's thesis about microaggressions. And the entire thing is an ode to her own underachievement (all the sports she didn't play, the charitable and leadership activities she didn't get involved with). A self-deprecating anecdote about preferring to watch the "Real Housewives" to making use of "the wonderful gifts I have been afforded" might have worked in some other context, but in a rant about not getting into nice enough colleges, it falls flat.

Among those taking the opportunity to hurl YPIS at Weiss were students who had fared a bit better in the admissions process: "During the three minutes I wasted reading this piece, a word continuously screamed and shouted in my head: privilege,"[92] wrote Steven Gu of Swarthmore. *The Huffington Post* found a high school senior who'd been "accepted to Harvard, Yale and Princeton," who was none too impressed by Weiss's "privilege and sense of entitlement."[93] Morgan Jerkins of Princeton had much the same take: "[F]or a young woman who gloated about being accepted in the big 10 schools, receiving a 2120 on the SATs and achieving an astounding 4.5 GPA, it baffles me how blind you are to a term that perhaps may or may not have crossed your mind before you wrote your letter. Would you like to know what it is?" I would, but I have a guess. "It's privilege."[94] What else?

There's something about the mix of academic mediocrity and entitlement that's off-putting in that narrow way where "privilege" seems appropriate. Students like Weiss, Fisher, and Krems—seemingly unashamed of their unexceptional academic records, and all too delighted to blame society's have-nots for their own minor setbacks—are certainly unsympathetic and entitled. However, it's quite likely that *their* spots, at least where private universities are concerned, went not to the underdogs they're happy to trample, but to the still-more privileged. According to a 2014 *Harvard Crimson* survey, "about 15 percent of the incoming freshmen said their families earn above $500,000 per year, putting them among the top 1 percent of earners in the United States."[95] What this—along with the accompanying stats on legacy admissions—conveys is that it's possible to exude all manner of suburban white-privileged entitlement . . . and still fall far short of that stratosphere.

The issue for bitter, upper-middle-class students, in other words, may be the opposite of what's generally assumed. It's not (just) that they've failed to acknowledge the privilege they do have. It's that they've *overestimated* their privilege, mistakenly imagining that they're competing in some kind of general privileged-person pool, and not realizing that if they were *really* privileged—that is, if they were members of political dynasties, or so well-off that their parents could offer up a new gym—they wouldn't have to face rejection from Harvard, let alone the University of Texas. The "ugh-privilege" reaction such students inspire (and they inspire it in me) isn't entirely warranted. It's emotionally unavoidable, I suppose, but it still involves redirecting class rage away from the super elites, who will get into the top schools regardless, and toward the sheltered but hook-lacking middle and upper middle class.

Rejecting applicants on the basis of "privilege" has become a convenient stand-in for actually addressing all the unfairness that enters into the college admissions process. It *seems* progressive to picture a bunch of gatekeepers in a sealed-off room, all putting some mediocre-yet-entitled kid's essay in their desktop trash cans in a fit of righteous disgust. Yet it isn't substantively changing anything. It isn't opening up slots for more than a handful of underprivileged applicants. All it's doing is penalizing students who write crummy essays, or essays in which they display poor judgment. Which is to say, it's just one more means of keeping a college elite.

TWO STEPS BACK

IN RECENT YEARS, elite and elite-adjacent colleges have explored ways of changing the process. I want to say, "of addressing systemic inequality in college admissions," but that's not quite it. Basically, the system is unfair, as everyone agrees, albeit for a range of contradictory reasons. In order to address concerns, if not necessarily realities, these schools have sought out ways to ramp up their emphasis on "holistic" assessment.

Sometimes the hypocrisy's really over the top, like when Wesleyan framed its decision to go from need-blind to need-aware (admissions-speak for, it's *officially* easier to get in if you're rich, as versus just an unstated likelihood) as a noble effort to keep disadvantaged students out of debt.[96] I'm not entirely clear on how this works—wouldn't getting rejected from Wesleyan just mean taking out loans to go to a different college?—but it's hard to see how else they'd have presented the move.

Mostly, though, we're looking at the sort of changes that seem on the surface to be helpful, but that, upon closer examination, either wouldn't improve matters or would plainly help the rich.

The brochures have gotten even glossier, and by "glossier" I mean that their promises keep expanding. The Web site for the Coalition for Access, Affordability, and Success[97]—a group of largely elite colleges seeking "to improve the college application process for all students as they search for and apply to their perfect college" via an alternative to the Common Application—opens with an image of, well, perfection. A group of five young women of color (plus a sixth, of indeterminate ethnicity) are standing, in graduation robes, smiling. Every major nonwhite ethnicity is represented, but the camera's focus is on a dark-skinned black woman. Well done! With the brochure, that is. The reality sounds substantially less impressive. In a column ambivalent to what he appears to view as a well-meaning development, Frank Bruni summarizes critics' objections:

> They predicted that privileged kids with hovering
> parents would interpret the coalition's suggestion about
> beginning to fill a [virtual] locker [of "creative work"] in
> the ninth grade as yet another reason to turn the entire
> high school experience into a calculated, pragmatic
> audition for college admissions officers. Meanwhile,
> underprivileged kids, lacking the necessary guidance
> and awareness, might never take advantage of the
> platform.[98]

I'd dispense with all of that hedging, and say with confidence that this is exactly what would happen. Yes, making admissions procedures more complicated would keep out, rather than attract, students from less-advantaged backgrounds. And then there's Turning the Tide,[99] a Harvard-based effort at (further) emphasizing community service, essays, and general holistic-ness, which has met with the same sort of criticism, for more or less the same reasons.[100]

And then there's the new SAT, a shift with the potential to impact even more students. Aimed at improving socioeconomic diversity,[101] it, too, has flaws that make it seem as if it probably wouldn't help, and could hurt.[102] In any event, there's already a page devoted to it at the Princeton Review test-prep Web site: "The New SAT. We're ON IT."[103]

More and more colleges are going "test optional," or allowing students to apply without providing standardized test scores.[104] This move, too, gets justified in terms of privilege. SAT scores correlate with family income.[105] So surely a college that abandons that metric is doing so in order to make the student body more socioeconomically diverse. Or so the schools would have applicants believe, even if nearly all evidence points to other motivations.

In a piece about George Washington University's decision to scrap the test requirement, journalist Sarah Kaplan writes, "The ironic thing is that the test was invented for exactly the same reason that GW is moving away from it: a hope of creating a more merito-cratic admissions process, one that evaluated applicants based not on their privileges as children, but on their promise as adults."[106] Kaplan does indeed offer a quote from the school's dean of admissions, some platitude about students "'from all different backgrounds'" be-ing encouraged to apply, but there's reason to be skeptical. As journal-ist Kate Groetzinger pointed out in Quartz, George Washington had recently got called out for wait-listing students for requiring financial aid:[107] "While not technically a lie, [a GW administrator's] claim that the new admissions policy is aimed at increasing socio-economic diversity in the student body is misleading, when students are cur-rently being turned away based on their ability to pay." Writing in *The American Interest*, Jason Willick noted, correctly, "If anything, making the admissions process based more on subjective factors like essays, extra-curricular activities, and applicant 'personality' will tilt the process *even more* in favor of students who know the ins and outs of what admissions officers want to hear—students that are disproportionately rich and white."[108] A *Daily Caller* headline put it more bluntly: "Fancypants Rich Kids School That Wait-listed Poor Kids for Being Poor Dumps SAT, ACT."[109] Along simi-lar lines, it sounded promising when a Wesleyan University dean, when asked about the reason for that school's test-optional policy, cites the relationship between income and scores.[110] Yet as long as Wesleyan remains not just pricey but need-aware—that is, it's actu-ally easier to gain admission if you can pay the full tuition—the phrase lip service will come to mind.[111]

There's some evidence that scrapping standardized tests could promote diversity, but nothing conclusive.[112] The overlap between schools that are need-aware[113] and ones that are test optional (Wes-leyan, but also Bryn Mawr,[114] Pitzer,[115] Bates,[116] and then there's Trinity which is "test-flexible"[117]) does raise the possibility that when schools claim to be moving away from standardized tests as a way of reaching out to bright kids from underserved communities, what they're actually doing is courting the reverse demographic.

Consider the case of Bard College in upstate New York, heralded in 2013 and more recently for offering an essays-only admissions option. Rather than subjecting themselves to the tyranny of standardized testing (or, realistically, in addition to taking those tests, given that other schools still tend to demand it, and students apply to multiple colleges), an aspiring Bard freshman would have the option of writing a mere four 2,500-word research papers. Ones with no relevance to any project other than this one college application. In *The New York Times*, reporter Ariel Kaminer described the new exam, and its ostensible accessibility:

> Bard's audition is open book: Along with the menu of 17 questions, the college's Web site will provide all the relevant source materials—from a Nobel lecture about prion disorders to the United Nations Charter to an Aeschylus play—with which to address them. (Additional research is permitted if properly documented.) Mary Backlund, Bard's director of admission, said that that access will place students who may not have encountered the subjects in school or do not have good local libraries on equal footing with those who attended elite high schools."[118]

I realize this is a book protesting YPIS. However, let's just pause for a moment and ask whether providing source materials and merely "permitt[ing]" further research is enough to mitigate the tremendous disadvantage an assignment like this would place on students who didn't have exposure to topics like these in high school—a point made in the piece by Stuyvesant High School English teacher Walter Gern (my own former English teacher)—not to mention ones who have the leisure time to devote to a project along these lines. And then there's the question of tutoring, or the euphemistic sort of tutoring that involves someone else (a tutor or parent) writing an applicant's essay. Eliminating test prep hardly removes the potential for corruption or "help" along those lines. As journalist Jordan Weissmann pointed out in *The Atlantic*, "Bard's new admissions option isn't just vulnerable to cheating; it's vulnerable to cheating from undeserving students who can afford to cheat."[119] A lot seems to hinge on the belief that admissions committees *just know* if an adult is the real author, which is a level of confidence anyone who's ever read fiction with a convincing adolescent narrator should find suspicious. The stakes become that much greater where essays are the only metric.

However, even setting aside the possibilities for outright cheating, a switch to emphasizing essays would so obviously benefit privileged students; any denial of this reads as obliviousness, willful or otherwise. Yet it's being marketed as not just privilege neutral, but as a progressive measure. After all, as Kaminer reminds in her piece, "new evidence shows that few low-income students attend elite colleges, despite the financial aid they offer, a problem that Bard hopes its new approach can address." A note, then, on "the financial aid they offer." As of August 2015, according to the college's Web site, "Bard has a need-aware admission policy."[120] Furthermore, "Applicants should be aware that not every student will receive assistance equal to his or her demonstrated financial need."[121] And yet we're supposed to believe that offering applicants a chance to write 2,500 words on what Ezra Pound mused about Chaucer will somehow level the playing field.[122]

The refrain that subjective measurement is the way out of perpetuating privilege keeps getting repeated. In a *Slate* piece praising Bard's policy, higher-education journalist Rebecca Schuman suggested other colleges embrace the approach and extend it beyond just essays:

What about submitting a spectacular and original science or math project? The detailed business model of a company you invented? I wish more American colleges and universities would stop asking students to jump through a series of increasingly privilege-reifying hoops (the current admissions process favors higher-income students) and start asking for applicants to show their *real* potential.[123]

Somehow, the corrective for a system that, as Schuman puts it, "determine[s] a young person's entire future based on her choices as a 14-year-old" is to reward teenagers whose accomplishments are so great as to suggest they may as well just bypass college altogether. It's as if we've all forgotten the proportion of kids with achievements along those lines, who were helped or "helped" along the way by parents or family friends. I'm thinking of "The Care and Feeding of Parents" episode (from 1972, but timeless) of *The Mary Tyler Moore Show*, in which unfulfilled, overeducated housewife Phyllis decides that her twelve-year-old daughter Bess's "A" on a homework assignment is proof of literary genius.[124] Phyllis starts by trying to finagle connections to get Bess's composition published in a teen magazine, but things escalate, and by the end of the episode, the beleaguered Bess is "writing a book," although it's of course Phyllis writing it, with Bess struggling in vain to get her mother to lay off, and to just let her be a kid. Any time children are judged by adult standards, this is only going to (further) encourage parents to do their kids' work, or to pay other adults for this service.

The hypocritical tensions built into the privilege project are at their most obvious in higher education. Tremendous effort goes into a cosmetic appearance of commitment to social justice (look, a black woman on the cover of a brochure!), while the old ways (white men lecturing students about the achievements of white men, all within the context of a hyper-rigid hierarchy) remain. Seminars explore the minutiae of symbolic violences and socioeconomic marginalization, while adjuncts make do on less than a living wage. Campus life is on the one hand progressive enough to inspire a regular drumbeat of conservative outrage (Queer Studies is a thing!), and on the other, so terribly expensive that gay students with homophobic parents wind up staying in the closet for much of their young adulthood.[125] A veneer of hypersensitivity allows tremendous on-the-ground insensitivity to flourish.

American colleges and universities are intensely privilege aware, at every level. And they become more privilege conscious by the day. Further privilege sensitivity has become the default answer to all problems, yet winds up making things worse. It does so by increasing the cost of college; by constantly alerting less-privileged students to their status; and by creating this new trait, "privilege awareness," which is, by definition, only available to those *with* privilege about which they may be aware. A focus on "privilege" is convenient for the schools themselves, because it means, in all kinds of ways, an increase in demand. However, it also creates problems for the schools, because it keeps placing them in the news as sites of grievous harm.

3

THE "PROBLEMATIC FAVE"

IS IT STILL OK TO ENJOY WOODY ALLEN MOVIES?

IN MAY 2016, the humor Web site *ClickHole* published an item that should probably go into whatever the Internet-age equivalent is of a time capsule, as it so thoroughly sums up the then-current state of pop-culture criticism.[1] The post consists of "seven of the many reasons why George Clooney is the greatest Hollywood star ever, although if he ever says anything racist, use the sliders to turn this list into seven reasons why George Clooney is a repulsive piece of shit who needs to crawl into the ocean and die." Clooney's purported sins are presented via seven "slider" images, where you can switch back and forth between images of Clooney, with accompanying text. So in one version, it says, "Another reason why George Clooney is absolutely flawless: that gorgeous smile!" Yet slide the "slider" to the left, and the caption now reads, "Another great reason for this racist asshole to go die in an ocean: his infuriating, shit-eating grin. No one forgets what you said, George Clooney. No one." The point of this item wasn't to reference any actual racism scandal involving this actor—he's by all accounts an untarnished progressive; otherwise the joke wouldn't have worked. Rather, it's a play on the frequent media cycles where an otherwise likable celebrity will *cause controversy* for saying something offensive, or that could be taken out of context as offensive, and for this incident to dominate the "trending" news cycle for days to come.

There's a standby on Twitter, popular among journalists and others wishing to lend an air of seriousness to their bios: RT≠endorsement.[2] Its purpose is to draw a distinction between the articles someone deems shareworthy (and thus retweets) and this person's own beliefs. It's in many ways a silly disclaimer, both in its presumptuousness, and in the obviousness of the fact that unless otherwise specified (that is, unless prefaced with some version of, "Can you believe this idiot?"), a retweet is certainly promotion of some kind. However, what RT≠endorsement allows for, rhetorically, is a discrepancy between media consumption and presumed stance. As in, you get to be a conservative who reads the liberal news, and vice versa, without having suddenly outed yourself as being on the opposing camp. It's a way out of the echo chamber, and, perhaps, a way to signal support for the airing of diverse viewpoints. But it's also, in broader terms, a way out of the assumption that everything we find interesting is something we *support*. The disclaimer is necessary because the presumption is that these things would be identical.

What attracts us—aesthetically, intellectually, comically—isn't necessarily what we think *deserves* our appreciation. Yet we live in an age where admitting this discrepancy is becoming impossible. At the very moment in time when cultural consumption has gone hyperpublic—when the enjoyment of a show or song implicitly entails the public endorsement of the same via social media—the mere act of liking something has become fraught. The great *signaling* question—so recently all but limited to the desire among hipsters to like things before they got cool—has gone political. Very political.

There's a meme for this phenomenon: "your fave is problematic."[3] Comedy gets divided into that which punches up and punches down. Fashion criticism—despite the occasional pleas from experts[4]—has morphed into a tired conversation about cultural appropriation. (Much of this conversation hinges on the appropriateness of white British women and girls wearing Native American headdresses to music festivals . . . in the United Kingdom. The extent to which US-centrism enters into this is generally ignored.) Historical dramas get taken to task when they fail to live up to (often anachronistic) diversity standards. It's not just that outright bigoted entertainment has fallen out of favor. (Except when it manifests itself as a Republican presidential nominee with a reality-show past.) Everything, even entertainment that seems to be *coming from a good place*, is forever hovering on the cusp of that disastrous scenario: causing controversy, or getting it wrong.

The podcast *Serial*, according to a piece in *The Awl*, was definitive "of white privilege in journalism," because what else would there possibly be to say about a cultural product one has consumed?[5] Or, for that matter, one that one hasn't: A *Guardian* headline announces, headline-generator style: "Trans Rights Activists Launch Petition calling for *Zoolander 2* Boycott." The piece itself clarifies, "More than 9,000 people have now signed the Care2 petition saying they will boycott the film on the basis of the trailer's portrayal of [Benedict] Cumberbatch's character in the highly anticipated sequel."[6] Yes, sounds about right.

The privilege lens does not spare works from the pre-awareness era. In a 2015 essay with the (accurate) subhead, "Why *Seinfeld's* Comedic Brilliance Relied on a Privileged Perspective," in Canadian magazine *Maisonneuve*, film critic Adam Nayman took on the urgent question of whether one is allowed to enjoy reruns of a 1990s sitcom. The answer is, I regret to inform you, that you may not:

> [W]hile critics frequently made reference to the show's use of satire—as in its skewering of social rituals (dinner parties, workplace meetings) and public figures (George Steinbrenner, J. Peterman)—the jokes fall far short of Northrop Frye's contention that satire is "militant" irony, exercised in the hope of instigating change.[7]

Alas, the only "change" *Seinfeld* instigated was, for approximately thirty-minute intervals, improving the lives of those who watched the show without proverbial sticks in the proverbial stick location.

THE PRIVILEGE CULTURAL CRITIQUE, AND THE BACKLASH

PRIVILEGE CHECKING, WHICH began around 2009 as a relatively straightforward way to mock ostentatious kale consumption (and oblivious posts about flying first class), has morphed into a more general privilege critique of cultural products beyond the vegetable aisle. I'm referring to the trend—no, the quasi requirement—in arts criticism that involves subjecting every book, movie, and television show to a privilege critique. By "a privilege critique," I don't simply mean questions of representation, like calling out *Saturday Night Live* for not having any black female cast members.[8] I mean a full checklist: Who's the artist? Who are his or her parents? Is the work punching up, which is to say, are powerful people (or, at least, white men) the butt of any jokes? Is the artist (or the protagonist, who may, these days, be freely conflated with the artist) sufficiently self-aware? What's the movie/book/television show *arguing*, and is it flawlessly in line with an of-the-moment think piece on that topic? And are there any topics it didn't address, and can it be faulted for not addressing them?

Because of its focus on self-awareness, representation is if anything secondary. Political correctness was—yes, *was*; this is something different—about diversity and slur avoidance. "Privilege" is anointing Louis C.K., a straight white male comic, a hero for privilege awareness. As TV critic James Poniewozik has argued, "The privilege-check has . . . been a feature of some of Louis C.K.'s most caustically funny standup.[9] It's true—he's good! Poniewozik allowed that "in the end, we're listening to Louis C.K., the guy who has the privilege"—a point no privilege critique can ever really avoid—but concludes that the gets-it-right-ness cancels this out. Media site *Upworthy* took a less subtle approach in its aggregation of the comic's routine: "Sometimes it takes a white dude to get real about racism."[10] Does it, though?

It's easy for conservatives to dismiss this turn in criticism. Yet even on the left, it's now regularly lamented that there's no longer any space for celebrating works that aren't in line with one's politics, or—more importantly—for ways of taking in culture that aren't explicitly political. The complaint was perhaps best summed up in a blog post by Freddie deBoer, who, reading *The Atlantic*, "was struck by the degree to which I just expect all of our cultural criticism to function as a checklist for socially liberal politics—knowing when I sit down to read a piece on a movie or book or music, particularly when addressing some sort of controversy, that such a piece will undertake an obligatory exploration of the degree to which the art in question satisfies contemporary progressive political expectations."[11] He was joining a conversation already well underway. In a 2014 *Observer* piece, liberal journalist Lindsay Beyerstein defended *Serial* against the dual "privileged" and "problematic" accusations, and came to the following conclusion:

> Calling a show "problematic" is a way of insinuating that it's racist, sexist, or exploitative without actually having to argue the point. Conveniently, since everything's problematic, there's no need to boycott *Serial*. Which means the morally serious critic can keep right on listening.[12]

And *Slate*'s "2014: The Year of Outrage" roundup included an entry by (morally serious) television critic Willa Paskin, called "The Cultural Outrage Audit," which addressed head-on the fact that "Identity politics has become an increasingly powerful lens for critiquing television (and podcasts, and pop music, and movies)."[13] Paskin came out in very hesitant defense of the practice, noting that things are, at least, looking more diverse, likely because of the outragathon directed at the industry. Still, she argued, "Auditing cultural products for their treatment—or lack of treatment—of marginalized groups of people can seem like an antiseptic way of consuming culture, more head than heart." Moreover, "sometimes, especially when you aren't aghast yourself, all this outrage can feel like a reductive way to consume art."

It's tempting to say that these days, everyone is outraged—or, in more positive terms, that everyone is simply freer to express outrage than ever before. The reality is not so straightforward. This is as much a story about sensitivities as one about the state of journalism. As pop culture critic Alyssa Rosenberg wrote, in a *Washington Post* response to deBoer, "The problem with the current state of political art criticism isn't really that it's *political*, but that it's predictable."[14] And that predictability can't solely be blamed on critics themselves. For content to go viral—which is, these days, the business model—it needs to be framed as outrage. It needs to be that the author is *very sad* about the topic at hand. This implicit requirement drives journalists (particularly those whose identity matches up with the controversy of the moment) to produce reflections on being mildly offended, and to ramp up "mildly offended" to fury, because nuance doesn't sell.

Moreover, nuance takes *time*. If your job—as it now often will be, in "journalism"—involves churning out aggregated content, maybe you *could* have some complex political and aesthetic response to whichever new television show, if you weren't responding to it in quite such an assembly-line manner. Publications prompt writers to express outrage about things that they hadn't even been thinking about, and demand "takes" that keep up with the news cycle. A mini-scandal erupted in the summer of 2015 when it emerged that the coauthor of a really out-there (even by YPIS standards) *Washington Post* piece[15] calling comedian Amy Schumer a racist and connecting her stand-up to a recent racially motivated massacre was—lo and behold—unfamiliar with Schumer's work, and hadn't so much as browsed a YouTube clip before declaring the bawdy feminist comedian a white supremacist thought leader.[16] Coauthor Stacey Patton, a journalist and academic, told Debra Kessler of the *Interrobang* that she had read about it, which was, yes, pretty weak. Yet Kessler's more interesting revelation was that, contrary to a *Post* editor's off-the-cuff claims, "Dr. Patton hadn't 'pitched' the article to *The Washington Post*. She said it wasn't her idea at all, and in fact she initially turned down the story, because, she thought there wasn't much there." So is this a story about cultural hypersensitivity? How can it be, when Schumer's comedy hadn't even been on Patton's radar?

Meanwhile, the thoughtful criticism that does get produced and make it past self-appointed gatekeepers ends up getting framed—through a headline a writer won't generally choose—as activist outrage. Take Amy McCarthy's *Dallas Observer* piece from September 2015, which used the moment's news story about musician Ryan Adams covering a Taylor Swift album, and the attention this new cover album had received, as a starting point for a discussion of female musicians getting insufficient critical respect. Political? Yes, but hardly hysterical. The all-caps headline sends quite a different message: "THANK YOU RYAN ADAMS FOR MANSPLAINING TAYLOR SWIFT TO THE WORLD."[17] Apart from being misleading—if anyone was mansplaining Taylor Swift to the world, according to McCarthy, it was *Boston Globe* critic James Reed, whose far-shallower piece she was responding to[18]—there was really no overlap in tone.

It's likely, then, that the ranks of the outraged have been overestimated. Yet the influence of privilege criticism remains, regardless of the sincerity of each individual critic. Readers—and I include in this category the people who get their criticism mainly from social media—end up with a severely limited outlook on what could not just be said but *thought* about a work or an artist.

FROM POLITICAL CRITICISM TO THE DEATH OF THE APOLITICAL VARIETY

TO BE CLEAR, there's nothing new about art—or criticism, for that matter—being political. The *roman à thèse*, or didactic novel, is an old form, and Marxist literary theory wasn't invented by the Tumblr crowd. Criticism and entertainment alike have always reflected the values of the time. Those who look at the current landscape and lament the loss of timeless art, or of purely aesthetic assessments, are—to put it generously—misremembering. And it's no more inherently political for a cast to be multiracial than for it to be all white.

What's new, then, is—here as elsewhere—the all-encompassing "privilege" framework. The question ceases to be whether a work is good, new, interesting, enlightening, or even—as with old-school political correctness—whether the work offends outright. It becomes instead one of how it falls according to various preordained privilege categories. To critique a work is to hold it up to the scrutiny of the privilege axes: gender, race, class, sexual orientation, gender identity, able-bodiedness. The questions asked become whether ground has been broken, or, conversely, whether any insensitivity to these hierarchies was exhibited. A work gets called brilliant if it brilliantly skewers someone from one of the official have categories. Each artist, meanwhile, gets assessed—in the manner of a college applicant—according to whether his or her achievements are a) surprising, or b) predictable, given his or her background and identity categories. (Taylor Swift, *Salon* helpfully revealed,[19] did not grow up on a favela. So really, why *is* she making music?) But there's a bit of leeway. Self-presentation is, in a sense, *all*. "Privilege," in the personal sense, can be owned, as a brand, or rejected, for the same reason.

The privilege turn cuts across all genres. Writer Arielle Bernstein's 2016 *Atlantic* essay, "Marie Kondo and the Privilege of Clutter,"[20] is a fine example of a potentially fascinating story held back by a "privilege" framing. In it, Bernstein describes her family's "fraught" relationship to material waste, a relationship stemming from a history of fleeing Nazism and then Communism:

> In the U.S., my grandparents and mother responded to the trauma they'd experienced by holding on to things. My grandfather was a collector who was prone to hoarding. He'd often find random trinkets on the street and bring them home, and he kept everything, from books to receipts to costume jewelry. . . . In my home, we didn't throw out food or plastic bags, or clothing that was out of style but that still fit us. We saved everything.

The piece might have been an essay along the lines of Roz Chast's graphic-memoir rendition of her late parents' hoarding tendencies, *Can't We Talk About Something More Pleasant?* It might have been a meditation on what it's like to be the relatively pampered American child or grandchild of struggling immigrants. And it *is*, in a way, at least until Bernstein segues into remarks about Syrian refugees: "It's particularly ironic that the KonMari method has taken hold now, during a major refugee crisis, when the news constantly shows scenes of people fleeing their homes and everything they have." Is it ironic, though? How is this different from pampered Westerners cutting carbs while other parts of the world deal with famine? What did mentioning Syrian refugees in this context do, either for Syrian refugees, or, more immediately, for Bernstein's story? It was a thoughtful tie-in with current events, but it was also out of place in a highly personal, highly specific story.

It's difficult to read privilege-centric criticism through anything other than a privilege lens. Once the word is planted, it's hard to avoid. Thus, I suppose, deBoer's snarky Twitter response: "If it's privileged to get rid of clutter, how privileged is it to write thousands of words on the political ramifications of the same?"[21] While I can't say I find the fact that someone had an article in an online publication a sign of noteworthy privilege, I did find myself frustrated by Bernstein's imprecision over whether it's her *parents* who lack the privilege of throwing stuff away, or whether this lack of privilege extends to the entire "families," that is, to Bernstein herself. How is she—going by the information she provides, I don't know her personally—any less privileged than anyone else in Kondo's target demographic? An *Atlantic* commenter had a response along those lines:

> You do realize that most Americans alive now have the same, equally important or vague ties—depending on how much they want to justify themselves—to previous generations that held onto things by necessity, yes? (You know, that whole Great Depression thing?) Many, if not most, of us are the children, grandchildren, and great-grandchildren of immigrants.[22]

What this critical comment tells us, though, isn't that Bernstein is privileged and therefore wrong. It tells us that this privilege *argu-*

ment was a flawed one. Because there is an interesting point to be made about minimalism and privilege: The rich people who embrace minimalism do so in a way that suggests *they're* somehow scrappier than poorer people who are more attached to whichever possessions. This tendency is hypocritical, annoying, and worthy of mockery. Yet to just point out that showily getting rid of your stuff requires a certain amount of privilege, while true, doesn't get at that question. Obviously Kondo's readers, in Japan and beyond, include people whose forebearers dealt with hardships. If there's something particular about Bernstein's relationship with the decluttering craze, it relates to her own specific family history and dynamics. Any broader awareness theorizing winds up making a writer seem out of touch.

In a certain sense, the privilege turn in criticism was unavoidable. We want art and entertainment—at least the mainstream sort—to be relatable, and it's no longer tenable to assume relatability is achieved by putting a white guy at the center of the action. Some of what reads as gratuitous (or media-fanned) outrage to the general population may simply be the open expression of objections marginalized communities have held all along, and are only now feeling empowered enough to express. Yet the all-encompassing nature of the critique—and the extent to which the approach is demanded most stringently of precisely the creators and consumers who are *not* white men—has backfired. Rather than opening up paths to recognition for all, it has created two conceptual tracks: groundbreaking and actually *good*. In doing so, it has somehow managed to make the works that couldn't possibly be described as groundbreaking—that is, the ones without any of that pesky "identity" stuff going on—seem as if they must have *something* going for them.

BUT IS IT APPROPRIATION?

A S I W R I T E this paragraph, the scandal of the moment is a yoga class at the University of Ottawa, which may or may not have gotten canceled because it occurred to someone at the university's disability center—the class's host—that yoga is culturally appropriative. The story—however dubious[23]—went viral in the fish-in-a-barrel sort of way, with even *Jezebel* wondering whether canceling yoga due to cultural appropriation concerns was maybe a bit of sensitivity overreach.[24] As *Jezebel* writer Ellie Shechet put it, "Yoga—like coffee, tea, math, syringes, and many other things people put to good use on a daily basis—has its origins in a culture that was infected by the long, sickly arm of Western colonialism." The Ottawa yoga story—at least before it got somewhat debunked—became quite the unifier, which is, as these things go, the exception.

No form of cultural criticism is better suited to the privilege lens than the much-debated[25] concept of cultural appropriation. The line between exchange and appropriation is drawn according to whether the cultural borrowing reaches down. *Punches* down, one might say, except that even clumsily expressed admiration isn't exactly a punch. With the glaring exception of blackface, it's difficult to single out an unambiguous case of cultural appropriation of the nefarious variety. Take drag. Is this an example of gay men bravely defying gender norms? Or is prancing around in imitation of a cisgender woman actually a mean-spirited thing for a cisgender man—yes, even a gay one—to engage in? As is so often the case, the answer is: both.

So, too, with the notorious kimono exhibit, in 2015, at the Boston Museum of Fine Arts. The exhibition urged visitors to try on a kimono, inspired by a painting of Monet's (yup, white) wife wearing one. There were various levels of problematic-or-maybe-not to sort out: Was the painting actually mocking white people for being into Japanese stuff? Were the museum's visitors necessarily white, or necessarily from cultures that fall below Japan's on the privilege hierarchy?

While it squicked out certain Asian Americans to see white people trying on kimonos (thus the protests[26]), by all accounts, kimono wearing by non-Japanese people isn't fraught in the same way as headdress wearing by non–Native Americans, and is actually something that makes the Japanese people who sell kimonos to foreigners quite happy. According to news reports, Japanese observers were partly baffled, but also annoyed at having their plight, not so much appropriated, as invented by other East Asians.[27] Can Chinese Americans be offended on behalf of Japanese people who, when consulted, are not actually offended?

Yet a further, ignored, angle is the question of whether it's offensive (or even inaccurate) to suggest that Japanese people are somehow underdogs with respect to white Americans in the twenty-first century. But is a culture that's produced kaiseki cuisine, competitive poodle grooming, and electronic bidet toilets really one to which the "punch down" framework necessarily applias? Part of the Japanese refusal to find the kimono exhibit offensive may have stemmed from the fact that it was, for them, *problematic* to suggest that anything other than sincere admiration was at stake.

The appropriation discussion is thus a microcosm of the privilege critique more generally. Despite being ostensibly about social justice, it ends up reinforcing and maybe even inventing hierarchies, and therefore further centering whiteness, maleness, Westernness, and whichever other forms of have-ishness I've forgotten. It's about obsessing—to the inclusion both of bigger issues and, conversely, of apolitical ones—over politicized minutiae.

OUTRAGE BAIT AS MARKETING STRATEGY

IT ISN'T QUITE right to say that privilege awareness and think pieces merely restrict cultural production. They also, paradoxically, *encourage* many creators to offend, which is limiting in its own way, and which hardly contributes to progressive aims. Intentional outrage bait is perhaps most prominent in the fashion world, a place where there are, in the most straightforward sense, objects getting sold. The eternal question of why, despite so many bloggy reminders, fashion magazines keep offering up spreads showcasing white models in blackface (or in American Indian headdresses, or dressed as Syrian refugees) can readily be answered by the free publicity these choices elicit. It doesn't take a tremendous amount of cynicism to wonder if maybe, when Bloomingdale's ran—then briskly apologized for—a 2015 holiday ad suggesting that you "spike your best friend's eggnog when they're not looking," they knew what they were doing, and were going with an all-publicity-is-good-publicity strategy. "What a Creepy Bloomingdale's Ad Tells Us About America's Understanding of Rape,"[28] went a *Washington Post* online headline, for a piece that—through its use of social-media examples—wound up reprinting the ad image itself three separate times.

And where even to begin with the concern-drooling industry surrounding the existence of ever-younger, ever-thinner fashion models? Brands hire preadolescent-looking girls to strut the catwalk, and *very concerned* publications get to publish feminist talking points alongside photographs of symmetrical, emaciated-yet-voluptuous fifteen-year-old children, thereby reminding otherwise sensible adult women that we are neither as thin nor as smooth-skinned as we might be, which—through some mechanism I will never entirely outsmart—drives us to shop.

However, outrage-bait marketing isn't just about selling stuff in the widget sense. If you or your work manages to cause controversy, you gain not only the attention of whichever fledgling journalist has been given the be-offended prompt, but also the adulation of the *other* side of the outrage wars. (The libertarian publication *Reason* ran a piece defending the Bloomingdale's ad from the "Culture Police."[29]) Just as, in politics, a hypersensitive mood may have brought us

Donald Trump. In the creative realm, outrage policing ends up encouraging the unsubtly outrageous.

"MUCH-NEEDED DISCUSSION"

IN A WONDERFUL early-2016 piece on the *Fusion* Web site, writer Charles Pulliam-Moore traced the history of the expression "stay woke," from "socially-minded, black social media" around 2013 to broader social-justice alertness to literally meaning staying awake.[30] "Woke," as Pulliam-Moore explains, gets employed as a way of sincerely promoting alertness to injustice, but also ironically, as a way of having a go at the hyperaware, as well as at those whose proclamations of awareness somehow announce their cluelessness:

> "Woke" can also refer, mockingly, to (white) people whose perspectives on race change suddenly after learning about historical injustice. (e.g. "You talked to Brad recently? He read some Ta-Nehesi [*sic*] Coates and now he thinks he's woke.")

Pulliam-Moore gives an example of "woke" used in this context: "When *Jezebel* writes about a 'Woke Hungarian Who Did 7 Types of Blackface to Save Africa From Going Extinct,'[31] they're mocking a white woman who acted a damned fool in her self-righteous quest, not praising her for racial awareness." Precisely.[32]

One could place Justine Sacco, the notorious Twitter-gaffe committer, into this category as well. The tweet that sparked controversy—"Going to Africa. Hope I don't get AIDS. Just kidding. I'm white!"—was widely interpreted as racist, but may also have been, as Ronson writes, "a reflexive critique of white privilege."[33] Whether out of earnest anti-racism; a desire to save their own reputations; or some mix, a white opponent of racism might want to think twice before ostentatiously demonstrating that sentiment. What this usage of "woke" reveals, for our purposes, is that there's a backlash against white hyperawareness *from some progressive journalists of color*[34]: the very people the "woke" white ally believes him- or herself to be supporting.

And, with the necessary caveat that a letter to an advice columnist is not the most authoritative resource, consider this 2016 letter to *The New York Times* columnist Philip Galanes:

> I am a member of a racial minority. Often, a person I do not know will take pains to bring a matter to my attention (a news article, movie or lecture) that features the subject of my race. I don't pretend that people are color blind. But I am put off when a person I have just met tells me that I should read a book on my group's experience with the American justice system. How should I respond?[35]

To which Galanes (who is, he admits, "not a member of a visible minority") responds that while the letter writer's annoyance is understandable, the thing to do in this situation is to suck it up and have that conversation: "[I]f this dynamic creates opportunities for much-needed discussion about the racism that is baked into so many of our culture's institutions, think again about taking them up."

Not to get too meta, but isn't it also kind of troubling, if not racist, to assume people of color owe white people education on these matters? I ask not because I have any more personal insight than Galanes does into how it feels to be, say, a black person asked to expound upon *12 Years a Slave* while waiting in line at the post office, but because that's what the letter writer herself is telling us.

Two days later, the *Times* would run another piece by Galanes, a "Table for Three" column entitled, "Lupita Nyong'o and Trevor Noah, and Their Meaningful Roles."[36] In it, Galanes asks the Oscar winner and *Daily Show* host, respectively, about Hollywood diversity. The conversation sticks to that topic for a good long while, until Noah points out, "But you know the irony of #OscarsSoWhite? If you were talking with two white people, they would get to discuss their achievements, their hopes and dreams, maybe a passion project." Nyong'o then agrees, adding that the focus "cuts down on human experience." Galanes changes course and asks them about their work, only to ask Noah, soon after, "Growing up under apartheid, were you in a big rush to tell the truth?" His answer? "Not really."

My aim here is not to pick on Galanes. On the essential point, he's right. These issues *are* important, and it *is* crucial to hear about them from black people. As for whether the issues are, as he claims in the Social Q's column, underdiscussed, there we'd have to part ways. Indeed, say what you will (and should) about the flaws of the "privilege" approach specifically, but white people with deep commitment to the "white privilege" framework are probably going to be *less* racist than average, a point Hua Hsu notes in his *New Yorker* review of an MTV show on the topic: "As I watched 'White People,' I fantasized about all the other, far more oblivious-seeming white people I would rather hear from than these fairly bright young kids, who had, after all, agreed to appear in a film called 'White People.'"[37] There *is* real racism and it doesn't manifest itself as hypersensitivity.

Indeed, privilege accusations have a way of sparing the very people who'd most need to hear them. In a piece called "The Real Problem with 'Check Your Privilege': It's Too Generous,"[38] feminist writer Amanda Marcotte explains that she "find[s] the concept of examining your privilege to be limited, because it assumes that the only problem that those fighting for social justice face is one of education." In fact, as she makes clear, some people are the joyful beneficiaries of systemic injustice:

> There's another possibility besides unexamined privilege, usually just shortened to "privilege." It could be

that they have looked at their privileges, find them
appealing, and would like to preserve them at the expense of basic decency and keeping the peace.

Or as she puts it more bluntly, later in the piece, "it's not about unexamined privilege. It's about being an asshole."

Writing in *Salon*, philosopher Myisha Cherry offered an even
more pessimistic take:

When I look at people who refuse to accept that they
have privilege, after they've been schooled about its
existence and its problems, I no longer see an ignorant
heart in need of enlightenment. I see a greedy soul
holding on to anything that can put it ahead of others.[39]

The main problem with fashionable notions of allyship (that is,
of privilege awareness) isn't that its proponents are *just as bad* as bigots. Rather, it's that privilege awareness has made it more difficult
for baseline-well-meaning men, white people, etc., to treat members
of marginalized groups as *people*, and not as anthropomorphized
discussion points.

In his *New Yorker* piece, Hsu, like Tolentino in the *Jezebel* post
discussed above, casts doubt on the power of awareness to bring
about change:

[T]he show, emblematic of one version of our "conversation on race," presumes that the solution is conversa-
tional. The problem with dwelling on the sullen vibes or
narcissistic guilt spirals of white people is that feelings
can change with relative ease. The scenes of American
injustice that we see on a regular basis are not failures of
people being insufficiently nice to one another.

Progressive-minded white critics will also sometimes grapple with the question of how useful all the self-awareness is, *really*. When *New Yorker* television critic Emily Nussbaum opens a review of *Broad City* by calling the show "[a] stoner comedy about two woke girls," she isn't just riffing off the title of another show, *2 Broke Girls*. She's also setting up a discussion of the "characters' well-intentioned but barely informed fourth-wave, queerish, anti-rape/pro-porn intersectional feminism." The review hints at a growing understanding on the left that *aware* can, paradoxically, be worse than the alternative.[40] This understanding coexists (often in the same writer, even the same article!) with an impulse toward self-awareness confession. Soon after Pulliam-Moore's "woke" piece appeared, *The Guardian* ran a sweeping essay by Canadian writer Stephen Marche called "The White Man Pathology." While ostensibly a reported piece on the US presidential elections, it was also an explicitly Coates-inspired apologetic gaze at Marche's own "white and male body."[41] The "body" rhetoric, so of the moment, gets repurposed here, in what seems at first glance to be classic "privilege" form, to allow for a privileged self-examination. "It is hard to have a male and white body and to conceive of its weakness," writes Marche, in one of the many places in the essay where it's not entirely clear if this is a heartfelt confession of white privilege or a parody of the same. In a twist, it isn't *quite* that Coates's work has inspired Marche to think about his own white privilege. He sneaks in a reference to the way white people use references to Coates's book as a way to signal awareness:

> You can say to yourself or to others that black people are stupid and lazy; you can say that you don't see color; you can call your uncle a racist so everybody knows you're not; you can share the latest critique of brutality on Twitter with the word THIS; and now you can tell a friend that she really has to read *Between the World and Me*."

Marche equates I'm-not-a-racist posturing *with racism*, classifying each of these phenomena as an "alibi from . . . whiteness." He skewers the genre, in other words, while simultaneously taking part. Or not exactly—maybe what he's skewering is the thing where white people point to *other* white people and declare them the true racists. Maybe he's offering up an alternative, one that involves *still greater* self-awareness. In which case, how frustrating: the white navel is already overexposed.

The next, unstated step in the progression Marche describes, from casual racism to anti-racist signaling, is, without a doubt, the white-privilege confession. His piece opens with a classic #woke scene, a #CrimingWhileWhite moment where he's treated decently by a guard at the US–Canada border, and knows that he owes his decent treatment to his race. Sure, he offers no corresponding anecdote about what happens when nonwhite people enter the States, no anecdote (personal, or even something he'd read about in the news) of someone nonwhite having problems there, but he doesn't need to. The point—which in this case is Marche's Tocquevillian (Knausgaardian) observations at Trump and Sanders rallies—is always that the author *gets it*. And getting it, like all the rest, has a way of coming full circle. At one point Marche cites a passage where bell hooks calls white men emotionally stunted. Marche calls hooks's assessment "inaccurate," explaining, "No one is more emotional than a piece-of-shit white man." And back into the privileged loop we go, to the place where self-awareness mingles with self-centeredness.

It wouldn't be accurate to label all criticism of white "wokeness" from writers of color as "privilege"-critique. I'd thought that was where Rebecca Carroll was going with a *Guardian* column (headline: "Macklemore Raps About White Privilege—While Reaping Its Rewards") about Stephen Colbert, Macklemore, and other white male celebrity's much-heralded (in white progressive circles) discovery of white privilege.[42] Carroll, who is black, referred to these public awakenings as "legitimate first-step efforts," but nevertheless a form of "white liberal microaggression racism, vis-à-vis an extreme lack of racial conversancy—a language that reflects white privilege as culturally inherent, not novel discovery that warrants praise and a membership card to the Down White People Club."

I was expecting, then, another piece about the insufficiencies of discussing white privilege. Carroll's solution, though, was for white people to discuss white privilege even more:

> And so, Stephen Colbert, the way to turn this around is not by living deeper in that legacy by giving your host seat to a black guest for five minutes in front of three million viewers, but by establishing a recurring segment in which you talk with all of your guests about white privilege and how it is perpetuating systemic racism nationwide—in our economy, in our neighborhoods, and in our everyday lives.

There is, needless to say, no official consensus on this matter, among writers of any background. The closest thing to one, though, is that privilege awareness, on its own, isn't effective. And yet the freestanding declaration remains ubiquitous.

THE YPIS OF JEALOUSY

A LOT OF "privilege"-based cultural criticism stems from the fact that being a rich and famous artist is an enviable position. As writer and blogger Maria Popova has argued, and as I, too, have pointed out on occasion, a lot of the privilege accusations hurled at creative types come from confusion over unearned advantage and the earned variety.[43] Jealousy leads critics to overestimate the privilege of artists whose work they find unimpressive. The idea being, what, if not some kind of extra-special privilege, explains why this idiot has a novel or TV show out, while I toil away at the office, on a computer game, or whatever?

In a 2011 *Slate* essay,[44] the writer Katie Roiphe took aim at Internet trolls, a topic that was, at the time, new-ish: "There are several common fantasies about the writer that fly through comments sections. One," she explained, "is that the writer is 'privileged,' and/or getting rich off of their insipid and offending article."

This accusation, Roiphe claimed, was absurd:

> If the writer has come from a place of privilege—and as in the rest of the world, some have and some haven't—they are most likely frittering away whatever they do have by entering an insecure and unlucrative profession like writing. These demographic realities, though, make little impression on the angry commenter, who, one notes admiringly, sticks to her guns. We are clearly in a season of class war, and one can understand the class war against a hedge-fund guy, but a *writer*?

On the basis of who knows which unpleasant interactions, Roiphe continued along these lines, protesting the apparent tendency of commenters to treat proper spelling and grammar as "kind of a show-offy part of the writer's 'privilege.' We all do have spell check on our computers, so clearly if the angry commenter wanted to she could spell correctly too, but spelling correctly would be giving in to the whole hierarchy, namely the idea that some things might be more interesting to read than other things, that has angered her in the first place."

Touché, in a sense, although it isn't such a stretch to imagine that famous writers who are the children of other famous writers—that is, the sort of people who've been fielding privilege accusations since at least 1993[45]—would get this sort of thing more than most. Yet as it so happens, Roiphe was basically right. How else to explain the obsession, in feminist comment sections,[46] with teen fashion blogger-and-more Tavi Gevinson's supposed socioeconomic "privilege"? The thinking there is that she can't possibly be a middle-class white kid from Chicago. There has to be some explanation, some secret rich relative, *something*.

THE RUSTY-CAR MOTIF

WHILE WALKING MY dog one day in Toronto, nostalgic, perhaps, for my hometown, I found myself listening to a WNYC podcast. Host Leonard Lopate was interviewing a surfer-slash-war-reporter. Despite the audio-only nature of the program, some part of my hetero-female brain was surely intrigued. Or maybe I'd just run out of podcasts. In any case, the interviewee, William Finnegan, turned out to be a *New Yorker* staff writer, who, after covering conflicts in Africa, decided to turn inward, and to write up a memoir of his lifelong love of surfing. These two seemingly contradictory interests make for a compelling story (Who wants the memoir of a surfer who isn't *also* a talented journalist? A photo would do . . .), but they also amount to the same: a man driven to see the world, unencumbered by such bourgeois, soft concerns as, does the house have a dishwasher? Sun-damaged, but (we learn) six feet two, Finnegan laments the fact that some remote surfing locale he and a friend discovered is now a resort. The theme of the interview was that *real* surfing isn't all Beach Boys and the boho-chic lifestyle. I thought about a profile I'd read a while back on cool-girl beauty blog *Into The Gloss*, of a nineteen-year-old female professional surfer, who revealed, among other things, that she gets highlights in the off-season, when being out in the sun isn't enough to keep her properly blond.[47] Somehow I doubt if this would meet Finnegan's authenticity standards.

What struck me about the WNYC interview was as much what was discussed as what wasn't. We learn that Finnegan got seriously into surfing because his father was a television producer working on a set in Hawaii. A moment's Internet research reveals that William Finnegan, senior, was something of a big deal, a five-time Emmy nominee who'd produced numerous well-known movies and television shows.[48] Lopate asked Finnegan how he'd supported himself at various points in his adult life when he chucked it all to just follow those epic waves, and the answers (worked at a bookstore, taught at a black school in South Africa) all sound reasonable enough, if not noble and fascinating. Yet what's never so much as hinted at is the possibility that his privileged background played a role of some kind in his trajectory from Hawaiian surfer and college dropout to *The New Yorker* and WNYC.

Put another way: If Finnegan were a woman, I can't imagine the family-privilege angle wouldn't have come up. Consider that what sure sounds like a rich-kid hobby—hanging out at the beach full time—gets described as if it were some kind of *science*. Which I'll accept, but please do tell me when a woman who periodically ditches work and family responsibilities to devote herself fully to sample sales gets presented on the Leonard Lopate show as an amateur economist.

The privilege turn has not made much headway in changing who gets to enter the arts in the first place. What it has done is introduce a log-cabin-narrative requirement for writers and performers of all genres. A scrappy origin story is always needed, not just for politicians, but for anyone in the public eye. In a 2014 *Harper's Bazaar* interview with fellow actress Chloë Sevigny, Natasha Lyonne remarked, "You and I have that in common—we were both outcasts in school in privileged communities where we were not the richest."[49] Or take Louis C.K.'s description of his childhood. When an interviewer brings up the fact that his parents had met at Harvard, the comedian launches into an explanation of why this biographical detail isn't what it seems. Below, his response to journalist Jonah Weiner:

When I was doing *Lucky Louie* and I had this blue collar
profile, people were like, "Yeah, but his parents met at
Harvard," which is funny to me. My dad's upper class
[from] Mexico, and his father was an immigrant from
Hungary. My mom was from Michigan, she lived on a
farm in Michigan, and she grew up with nothing. She was
just, academically, really bright, and she went to Harvard
summer school to take some courses, and my dad was
there going to grad school. They weren't undergrad,
that's the thing to remember. If you go to Harvard
undergrad, you're a spoiled brat, and you probably got in
through some legacy, and you're not even getting that
good of an education, most Harvard people, but Harvard
grad school is where serious professionals get their
degrees and licenses. My father was there studying as
an economist, and my mother was doing some post-grad
stuff.[50]

The *feeling* this passage conveys is that Louis C.K. came by his
blue-collar persona honestly. Something-something "Mexico,"
something-something "immigrant," something-something "farm." And
then there's the juxtaposition of Louis C.K.'s parents with Harvard *un-*
dergrads, a group whose copious privilege no one is going to deny.

What's so clever about Louis C.K.'s response is that he doesn't
simply point out (as he might have, and as comes up elsewhere in this
same interview) that his father left the family when he was ten, and
that Harvard or no Harvard, he had a tough childhood. He has the
audacity to spin *the Harvard part* of his family history as conferring
underdog status, as well as the rhetorical skill necessary to pull this
off. And there really is an art to self-depiction as self-made. Consider
the opening sentence of Finnegan's *New Yorker* excerpt: "The bud-
get for moving our family to Honolulu was tight, judging from the
tiny cottage we rented and the rusted-out Ford Fairlane we bought

to get around."[51] For some reason, privilege denial always includes a rusty car. All that rust—the car is literally *scrappy*—obscures a bigger truth about an artist's circumstances.

LENA DUNHAM REPORTED TO POSSESS PRIVILEGE

PRIVILEGE-CENTRIC ARTS CRITICISM began to take off around the same time as online social-justice YPIS. The two phenomena act in synergy with cultural production itself, which now must preemptively deflect these accusations. Privilege checks have been appearing for a while in A. O. Scott's movie reviews. In 2010, he took on the *Sex and the City* movie sequel in explicitly YPIS terms:

> [T]he ugly smell of unexamined privilege hangs over this film like the smoke from cheap incense. Over cosmos in their private bar, Charlotte and Miranda commiserate about the hardships of motherhood and then raise their glasses to moms who "don't have help," by which they mean paid servants. Later the climactic crisis raises the specter either of Samantha going to jail or the friends having to fly home in coach, and it's not altogether clear which prospect they regard as more dreadful.[52]

It's not clear what it means to accuse escapist entertainment of "unexamined privilege." Nor is it evident who Scott hoped would do this examining. But so it goes with the dubious awareness requirement.

Scott went for a deeper privilege critique in his December 2012 review of Judd Apatow's *This Is 40*, which, as he describes it, "is all about Pete and Debbie, who, along with their two daughters, occupy a big white house in one of Los Angeles's nicer ZIP codes and who, in the course of a hectic week, undergo—well, what, exactly? A matched set of midlife crises? A rough patch in their marriage? A flurry of 'first-world problems' so trivial as to be an insult to the planet's struggling masses?" Scott spells out that "for all its crude jokes and on-the-money observations of the tastes and consumer habits of aging white Gen X-ers (we still love the Pixies!), *This Is 40* should not be mistaken for satire."[53] The film's problem, in other words, isn't its depiction of privilege, but its lack of self-awareness. It's good and well to make a movie about rich white people with nonproblems, as long as you, perhaps, affix a disclaimer?

While variants of it appeared slightly earlier, the "privilege" critique as we know it today—where "privilege" is the only lens through which a work can be discussed—began in the spring of 2012, with the backlash to Lena Dunham's HBO series, *Girls*. Just about everything written about the show—and even in its defense—addressed the "privilege" question, which had not really been a question until that point.[54] Dunham, it was generally agreed, should be, *must* be, referred to as "privileged"; failure to mention Dunham's privilege, and to do so with the term "privilege," was tantamount to declaring one's support for injustice. Dunham's *Fresh Air* interview about the show, the month after *Girls* first aired, wasn't the usual promotional introduction, but was presented, instead, under the heading, "Lena Dunham Addresses Criticism Aimed at 'Girls,'" that criticism being "that the show is narcissistic, lacks racial diversity and showcases whiny, privileged millennials complaining about topics only relevant to whiny, privileged millennials."[55] The only thing everyone could agree on about the show was that it and its creator embodied "privilege," and that to discuss the show was to discuss that aspect of it.

Given that *Girls* was the ten-trillionth show about a group of white friends living in New York and trying to make it in glamorous professions, it's not immediately obvious why this one set forth the privilege critique. If we want to pin this on Dunham's own "privilege"—and what notorious "privilege" it is[56]—we still come up short. In an industry filled with nepotism, the specific variant she benefits from—she's the child of successful artists—puts her ahead of most, but hardly makes her success predestined. And the show's New Brooklyn setting, while overrepresented in the cultural sphere, is far from the most posh onscreen setting. (Half of American entertainment takes place in enormous California beach houses.) If "privilege" is spectacular wealth or unearned advantage, surely better examples could be found, even in 2012 alone. (The "Housewives" franchise comes to mind.)

The explanation for the *Girls*-as-privilege meme lies in a convergence of the content (especially of the pilot); the marketing of the show; and the broader culture in which it first appeared, namely a postrecession America not inclined to sympathize with the nonproblems of a group of broke but safety-net-having young Brooklynites. The show opens with Dunham's character, Hannah, learning from her parents—at an upscale New York restaurant—that they're about to cut her off. A no-longer-so-recent college grad, her parents had been supporting her as she interned for free at a publishing house. An indictment of the times, but mainly one of the sort of recent grad who doesn't at least try to find paid work. We watch Hannah whine and plead for her parents to keep supporting her. The episode ends with a still-more-cringe-inducing version of the opening scene: Hannah notices and pockets the money her parents have left for the hotel housekeeper. Insofar as "privilege" is brattiness, it's certainly privilege being depicted. Some kind of messy conflation of Hannah the character and Dunham the person, and of the portrayal of a behavior and the celebration of the same, led to a collective— mistaken!—belief that the show was not just about but created by the unapologetically spoiled.

The show was presented as an anti–*Sex and the City*, offering a grittier, more authentic portrait of single female friends in New York.[57] This promise of social realism set the show up for a certain kind of criticism. Without the scrappiness promise, it seems unlikely anyone would have found the show all that "privileged." As *New Yorker* television critic Emily Nussbaum pointed out in an early review, "like *SATC*, Dunham's show takes as its subject women who are quite demographically specific—cosseted white New Yorkers from educated backgrounds—then mines their lives for the universal." The difference, Nussbaum argued—justly—lay in the "very different stages of life" depicted, rather than in the two shows' socioeconomic worlds.[58] Something similar could be said about the furious response to the show's lack of nonwhite characters. As writer Anna Holmes pointed out in *The New Yorker*, some of the backlash was simply about the times ("this is 2012"), but I'd say it stemmed at least as much from Dunham's own self-presentation as a progressive, and the breathless treatment of "Girls" as "groundbreaking."[59] A female creator, and so young! And so clearly not chosen for her adherence to conventional beauty standards! Holmes wrote that the show's whiteness was "all the more surprising because Dunham, a self-described feminist, seems unaware that the progressive gender politics she embraces have a long and frustrating history of relegating race to the sidelines."[60] Indeed, if liking *Girls* hadn't been presented as almost a progressive requirement, it seems far more likely it would have been permitted to just be a show.

I'd pause, for a moment, on two words from Holmes's assessment: "seems unaware." The conversation about *Girls* ended up hinging not on the show, and not even exactly on the identity of the show's creator. Rather, the central concern was Dunham herself—her own relationship to privilege, and her ability to satisfactorily perform privilege awareness. The question, when it comes to Lena Dunham, is always this: Does she get it? Has she, Lena Dunham, properly reckoned with her place in the world, and properly conveyed the fruits of said reckoning to the appropriate commentators? The far bigger question, namely of who gets to make a show in the first place, took a backseat to questions of whom Dunham chose to cast, and what sort of *stance* the show was taking. Consider writer Max

Read on *Gawker,* posting in response to a tweet of Dunham's he felt didn't come across quite right:

> I *used* to think that [she] just hadn't learned her lesson about treating minority groups as subjects for the children of privilege to strike poses over at dinner parties or make jokes about on Twitter, and that eventually she would stop saying stupid things and hanging out with stupid people. But, no, as it turns out, she's just an asshole.[61]

For a time, it seemed as if social justice itself hinged on this one woman "learn[ing] her lesson." There's surprisingly little hint, actually, of this pattern letting up.

Dunham, herself, I'm not too worried about. She's made unexamined privilege (which is to say, painstakingly examined privilege) her brand. Maybe it helped that she was already getting this label in the years before her privilege went viral: A *New Yorker* profile of her from back in 2010, pre-*Girls,* ran with the subhead, "Lena Dunham Cheerfully Exposes Her Privileged Life." [62] She's the think-piece face of millennial entitlement, which, if nothing else, keeps her in the news. "Is Lena Dunham too privileged to fail?" asked a *Daily Beast* writer, in reference to does it even matter at this point?[63] "Lena Dunham apologizes for . . ."[64] is a veritable genre. To be the symbol of the issue of the moment is surely exhausting, but she has, if not sought that out, found a way to make being so profitable.

THE VANISHING DIVIDE BETWEEN THINK PIECE AND SITCOM

WHAT IS A concern, however, is the impact the privilege critique, in its ubiquity, has had on cultural production. The vast majority of artists and entertainers haven't, like Dunham, found a way to make teetering on the edge of obliviousness marketable.

Since the *Girls* backlash, new shows have been responding, pre-emptively, to the accusations that show received. This preemptive base covering has been the most obvious with *Broad City*, which—despite being hilarious and worthy enough on that count—got cele-brated in the press for *getting it* in a way that *Girls*, in particular, had not. For starters, *Broad City* features a diverse cast—Ilana's friend-with-benefits is a black man, and her roommate is a gay Latino. And there wasn't that same *Girls thing* where you never quite believe that the protagonists are broke, let alone struggling. Writer Jada Yuan's *New York* magazine feature on the show and its cre-ators, "The *Broad City* Hustle," is, as the title suggests, about the scrappiness—middle class, yes, but at least not *that* privileged!—of the protagonists.[65] In a 2015 *Slate* piece called "The Best Part of *Broad City* Is How It Handles Class,"[66] writer Heather Schwedel explicitly compares the two shows and declares *Broad City* the winner . . . on privilege-awareness grounds:

> The show is very much aware of Abbi and Ilana's privilege; it uses that old saw of making the characters seem clueless as a way to communicate knowingness to the audience to great comic effect. In the finale, that panhandler is able to guilt-trip them precisely because, "poor" as they may be, they are (unlike, say, the girls of *Girls*) aware of the air quotes around their disadvantagedness.

Schwedel makes the entirely accurate observation that "Abbi and Ilana's cluelessness is so ratcheted up, so clumsily apparent, that it's hard to mistake for cluelessness on the part of the show's writers." It's now taken for granted that a lack of subtlety in areas such as these is a point in a show's favor. And so *Broad City*, which is simply *a more fun show* than *Girls*, can't be assessed as such. There needs to be a privilege-lens explanation for why it's superior. It needs to be about which show gets it, and the "it" can't be something as simple (and apolitical) as cleverness.

Entertainment that can be readily shared, out of context, on social media holds a certain advantage in the current market. Journalist Noreen Malone couldn't have been more correct when she described the third season of *Inside Amy Schumer* as consisting of Schumer "taking the major hot-button feminist issues straight off the Internet and turning them into skits."[67] A show-ruining remark if there ever was one.

To Schumer's credit, this approach sometimes worked. Her Emmy-winning[68] parody music video, "Girl, You Don't Need Makeup," in which a (fake) boy band sings the praises of the Schumer alter ego's natural beauty . . . until seeing her makeup-free, at which point the lyrics switch over to an insistence that she put on more of the stuff, somehow managed to both *work* and make the relatively subtle point better it's ever been in made in print. Others, such as a sketch about aging actresses' plight, really did just have the feel of talking points transposed, gratuitously, into viral-video form. Which, perhaps, explains all the Amy Schumer gets-whichever-issue-right think pieces (such as this *Vox* headline: "Amy Schumer nails why privilege isn't the same thing as respect for women"),[69] but it goes further still. The official site announcing Schumer's Peabody Award win describes her contribution in righteous, noble terms that make it sound as if she'd be unwatchable: "The fleet-footed Schumer will satirically embody vacuous white privilege in one sketch before pivoting to comically interrogate rape culture, body image norms or sanctimonious savior narratives in the next—and then engage in crisp banter about sexual failures and disappointments in person-on-the-street interviews."[70]

If *Inside Amy Schumer* is *Jezebel* as comedy, Aziz Ansari's series, *Master of None*, is, perhaps, *Salon*. Dev, Ansari's protagonist, spends most of each episode demonstrating his awareness of one facet or another of his privilege, or, less frequently, of a systemic injustice of which he happens to be a victim. The friend group at the center of the show—which has gone with the innovative choice of being about a group of single, well-off, thirtyish friends in New York—has no chemistry whatsoever, and seems instead to have been constructed purely to anticipate representation-specific criticisms. There's a schlubby, white, male friend who, like the gratuitous upscale New York setting, signals that the series is, in fact, a comedy. Then there's Brian, the good-looking Taiwanese American man, who has no discernible personality, but who serves the purpose of reflecting negative media stereotypes about the sex appeal of East Asian men. Women *like* him, it's mentioned. In case you were about to point out that this group sounds awfully straight and male, and also, where are the black characters?—fear not! The remaining friend is a black lesbian! It is, at exactly no point in the series, convincing that any of these people are friends with one another. But Lena Waithe's Denise, while plenty likable, is perhaps the least convincing of all, seeming, as she does, to have been airlifted in from a far cooler clique.

In the episode "Ladies and Gentlemen," Dev learns about male privilege, while the audience gets a lesson in what the term heavy-handed refers to. In the opening scene, we see Dev and his friend—the white, schlubby guy—having drinks at a bar. Elsewhere at the same bar, we see a thus far unidentified black woman (TFUBW) getting aggressively hit on by a white dude. The show switches back and forth between these two situations: there's Dev and white schlub (WS) walking home, deciding to walk through the park (male privilege alert!), and then there's TFUBW walking home alone, visibly terrified of the ambient rape-culture menace, because—at least according to a certain brand of feminist think piece—that's what it's always like to walk home, at night, as a young woman. Except the thing is, the bar creep has actually followed TFUBW home! She has to call the police and everything! All the while, Dev is whining to WS about having stepped in a dog turd and ruined his "sneakies." Because there was apparently some microscopic chance that not every agenda item had been addressed, we hear the would-be assault perpetrator insisting that he's a "nice guy."

At which point the viewer—this liberal, feminist, Canada-dwelling viewer—wanted to say, OK, we get it. Women, young ones especially, have to deal with the ever-present threat of male violence. This point—a sound one—is the episode's argument. (Note: the sitcom episode has an argument.) But no, the show's hand was heavier even than anticipated. We are then subject to a *very serious discussion* among Dev's friend group, with the women educating the men about how getting followed home from bars by strange dudes is just how it goes for women, which segues into the next *very important plot point*, involving Dev voluntarily giving up some male privilege by encouraging women to have more airtime in a commercial he is (well, was) starring in. The episode even gracefully avoids the "cookie" accusation (that is, that the show wants us to praise Dev for being a decent human being), principally by having Dev (initially, because let's face it, he's a saint) disagree with his girlfriend and a female friend that it's sexist when men come up to a mixed-gender group and introduce themselves only to the men.

The show's best moments aren't necessarily the apolitical ones, so much as the ones that break free of the op-ed-ish constraints. The "Finale" tells an old story about marriage ambivalence in a fresh way, and while there are talking points sprinkled throughout (marriage is an outdated institution, people say weird things to interracial couples, etc.), the story finally seems more like that of two people informed by their backgrounds, rather than like a *Salon* tirade come to life.

And the "Parents" episode, which plunges viewers into the perspective of Asian immigrant parents, is brilliant, and seems as if it comes from another show entirely. First we see Dev and Brian, acting like entitled millennials, annoyed at their old-country parents.

We then get flashbacks, from both fathers' perspectives, and to their childhoods in India and Taiwan, respectively. While its thesis is the same as that of the other episodes—Dev is nice, niceness is good, and racism is bad (we witness both fathers, in flashbacks, experiencing racism upon arriving in the States)—this one doesn't linger quite so long in those realms.

It seems, in other words, that the show *gets it right* like none ever before. Perhaps not surprisingly, Ansari's own opinion essay on the topic of racism and the entertainment industry, which appeared in *The New York Times* as a bonus track of sorts to the show itself—a thoughtful look at what it means to be an entertainer from an underrepresented group, and on the challenges of diversity in casting—is ultimately quite a bit *better* than the show.[71] What works as a think piece falls flat as entertainment. Yet at least no marginalized groups were harmed (or even left unacknowledged) in the making, right?

Not so! Even *Master of None*—this show whose *entire selling point* is having *gotten it right*—has, apparently, failed. On *Jezebel*'s side blog, *The Muse*, writer Kara Brown took Ansari to task for not including enough female characters, nor enough "women of color in significant roles." How this squares with Brown's following sentence, which is a list of the three main nonwhite (or, in one case, mixed-race but white-reading) female characters on the show, I couldn't say. And at *New York* magazine's *Vulture* blog, writer Ali Barthwell hones in specifically on the question of Dev's love interests, who are mainly white women:

> For a show that so deftly takes on race and how it influences how we see one another, and where every actor's ethnicity informs his or her character, the decision to not engage with it romantically on any level feels like a missed opportunity. *Master of None* addresses how the world perceives Rachel dating an "ethnic," as one man

refers to Dev—wouldn't it be great if there were also a
conversation about Dev's romantic preferences?[72]

On the one hand, I want to scream. Must entertainment always
set forth, in digestible, sound-bite-esque terms, a "conversation"?
Can't the "conversation" just be the thing people who watch the show
have about it? Apparently not. Artists and entertainers are now expected to respond, in more or less real time, to journalists' criticisms
of their politics. On *Vulture*, writer E. Alex Jung took Amy Schumer
to task[73] for failing to properly consider a *Guardian* piece that had accused her of having "a shockingly large blind spot around race."[74]
"Rather than listen to the critique, she got defensive," wrote Jung, before offering up as an example of a performer who takes a "better approach," namely "to listen and take the criticism in rather than try to
shut it down": none other than . . . Lena Dunham. Reader, I give up.

The requirement winds up being that much greater for women,
particularly women of color, thus revealing another way the privilege
turn has backfired. Yes, the very people whose voices progressives
supposedly want to hear are expected to take on additional thought-
leader responsibilities, while also being entertaining, and while of
course, within that entertainment, getting it right. The prime example of this phenomenon has to be Mindy Kaling, whose sitcom, *The
Mindy Project*, is pretty defiantly unconcerned with identity politics
or getting things right, and who regularly gets taken to task for this.[75]
Kaling ended up responding, on NPR, to critics faulting her for not
being active enough in the conversation around her existence:

> I was on Twitter recently and a critic, who's been very
> critical of me and of the show, was talking about a round
> table that three South Asian women had done where
> they kind of criticized and dissected the show, and said,
> "Why doesn't Mindy respond to this?" . . . I'm an actor
> and a writer and a showrunner and I edit my show.

Crucially, she added, "And I think that it's insidious to be spending more of your time reflecting and talking about panels, and talking more and more in smart ways about your otherness, rather than doing the hard work of your job."[76]

Kaling's right, or at least, I wish we lived in a world in which she were. However, we're now in an age where entertainment has to be in the service of a greater good. And as such, if further *good* can come about through the entertainer moonlighting as an opinion writer, that's simply what's demanded.

In *The Atlantic*, writer Megan Garber celebrated the fact that comedians have—in her view—become the new public intellectuals. She argues in the piece that as comedy "became (slightly) less exclusionary to women and minorities," the genre "began to ask, and answer, the questions that newfound diversity will tend to bring up—questions about power dynamics and privilege and cultural authority." An opened playing field, it would seem, must lead to sanctimony:

> As comedy began to do a better job of reflecting the world, it began, as well, to take on the responsibilities associated with that reflection. It began to recognize the fact that the long debate about the things comedy owes to its audiences and itself—the old "hey, I'm just making a joke" line of logic—can be partially resolved in the idea that nothing, ultimately, is "just a joke." Humor has moral purpose. Humor has intellectual heft. Humor can change the world.[77]

A part of Garber's argument is right—the "just a joke" disclaimer, long pinned on the kind of casual bigotry that lacks any humorous component, is done, and good riddance. However, the notion that inclusiveness means an end to the sort of humor that lacks an explicit "moral purpose" is frightening.

The beginning of Ali Barthwell's remark about *Master of None*, that bit where she writes, "For a show that so deftly takes on race . . ." is key: The show is presenting itself not as entertainment, but as a shining beacon of privilege awareness. The disappointment—as with Schumer and Dunham—comes from the sense of a broken promise. With that said, it's not entirely clear that any of these creators ever quite had the option to not, as it were, converse. Any show that's by-and-about someone who isn't a white man ends up subject, in a special and all-encompassing way, to this sort of criticism. Consider this part of Barthwell's review: "The onus is not necessarily on minority showrunners to change our views on who makes a viable romantic partner. But a preference for white lovers is not the same as wanting a partner who likes hiking or has tattoos." Consider, the first word of the second sentence, that "But." There's always this underlying assumption that a show by someone who isn't a white man is, in and of itself, a political gesture, and must, to be consistent, follow through with impeccable politics. This places an extra burden on already-marginalized performers, and produces too much think-piece-mirroring entertainment.

All of this played out the most dramatically in the controversies surrounding *Unbreakable Kimmy Schmidt*, Tina Fey and Ryan Carlock's sitcom about a Midwestern woman who escaped kidnapping and imprisonment to start a new life in New York. A *Time* magazine headline labeled the series "TV's Most #Problematic Show,"[78] which is absolutely true, if a bit convoluted to explain. Basically, in season one, the show violated (or subverted) a rule about not casting white people in nonwhite roles when it was revealed that the Jane Krakowski character is an American Indian woman intentionally passing as white. Problematic! Tina Fey—already a problematic "White Lady" for more reasons than I can keep track of—got taken to task for not engaging with online critics.[79] Then in the second season, Fey, and whoever else at the show, decided to have some fun with the tendency of television shows to get called out for offending.

In the most problematic episode, Kimmy's roommate Titus—black, gay, and played by Tituss Burgess, who might be the actor with the best comic timing in history—puts on a one-man show, in which he acts out what he imagines was his past life as a geisha. In a nod to Boston Museum's kimono-gate, there's not just Titus in a kimono (and whiteface; had this been *blackface*, we'd have left problematic territory for the straightforwardly racist, and therefore less think-piece worthy), but also a plotline involving hypersensitive Asian American protesters. It was clever, but if it was *funny* (which, fine, it was), that's because Burgess has comedic superpowers. While I enthusiastically support Fey's resistance to sanctimonious media criticism, and think her wise for avoiding engaging with her online detractors, there's always something a bit limited about a think-piece plotline, which, ultimately, that plot was. Even when it's a think piece you agree with.

Predictably enough, the kimono episode sparked still-more think-piece controversy. In *The Guardian*, critic Eric Thurm spells out what, exactly, made the plot problematic, while taking care to add that other "elements of the season work because they meet the old test of 'punching up,' making fun of people who can take it."[80] What's barely mentioned is the fact that the show is doing quite a bit to increase onscreen diversity. It's only after explaining why the kimono plot was problematic that critic Allie Pape, on *Vulture*, admits, "[F]or what it's worth, [the show] clearly intends to address Hollywood's deficits—there's no other show on TV whose primary cast is three women (two of them over 45), two men of color (one of them gay, the other an immigrant), and zero white dudes."[81] The cast's diversity, though, is a side note. It's almost as if that diversity makes its occasional forays into provocation *that much more* problematic, since perfection seems within reach.

THE HARDER THEY TRY, THE FASTER THEY FALL

THAT SAID, PRIVILEGE-BASED criticism tends to reach its peak when responding to works from what might be called the sanctitainment genre: A new show or movie will come out, one whose entire purpose is telling a *very important story*, and it's only a matter of time until the articles start appearing about why this latest work is, in fact, the most offensive thing ever, how dare they, how *dare* they! Usually, around the time a civil rights issue reaches noncontroversial status in mainstream society, that's about the right moment to make a movie about the righteousness of the now-long-accepted cause. Thus, I suppose, is what happened with Roland Emmerich's widely panned 2015 film, *Stonewall*, about the 1969 Stonewall riots. And thus all the more so the Sarah Gavron's also-2015 *Suffragette*, about take a wild guess. Gay people should be allowed to go to gay bars and live peacefully! Women should have the right to vote! Yes, an enthusiastic yes to both, but who were the liberal-minded Westerners in 2015 who questioned either? But moving on.

Both of these movies attracted tremendous from-the-left criticism and even protests.[82] In a *Vanity Fair* review, writer Richard Lawson lays out the issues with *Stonewall*, faulting Emmerich for making his protagonist a "beautiful, blond angel from the Midwest, sent to the Village to marshall the nonwhite, gender-queer street kids into action. Which, y'know, is certainly not how the Stonewall riots, which were largely incited by drag queens and trans women of color and lesbians, actually happened." The movie's redeeming feature, Lawson argues, in a backhanded-compliment sort of way, is the awareness its flaws raise of—yup—privilege: "*Stonewall* at least does that bit of good: it illustrates how systems of privilege and prejudice within a minority can be just as pervasive and ugly as anything imposed from the outside. And that's an outrage."[83]

Yet the true "privilege" treatment came in writer Daniel Reynolds's defense of the movie, in *The Advocate*,[84] a fairly short essay that uses variants of the term six times (but that also, to Reynolds's rhetorical credit, includes the unforgettable admonition to "not throw the gayby out with the bathwater," to express the thought that the movie, for all its flaws, shouldn't be dismissed entirely). While Reynolds allows that "Emmerich's perception that the best point of entry for 'everyone' would be the steely blue eyes of a white, musclebound young man from rural America may well indicate his own unexamined privilege," Reynolds's privilege-focused take goes one step further, calling out "[c]ritics of the movie, who are privileged enough to have seen" highbrow LGBT-themed films for expecting art-house perfection from a mainstream picture. According to Reynolds, the audience *Stonewall* is there to help is the small-town American kid with a homophobic family. An argument along those lines is needed, if one is to defend the legitimacy of a work accused of privilege. Or, at the very least, there needs to be some sort of acknowledgment that one is aware of the privilege accusations and the reason for them. If you're going to praise a work that has already been called out in this way, you need to pile on the disclaimers. Thus the 2013 *AlterNet* piece, "Lena Dunham Privileged? Yes, But You Should Still Watch 'Girls,'" which begins with the sentence, "Privilege is a powerful and predetermined form of luck."[85] A definition of privilege, in other words, is the very first line of what is, ostensibly, a review of a television program.

As with *Stonewall*, the *Suffragette* criticism was about the erasure of nonwhite historical actors. It's a weaker case with the British suffragette movement of the early twentieth century than with the Stonewall riots, but as a *New Statesman* piece helpfully explained, not every last suffragette was white, so in principle, the movie might have acknowledged contemporary sensitivities without resorting to full-on anachronism.[86] If the backlash to the relatively minor grievance was higher profile, it may have had something to do with Meryl Streep being in the film. But the think-piece virality of the opposition to *Suffragette* wound up stemming, as it so often does, from a question-able T-shirt, in this case one bearing a quote from real-life suffrag-ette (and Streep's character) Emmeline Pankhurst: "I'd rather be a rebel than a slave."[87] The movie's four (white) female stars posed in this shirt for *Time Out London*, each with the flawless-yet-undone hair of a glamorous actress going for a casual look, and with expressions that suggested a blithe indifference to the associations that "slave" might have, particularly—if not exclusively—in the United States.[88]

Tasked to review the film for *The Stranger*, critic Ijeoma Oluo instead produced an essay about her refusal to do so, "because I'm no longer going to legitimize films that refuse to acknowledge the existence of people of color. And neither should you."[89] Oluo doesn't claim in the piece that the movie is overtly racist, merely that in some entirely different version of it that she'd have preferred, it would have had nonwhite actors.

The privilege critique tends to fall with the heaviest thud on art-ists and works with a progressive mission. Is it that works purport-ing to be progressive come across as particularly hypocritical when they fail to exhibit progressiveness on all fronts? That there's some-thing particularly irritating about the smug self-satisfaction of the marketing campaigns around good-cause movies, say, such that it's that much more irritating when they, the self-proclaimed official ar-biters of justice, screw up? Or is it, on the contrary, that these works are already vulnerable, given their progressive messaging, and are easier targets? After all, a movie about gay rights or women's suffrage will already have a built-in audience of detractors from the right, as well as of politically indifferent sorts whose eyes roll at earnest mes-saging of any kind. Ultimately, both are true. Progressive works that fall short are more annoying than mainstream ones that were never trying in the first place, but they maybe shouldn't be.

The problem is less that "privilege" enters into criticism than that it's become the *only* critique. All there is to say about a work is where it stands with respect to privilege. Where on the privilege hierarchy does the work's perspective sit, and what precisely is its attitude to those lower down? Might anyone have taken offense, even if no one actually did (asks a critic who is, in all likelihood, plenty privileged himself)? Criticism has thus overcorrected for patterns of earlier eras, when the whiteness or maleness of characters and creators would go unremarked.

HOW PRIVILEGE CRITICISM BACKFIRES

MEANWHILE, THE WORKS that end up spared are the ones that were never promising privilege awareness to begin with. And who gets to produce such works? White men. The conceptual space for *art* in the apolitical sense, but also for political art that isn't making an easily digestible, so-and-so-nails-such-and-such-issue sort of point, ends up excluding anyone with any sort of "identity." Consider the Jonathan Franzen–criticism dichotomy, as laid out by writer Mike Medley in *The Globe and Mail*, in a piece about the novelist's reputation: "To some, [Franzen] represents everything wrong with contemporary literature, a symbol of unchecked privilege and unexamined sexism; to others, he's the Great American Novelist, one of the most skilled sentence builders of his time, a writer who can internalize the foremost issues of the day and bring clarity to them through his fiction."[90] Such is the dichotomy: Either you're on team identity politics and you sit around policing whatever authors may or may not have left "unexamined," or you're able to appreciate their brilliance. Where's the room for those of us who think he's just OK? And that, yes, he's gotten a boost from being of the one demographic allowed to exist outside the identity sphere, but that his identity doesn't discredit his work?

What "privilege" has done is create two tracks: the good-but-dull artist, whom think pieces declare *gets it right*, and the *enfant terrible*, a Franzen (or a Karl Ove Knausgaard, or a Michel Houellebecq; an opinion writer or two also come to mind) who tells it like it is. But do they, really? Declaring your appreciation for PC-defying white male artists is ultimately as much of a boring political statement as sharing, sheeplike, whichever sketches your right-thinking friends have declared, on social media, to have "nailed" the issues of the day.

"Privilege" criticism leaves no conceptual space for enjoyment that isn't in line with politics or identity, particularly for any reader/ viewer who isn't a white man, and therefore able to go the antisensitivity route without getting accused of personal hypocrisy. Or, rather, it leaves two options—either you can stake your claim as being the "cool" woman (or black person, gay person, etc.) who laughs along with bigoted jokes that aren't even funny, or you can object. Which just isn't how cultural consumption actually works. Plenty of the books, movies, and television shows I like most are offensive not just to my politics but to Jews, to women, and—ahem—to Jewish women. It's tough to articulate exactly how this works, and there's certainly a threshold of offensiveness where a novel or program will lose me entirely. Yet part of cultural consumption is escape.

The privilege lens also more or less rules out a certain sort of unlikable character. And no, I don't mean those cases where "unlikable" is used to praise female characters for being feminist role models. I'm thinking of characters like Basil Fawlty, Archie Bunker, or George Costanza: straight white men who are privileged, by today's definitions, but convinced of their own victimhood. Hotel owner Basil has to deal with his nagging (but usually correct) wife and the Spanish employee he hired who speaks no English (but whom he hired, it's spelled out, because it meant paying a lower wage). And the guests at Fawlty Towers are a mix—a few make unrealistic demands (sweeping views from hotel windows; fresh-squeezed orange juice), but many others have the audacity to demand basic hotel services like checking in. Archie's a casual-bigotry *machine*, but his malapropisms, plus the juxtaposition of his sanctimoniousnessincarnate son-in-law, makes it seem classist to despise him outright. And there's George Costanza, who pretends to be disabled in order to have a private restroom at the office, and whose redeeming qualities the show never reveals.

The privilege approach forbids such characters. It allows obvious cases—Stephen Colbert, *South Park*'s Cartman—but once there's any complexity, any hint that the viewer might . . . *identify* with the lack of self-awareness, forget it. Thus the sheer *unacceptability* of Hannah's character on *Girls*. Such characters' self-pity and obliviousness are what make them funny, but also what make them relatable. That's where the humor comes from—that discomfort that comes from seeing a part of oneself in a character who's clearly *not* intended to come across as an especially good person. We don't get this from Aziz Ansari's Dev taking his parents to dinner, buying them gifts, and calling out *all the bigotries*. And the thing is, entitled obliviousness is both wrong *and relatable*. Relatable across ethnic and gender lines, or else why would I kind of see where Basil Fawlty is coming from?

Having reached the end of the chapter on "privilege" criticism, I'm meant to offer a way out. But is there one? We could, I suppose, have two separate tracks for criticism, two different sections, as it were: one for the quasi-academic, quasi-political discussions of how various works contribute (or don't) to social justice; and another where critics (of all genders! of all backgrounds!) are free to convey, RT≠endorsement style, what they actually think about the works. Some of the "actually think" responses would, of course, be influenced by the work's politics, but there wouldn't be that same political *default*. If I'm not declaring this the out-and-out answer, though, it's because I fear the "privilege" approach has now become ingrained in how we consume art and entertainment. It may have simply gotten to the point that all other possible responses to a work have been rendered incomprehensible.

4

PRIVILEGED IMPOSTORS

THE SOBA PRIVILEGE OF THE FEMINIST BLOGGER

LONG AGO, IN the pre-awareness days of the feminist blogosphere (which is to say, in 2009), Courtney E. Martin, of the blog *Feministing,* wrote a post called, "Day in the Life of a Feminist Writer/ Activist."[1] In it, Martin described a range of activities—blogging, yes, but also working on a grant application of some kind, and a conference proposal, and writing articles, and fielding a media interview, and responding to what sounds like quite a bit of e-mail, and just generally . . . *working.* A flexible workday, for sure, and a relatively enviable one, in that "feminist writer/activist" is, after all, a media job. Yet nothing compared to the sorts of accounts one reads in, say, a women's magazine, where a socialite will describe a day split between having her hair blown out and gesturing at designing a handbag. The most upscale dropped reference in the post is to takeout noodles. A day in the life of Carrie Bradshaw this was not.

For reasons that are not immediately obvious—but that fore-shadowed oh so many later episodes—the post caused controversy. The problem? Martin's privilege was, apparently, showing. As best as I can tell, with all my many blind spots and limitations, Martin comes across in the post not as *rich*, but privileged, if according to the then-fairly new definition of someone who isn't entirely destitute, but who has failed to ostentatiously acknowledge the existence of those with less. As did so many of us, circa 2009, before it was generally recognized that a reference to one's own life required such disclaimers.

Commenters—some of whom claimed to be less privileged than Martin, others of whom were merely speaking on behalf of such individuals—wanted her to be aware that not everyone gets to slowly ease into the day with yoga and fruit. (The first clear work task mentioned is some 11:00 a.m. blogging. A workday that starts late, even if it ends late as well, is, apparently, privileged.) A commenter identifying herself as a female lawyer and single mother chimed in to say that this daily routine seemed "immature." Another mentioned being unemployed, and having little sympathy for the plight of too much e-mail. The thread more or less turns into a YPIS pile-on about how some *other* people have much longer workdays, many more dreary responsibilities, or, conversely, not enough work to pay the bills. All true points. But what of it?

There were—and there always are—*just* enough details that a YPIS brigade might pick up on. The noodles, for example, were "soba" and came "from yesterday's overpriced sushi order." Ooh, fancy! Most people can't afford expensive Japanese takeout! Clearly she's a gazillionaire! Or not, but YPIS isn't about properly classifying people in socioeconomic categories. It's about picking up on clues that *suggest* someone is wealthy and oblivious, and just kind of going with that, free-associating until what emerges is a portrait of the author that's so over-the-top that she's baited into setting the record straight.

Which is what ended up happening with Martin, who wrote a follow-up post, citing another blogger's description of her as a "caricature" of bourgeois feminism. While she accepted the "privilege" charge with about as much enthusiasm and self-flagellation as one could expect, she took issue with some of the particulars. Specifically, with another feminist blogger accusing her of being that wealthy, coastal mom who's concerned with finding the right nanny . . . despite Martin not being rich, coastal, or a mother.[2] She knew better, it seems, than to use this mischaracterization as a jumping point for a denial of privilege. According to some greater truth, once you've been deemed privileged, you just sort of *are* That Person (more to the point: That Lady); any quibbling over details is the petulant rant of the privileged.

FEMINISM CONFRONTS "PRIVILEGE"

CONFLICTS WITHIN—AND about—feminism over the past several years have all revolved, in one way or another, around the notion of privilege. The concept has its origins in feminist academia, and took hold early on in feminist online activism.[3] Every sub-debate organizes itself along "privilege" lines—that is, with the different sides having different takes on who wins the privilege trumps. Take the eternally hot-button issue of sex work: Is it about male privilege, or is the relevant form actually rich-women-who-have-no-idea-how-it-goes-for-sex-workers privilege?[4] Or the relatively recent arrival, topicwise, of transgender rights: Should we be focusing on cis privilege (that is, the privilege of the not-trans), or the marginalization of those born, and currently presenting as, female?[5] And where even to begin with the issue of street harassment: Is it "privilege" to expect to be left alone in public spaces? No. Is there racism inherent in how the topic gets raised? Yes. Which leaves us where?[6]

All these topics converge over the question of whether a white, straight, cis, middle-class, or wealthy woman is nevertheless, by virtue of her gender, a member of a marginalized caste? The term "feminism" would suggest that yes, according to the feminist movement, she is. That would seem to be a given. Within feminism, however, there are doubts. So, too, in society at large.

Courtney Martin would, in 2011, be one of the first writers on the left to publish a piece critical of the privilege-acknowledgment phenomenon.[7] She's also one of the activists who Michelle Goldberg wrote about in her important 2014 *Nation* article, "Feminism's Toxic Twitter Wars."[8] The 2012 story that Goldberg opened with was basically a large-scale version of the 2009 YPIS-fest I've described: Martin and Vanessa Valenti, another feminist blogger, organized a feminist meeting that strove for inclusivity, but, according to critics, wasn't inclusive enough. Goldberg put this and other intra-feminist conflicts into what strikes me as an accurate and indisputable framework: "There's a shorthand way of talking about online feminist arguments that pits middle-class white women against all the groups they oppress. Clearly, there's some truth here: privileged white people dominate feminism, just as they do most other sectors of American life." Which should be challenged, Goldberg agrees, but it's not entirely clear that that's all (or most of) what online feminism's call-out culture is about. As she writes, "[I]t's not just privileged white women who find themselves on the wrong side of an online trashing." She cites the example of Katherine Cross, a Puerto Rican transwoman, who'd blogged about having had enough of the online accusations of "'being an apologist for this, that and the other privilege.'"[9] Goldberg also offers a damning anecdote about a black feminist who'd participated in that meeting getting called out online by white feminists who, among other things, wanted to school her in the "fact" that there hadn't been any women of color at the meeting in question. Oops.

Indeed, impatience with online feminism's call-out culture has been around about as long as online feminism itself. As far back as 2012, writer Roxane Gay published an essay (also appearing in her 2014 essay collection *Bad Feminist*) that, though supportive of the general idea of privilege checking ("if you cannot recognize your privilege, you have a lot of work to do; get started"), was quite critical of YPIS:

> Too many people have become self-appointed privilege police, patrolling the halls of discourse, ready to remind people of their privilege, whether those people have denied that privilege or not. In online discourse, in particular, the specter of privilege is always looming darkly. When someone writes from their experience, there is often someone else, at the ready, pointing a trembling finger, accusing that writer of having various kinds of privilege.[10]

In other words, Martin's day-in-the-life, in all its blogging-and-buckwheat-noodle-privilege was perfect fodder for a "privilege" pile-on.

IN FEMINISM AS ELSEWHERE, YPIS IS AN INTRA-PRIVILEGED DEBATE

THE PROBLEM WITH YPIS isn't—as is too easily imagined—that getting called out by feminists of color or trans activists causes thin-skinned privileged feminists to feel sad, and is therefore toxic. Rather, it's that YPIS takes on a life of its own, getting aimed in all directions, and winds up damaging *every* feminist cause. The buried lead in "Feminism's Toxic Twitter Wars" is that YPIS isn't about intersectionality or inclusivity. It's about a bunch of privileged "White Ladies" instructing one another on etiquette: "There are also rules," writes Goldberg, "elaborated by white feminists, on how other white feminists should talk to women of color." Goldberg has tough words for the "[p]reening displays of white feminist abjection" that have—and oh, they have![11]—come into fashion.[12] Yet this is what YPIS has amounted to.

The British feminist Julie Bindel—like Michelle Goldberg—used the word "toxic" to describe parts of contemporary feminism, and arrived at similar conclusions: "The focus on individuals, however vile they may be, signifies a shift away from the more difficult, long-term work of making institutions . . . accountable."[13] In 2013, looking at debates within British feminism, *Guardian* writer Zoe Williams arrived at a similar view of feminism's self-defeating purity competitions:

> [I]f only the authentically poor are welcome on the left, that considerably depletes our numbers. If only the truly marginalised can speak as feminists, that depletes our numbers too. And if people "with a platform" are disqualified for being part of the power structure, that leaves us without a platform. This criticism started on the right for a reason—because it withers the left. We should think a bit more strategically before we internalise it.[14]

Williams is very clear that feminism needs to focus on the most marginalized women. Her concern, which I share, is with the fetishization of powerlessness.

The privilege turn has not brought about an inclusivity revolution. It would be *wildly* inaccurate to say that intersectionality has somehow "won." It most obviously has not when it comes to discussions of feminist issues in mainstream society. We hear plenty about the plight of female CEOs. And stories about the more "photogenic" (but still legitimate) women's-rights issues—that is, the ones that can be illustrated with a photograph of a young, pretty white woman—continue to get disproportionate attention. (Models, too young and too thin. Female Ivy League college students, unsafe at parties.) And then, of course, are all of the nonscandals over which ingenue singer or actress identifies as a feminist, to be illustrated with a photo of the beautiful woman in question, ideally scantily clad. The feminism *story* hasn't budged.

What's happened is that a shared sense has emerged on the far left and far right that mainstream feminism has rendered itself obsolete, with many elsewhere on the political spectrum coming to that same conclusion: straight, cis, white, middle-class women, all can agree, are doing just fine. If anything, a bit *too* well, at the expense of equivalent men (say the far right) or of men and women of color, as well as gay and gender-nonbinary individuals (that would be the far left).

THE WHITE LADY

THE TRIUMPH OF "privilege" in feminism is most clearly seen through discussions of a fictional composite of sorts: the White Lady. "Like the late aughts' 'hipster,'" writes editor Ayesha Siddiqi in the online magazine *The New Inquiry*, "'white girl' is a label applied either dismissively or self-consciously. The tastes, habits, and concerns of the white girl, like those of the hipster, are often punch lines used as self-evident definitions for the label."[15] How true, how true. Except for the fact that hipsters are a subculture, not an enormous and internally diverse demographic category. Ah, but one can mock white women freely—it's a punch up! Well, depending on who's punching. "Only outprivileged by white men," continues Siddiqi, "the white girl's assumed universality lets us project onto 'white girl' our attitudes about race, gender, class, and the behavior appropriate within those parameters." Is this true? Do white women "outprivilege" nonwhite men? According to a YPIS framework, at least, I should think so.

The surprise, I suppose, is that Siddiqi grants that the White Lady is not, in fact, the most privileged of all. I think the White Lady gets at this more than the "white girl," because of the implied class component. The pros and cons of a White Lady mocking progressivism in some ways seem to mirror those of left-wing efforts to otherize white men: On the one hand, there's fun in turning the tables on a have, but on the other, you wind up keeping the focus on exactly the people who already get plenty of attention.[16] Except, however, the White Lady isn't quite that, because she's only partly a have. She does not—pardon the expression—have it all.

The White Lady, as is generally the case with abstractions, is a malleable concept. She may be rich, but middle class and college educated might suffice; it's more about obliviousness than wealth. And it's also, as Siddiqi notes, about cultural consumption. A middle-class White Girl may be more pumpkin-spice latte, her schmancier counterpart more green juice. The White Girl likes Ugg boots, sorority parties, and hooking up with an "exotic" European on study abroad. The White Lady of a certain age is more prone to pearl clutching (that is, to the prudish, easily shocked attitudes possessed by the sort of old people who were never actually young), and to petulance in customer-service situations. There's the White Lady striver, a copy of Sheryl Sandberg's Lean In downloaded onto each of her many devices, as well as the White Lady stay-at-home mom, whose main concern in life is whether it's organic. There's also the "Nice White Lady," who takes a self-sacrificing job at an inner-city school to "save" some troubled youths.[17] There's even the "woke" White Lady, encompassing everyone from the overly enthusiastic ally to that Hungarian woman who (moronically, need this be stated) had herself photographed in blackface in order to raise awareness of

African tribes.[18] (The genuinely anti-racist, enlightened White Lady is simply a white woman; no cliché necessary.) At any age, the White Lady is *probably* straight, but a femme-presenting[19] bisexual woman could very well qualify. She's definitely cisgender, although she may not be familiar with the term.

And she may not even be white, although this is less negotiable. Comedian Sarah Haskins's *Target: Women* sketch, the one mocking yogurt commercials, included the following (spot-on) observation: "Yogurt eaters come from every race, but just one socioeconomic class: The class that wears gray hoodies. It's that, 'I have a masters, but then I got married' look."[20] The yogurt lady is a proto-White Lady, for sure, but the sketch is from 2008, and therefore pre-awareness. The White Lady's icon, in more recent years, might be Gwyneth Paltrow, Amy Schumer, Taylor Swift, Lena Dunham, or Emma Watson. Her preferred politician: Hillary Clinton, *obviously*.

A HILLARY INTERLUDE

HILLARY CLINTON—MORE than any public figure— embodies the kind of second-wave feminism that feels stale, to some, in the Tumblr age.[21] It's not exactly that she fails on awareness grounds—if anything, she was viewed as the stronger of the two main Democratic contenders when it came to addressing racism.[22] It's more that there's something stale about the idea that electing a rich white woman—especially *this* one, ahem, Bill—as president would constitute a vital civil-rights victory. As of this writing, it hasn't happened, but it feels almost as if it has, given how *present* Hillary Clinton has long been on the national and global landscape.

In an October 2015 blog post, Sanders supporter Matt Bruenig hoped/predicted that younger women would share his views, and for the following reason: "The new feminist emphasis is not pushing the top 1% of women even higher, but instead lifting the worse off women out of the cellar of society."[23] Supporting female executives or ordinary women is, as Bruenig presents it—even before offering a dubious but earnest explanation, relying on Bill Clinton's record, for why Hillary Clinton is the enemy of the poor, as versus a Democratic candidate an inch to Sanders's right—an either-or proposition. There's something sinister, in his presentation, about *anyone* being too successful, and nothing remotely progressive about gender equity at the top. And so went the eternal question of whether younger women would embrace Clinton's candidacy. Or were we, the millennials, so over those concerns, so evolved in our thinking that we couldn't possibly conceptualize any sort of –ism hurting a woman like HRC?[24]

A lot has been written (and, gosh, tweeted) about the so-called Bernie Bro phenomenon—where Democrats who maybe supported Sanders or maybe did not (and maybe were young men, and maybe were not) were offering sexist reasons for opposing Clinton. Count me as a Bernie Bro agnostic. Yet Rebecca Traister's *New York* magazine piece, "The Bernie Bros vs. the Hillarybots"—despite what the title suggests—isn't really about accusing Clinton's opponents-from-the-left of harassment.[25] Rather, it's a case for . . . feminism. The boring, old-school, unqualified kind whose starting principle is that women are, as a group, oppressed. And given women's representation in US politics, political representation would be a fine place to make that point:

> Where is the reckoning with the fact that the dearth of female leaders in America isn't just some quirk of electoral politics, but a reflection of long-standing economic, political, social, and sexual inequities on which this country was built and which current representational inequity further exacerbates?

Traister's piece gets at the essential, which is the difference between being fine with a theoretical woman candidate as president, and seeing it as evidence of tremendous injustice that none has been thus far. And—crucially—she demolishes the argument that Clinton's privilege is such that there's no glass ceiling left to shatter:

> How do the men who confidently disqualify Hillary as a meaningful history-maker on account of how she's a wealthy white woman [there, she links to Bruenig] explain that we've never had a female president of any race or class?[26]

How indeed? Yet this indifference to sexism (except when it intersects with other forms of discrimination) is what the privilege lens has contributed. Being someone who "merely" experiences misogyny has gotten recast as a position not just of *relative* advantage (as is completely accurate), but of objective, tippy-top privilege. Supporting Hillary Clinton "without apologies" is something female progressives, like Joan Walsh, evidently felt that they had to do.[27]

In all arenas, "privilege" involves a permanent quest to sort out who's the most marginalized, but in a way that gives the impression that all the less-dire battles have already been won. This came through especially clearly in Harvard senior Molly Roberts's *Politico* piece, "Why Millennials Don't Care That Hillary Clinton Is a Woman."[28] The millennials, Roberts explains, are so over the tired, antiquated concern that was *sexism*, and have moved on to the really important concerns: "The focus on hardship has shifted from sex to privilege as the country has moved forward on gender equality."

First question: Since when does "sex" not fall under the "privilege" umbrella? Gender, on its own, is no longer enough to count. Second question: Is this really about the country having "moved forward"? Or—as I suspect—is this about a new framework that casts anyone who doesn't have it the absolute worst as privileged? What Roberts's piece reveals—perhaps inadvertently—is that "privilege" can now be given as the reason *not* to care about a particular form of injustice. And there's still quite a way to go on the "gender equality" front; a *Jezebel* post from that same day reported on a study with rather bleak findings for the respective prospects of fathers and mothers in academia, and that's just how it goes in the cultural elite.[29] Old-school sexism, the sort it's so last season to care about, the kind involving concerns that are, in one way or another, "bourgeois," may no longer be cool to call out, but the problems themselves remain. The "privilege" framework, then, is about referring to a state of it-could-be-worse with the very same term as one would use to describe absolute advantage. And so, rather than bringing about perspective, use of "privilege" winds up erasing a whole host of struggles that, for some reason, didn't make the cut.

The absurdity, in the case of Hillary Clinton and the 2016 elections is, or ought to be, obvious: How can the need for a female president have become obsolete *before we've even had one?* How does that work? We've somehow leapt from "being a woman is always an obstacle" to "women as such no longer face oppression," without pausing in the sensible, accurate middle ground, the one that would involve agreeing that white women have it easier than nonwhite women, but acknowledging that gender-specific obstacles face not just wealthy white women, but even *white women married to former presidents.* Again, it's not exactly that the privilege lens favored Sanders over Clinton. It's more that it has made it suspect to get too revved up about Clinton. It's not permitted to be excited about the possibility of a female president without painstakingly disclaimerizing. And then there's the debate where some view it as "sexist"[30] to vote for Clinton because of her gender, which doesn't make sense. Or, rather, it only makes sense if we've recast "woman" as a privileged category.

Women's support for Clinton gets filed under women being politically oblivious. If only they knew the *real issues* at stake. If only they knew some history, they'd realize what a disaster Clinton would be, which is about where I'd place the reasoning behind the following tweet from controversial academic Steven Salaita: "Supporting #Hillary on feminist grounds fully negates Black, Iraqi, Latina, Palestinian, Pakistani, Native, Afghan, Yemeni, and poor women."[31] There's been a sea of if-only-you-knew, as if the moment Clinton's supporters learned that she was to Sanders's right (or that in the 1990s, the Clintons failed to live up to 2015-era social-justice standards), they'd run screaming.

There's also—although it's generally implicit—a sense that Hillary Clinton's gender would not be a legitimate reason to vote for her. Not because an insufficiently left Democrat is *just as bad* as a Sarah Palin or a Carly Fiorina. It's more that gender, in and of itself, isn't seen as *enough*. Writer Hamilton Nolan's November 2015 *Gawker* post on the elections, called "There Are Only Two Issues," makes precisely that case.[32] The two issues? Economic inequality and climate change. An accompanying illustration, by Jim Cooke, depicted two businessmen, with smokestacks for heads, shaking hands. I'm not one to use the expression *phallic imagery* at whim, but . . . yeah.

It's not just that Nolan brushes aside reproductive rights and gender equality, including only "abortion" in the long list of also-serious issues that he's arguing, as side notes. It's that he doesn't even address the possibility that some would, for progressive reasons, go with the Democratic candidate who's a woman.

"WHITE FEMINISM™"

THE WHITE LADY is wrapped up, in all kinds of symbolic ways, with entrenched racism. "It was, and remains, necessary for white women to decry the violence that is done in our name," writes Chloe Angyal in a *New Republic* essay about the Charleston, South Carolina, massacre.[33] The white woman who protests that the White Lady is a stereotype, and that none of us white women *asked* that evil idiot to shoot black people in our name, is borderline buying into the notion that reverse racism is real.

The essential quality of the White Lady is that she must think she has it tough, when reality would suggest otherwise. The only struggle the White Lady knows is White Lady struggle: the plight of taking a small rather than an extra small at J.Crew, or of not being able to simultaneously take the dream job and stay at home full time with the dream children. *Something*—a rich father or husband; the benefits of an Ivy League education; or just society smiling on her and handing her one seemingly random stroke of good luck after the next—is keeping her in the lifestyle to which she feels entitled. She experiences public spaces as *hers*, except when faced with the omnipresent threat of a lower-class and/or nonwhite man hitting on her. The White Lady is ambivalent about social justice, convinced as she is that *those* men are invading her personal space. The essential is that she be oblivious to her whiteness. This whiteness, though, can be a stand-in for other forms of slight or extreme advantage—wealth, cis-ness, thinness, resemblance to a supermodel, actually *being* a supermodel . . .

And this obliviousness, in turn, informs White Feminism, often referred to as White Feminism™, the trademark symbol used (as in, Nice Guy™, for the men who think that because they held the door open on a date, or were unpopular in high school, they're owed sex) to indicate a reference to an irritating type.[34] White Feminism is not the feminism of women (or the otherwise gendered) who happen to be white, but rather, at least in principle a version of feminism that rejects intersectionality, and whose focus is on the relatively minor complaints of women who *almost* have it all. It's the Tumblr-era version of the expression "bourgeois feminism."

In a perhaps unsurprising twist, the cliché of White Feminism converges quite neatly with misogynists' grievances against women, specifically against the kind of women whose romantic attention they believe they're entitled to. So one winds up seeing things like, on noted misogynist blog *Return of Kings* (in the men's-rights/"game" end of the spectrum), a post entitled, "Why Modern Feminism Is White Woman's Privilege."[35] The title might suggest a from-the-left check on Taylor Swiftian/Sheryl Sandbergian feminism; the context reveals a site aimed at men who want to *pick up* white women, and who exchange creepy, hateful strategies for how to go about doing so.

Then there's the question of where White Jewish Ladies—my people—fit into the mix. On the one hand, many of the Ladies cited as embodying these traits are Jewish. Clearly, being Jewish doesn't prevent someone from appearing or identifying as "white" in twenty-first century America. Nor does Jewishness prevent a woman from being well educated, entitled, or into upscale or "basic" things. (I could dig this hole further if I were more the autobiographical sort.) On the other, why do White Feminists act as if there are on the one hand, women, and on the other, people of color, without getting that *half of those people of color are women?* I've heard/read too many "Jews" vs. "women" discussions not to see, in some small way, why this obliviousness to gender can get annoying. That, and there's a part of being a White Lady that involves a blithe ignorance of the fact that one can be hated for one's gender and race simultaneously, and in intersecting ways. If you've been called a JAP (Jewish American Princess), that sort of ignorance is not really an option. And on that note, there's substantial cliché overlap between the White Lady and the JAP. Which gets confusing. The traits for which I'm to invite a gentle punch up are the very same ones that, in a slightly different context (and context won't always be clear) constitute a slur. I suppose what I'm getting at is, I have my own specific, if not altogether *personal*, reasons for balking at the cliché, and for not viscerally receiving it as progressive.

However, my main beef with White Lady rhetoric is more general. Any and all sexism becomes suddenly acceptable once the entity one opposes isn't *women*, but the White Lady. A woman should be ambitious, should demand equality and equal pay, of course! And sure, that includes white women. But the moment it's a White Lady we're talking about, any criticism goes. Women shouldn't be dismissed as vapid whiners. White Ladies, however, are fair game. The entitled White Lady, for whom feminism means ambivalence toward changing her name upon marriage to Douchey Muffington III, is the ultimate villain for all. As with Siddiqi's hipster analogy, no one thinks they *are* that thing, so white women get to join in the fun. There are all sorts of White Lady self-parody and self-critique, crossing various genres.[36]

And the concept of White Feminism, in its various incarnations, does get used by white feminists, and not just self-proclaimed allies who see themselves as the *aware* exceptions. There's also a growing discontent among, for lack of a better umbrella term, contrarian feminists with a feminism that's too focused on the frivolous, although opinions differ on what frivolousness consists of. The libertarian feminist writer Elizabeth Nolan Brown used "White Feminism" in a somewhat tongue-in-cheek way, explaining that "progressive circles" use the term "as a pejorative to critique the sort of bougie, classist, navel-gazing activism favored by folks like Sheryl Sandberg and those who think cat-calling should be criminalized."[37] Brown invokes the term to explain the problem with focusing on Twitter hate that female British politicians received for suggesting bombing Syria, rather than paying attention to the actual *bombing of Syria* question.

Anti–White Lady complaints are standard-issue online, but it's often ambiguous where they're coming from. Where they're coming from, that is, both in the identity sense—that is, the race and gender of the person making them—and in terms of the politics involved. Sometimes, it'll be clear enough—a black woman has, understandably, had it with White Feminism. For example, in a *Dame Magazine* piece, "White Women, Please Don't Expect Me to Wipe Away Your Tears,"[38] Stacey Patton expresses frustration with certain white female friends and acquaintances on Facebook (not all, she spells out) whose response to black anti-racism is to get dismissive. The headline is, as is often the case, not so nuanced, but it's clear form the piece itself that the reason Patton singles out white *women* is that she's encountered more of this behavior, anecdotally, from white women than white men. She's referring to specific white women in her life.

I'm thinking, too, of writer Jamilah Lemieux's *Gawker* post, "Sandra Bland: A Black Woman's Life Finally Matters."[39] In particular, the following passage:

> There's no joy in watching white folks and black men demand justice for Sandra Bland (white feminists are still M.I.A., but that train is always late, if not absent), nor should there be joy following a senseless loss of life. Yet, for me, there is this strange—*satisfaction* may be an overstatement—awareness that finally, *finally* a black girl lost matters to a great deal of people.

These are criticisms that may sting, that may inspire defensiveness, but that need to be heard. And the disproportionate attention paid to white *feminists* is, if not always fair (in Lemieux's case, it would seem she was referring to what she'd observed, not to *every last white feminist*), understandable. It's not that there's a greater problem with racism within feminism than without. It's that the same level of insensitivity that seems *normal* when coming from someone conservative, or just politically apathetic, reads as hypocrisy from a self-identified progressive. If you're all about representation and righteous causes and so forth, but your conception of justice ends where your own personal grievances do, you can't be surprised if you get called out for self-centeredness or hypocrisy.

THE REACTIONARY CRITIQUE
OF WHITE FEMINISM

THERE ARE, THOUGH, these *other* criticisms, appearing in left-leaning threads, but where it's unclear why, exactly, white women are being singled out. "White women never acknowledge the ridiculous privilege they have. They are every bit as privileged as white men. They'll never admit it though," writes one *Salon* commenter. "They're far more privileged," counters another.[40] And here, from a *New York Times Magazine* reader: "It's endlessly amusing to me how unaware white women are of their own special privilege that eclipses even that of straight white men."[41] The most out-there—not surprisingly—comes from a *Gawker* thread that exploded into a White Lady bashathon:

> [W]hat the heck happens to the perky, upbeat 18–28 year old white ladies to turn them into retail anger-o-holics after they marry, get some cash money and shit out a kid or two?? And the best part is that they call themselves liberal too. And liberal white middle/upper middle-class women have this big stick up their ass about "compassion". But this demographic is consistently the most snotty around service workers.[42]

Let's attempt a close reading of . . . whatever that was. Was it a protest against liberal hypocrisy? Or was the complaint that women begin to droop (that is, to become less "perky") after age twenty-eight? Because it was clearly both of those things. And so it becomes that much more confusing whether, in any given case, one is looking at a progressive or reactionary White Lady critique. As well it would (just as critiques of Clinton that looked like they were from the left were actually coming from the right[43]).

A further reason I prefer "White Lady" to "White Girl" is that the real (purported) "privilege" only ever kicks in when the woman in question ceases to be conventionally attractive, if indeed she was ever thus. The White Lady, crucially, isn't as hot as she thinks she is. That's central to the concept's underlying misogyny. It's about condemning the entitlement of the woman who has some sort of money or power or influence but is *not even a swimsuit model*, so how dare she! I'm thinking, of course, of conservative writer Kevin D. Williamson's grotesque and grotesquely illustrated *National Review* article, "Pathetic Privilege." The piece opens with "a list of things in Lena Dunham's life that do not strike Lena Dunham as being unusual," the gist of which is that Dunham grew up relatively wealthy in New York and has failed to demonstrate, to the universe's satisfaction, that she's aware that not everyone else did.[44]

Yet the clincher in this regard has to be Jonathan Franzen's *New Yorker* article about Edith Wharton, who was—at least according to Franzen—not much of a looker. (She looks fine enough in the accompanying photo, the one with the caption that reads, "Wharton's many privileges make her hard to like." With that said, it would never have occurred to me to wonder what Edith Wharton looked like.) In the piece, Franzen observes:

> An odd thing about beauty . . . is that its absence tends not to arouse our sympathy as much as other forms of privation do. To the contrary, Edith Wharton might well be more congenial to us now if, alongside her other advantages, she'd looked like Grace Kelly or Jacqueline Kennedy; and nobody was more conscious of this capacity of beauty to override our resentment of privilege than Wharton herself.[45]

It's a curious passage, because it's not entirely clear if Franzen's simply stating facts (namely, that YPIS gets hurled more at the plain) or if he's saying that *he* judges Wharton more harshly for her "privilege" because she wasn't gorgeous. Another line that jumps out: "No major American novelist has led a more privileged life than Wharton did." True? Impossible to fact-check, since Franzen admits that "she was seldom entirely free of money worries," and is using a subjective definition of privilege. One that—oh so coincidentally—places a woman at the top of the privilege hierarchy.

The concept of privilege is, it starts to seem, gendered female. A man or woman can be rich, but to be *privileged* is to lounge, to leech. Critic Ginia Bellafante got at this phenomenon brilliantly, in her *New York Times* response to the mini-controversy surrounding Wednesday Martin's book, *Primates of Park Avenue*:

> Making fun of women who don't eat carbohydrates and buy lots of handbags seems to get a far wider cultural buttress than making fun of, let's say, the guys who came up with mortgage-backed securities. Sexism, in many cases, has become our preferred mechanism of venting frustration toward the rich.[46]

On June 3, 2015, Bellafante took Martin and her fans to task for aiming at rich housewives and not the husbands. On June 4, Wednesday Martin herself appeared in *The Huffington Post* making effectively the same argument, speaking out against "an entirely unexamined, reflexive contempt for and anger against women who are or seem privileged." Evidently not seeing her own work as part of the housewife-deriding genre (a fact not lost on the commenters), she offered the following:

> [O]ur zeal in seeking out modern-day Marie Antoinettes is an insidious, widespread, and totally accepted form of misogyny, one that masquerades as engaged cultural critique while rehearsing and repeating the very same

sexist salvos most enlightened men and women have
long banished from their vocabularies.[47]

Well, yes. Setting aside Martin's own role in perpetuating this
sort of thing (note that she, like Franzen, uses that ambiguous first-
person plural), she's right, but she could have been even more so. She
briefly alludes to the fact that not all targets of these campaigns
actually *are* privileged, but she then segues into a full-on defense
of the maligned One Percent-ettes. And while I do think she and
Bellafante are right about rich women (self-made or otherwise) drawing more hate than rich men, if this were simply about a gender
disparity in the resentment inspired by the equivalently, fabulously
privileged, that would still be a problem, but not one that all too
many people could get worked up about. The bigger issue, I think, is
the readiness with which "privileged" gets applied to women who
aren't all that privileged. The privileged girl is a *type,* in the way that
the privileged guy is not.

THE AWARENESS DISCLAIMER

WRITER JESS ZIMMERMAN'S *Hazlitt* magazine essay
about leaving her husband and starting over at thirty-two, "A Midlife
Crisis, By Any Other Name," is by no means a privilege confessional
of the what-my-summer-job-taught-me-about-my-privilege variety.[48]
Its literary value is clearly of a different order, and it's far more nuanced than the self-flagellations churned out on the online magazine
xoJane and the like. It is, in other words, *good.* Yet the privilege turn
still guides the piece, and the prospect of YPIS hovers in the not-so-
distant background. The essay is Zimmerman telling the story of
leaving her husband in her early thirties, at the very age when society (or, at least, lifestyle media and inquiring distant cousins) expects
women to be settled down or striving to get there. It's an interesting

story told well. However, it wouldn't do to just point out that it's new and unusual for a woman to have a midlife crisis, for a woman to voluntarily chuck the stability of a good-enough marriage so as to see what else is out there. Leaving it at the novelty of the situation would be evidence of a blind spot, and those won't do, so we get this interlude:

> [M]aybe the classic midlife crisis really is the province of a certain kind of privileged, sheltered male. As defined by psychologist Elliot Jacques in 1965, the midlife crisis stems from recognizing one's mortality for the first time—a position arguably reserved for those lucky enough to have avoided facing mortality from an early age. (Imagine a black man living anywhere with a police force who makes it to 40 without realizing he could die.) Concerning yourself with existential problems like, "Have I done enough with my life?" also suggests that you don't have more pressing, acute concerns: feeding children, keeping or finding a home, avoiding being physically brutalized for being the wrong color or expressing the wrong gender at the wrong time. Even the ability to indulge a crisis is a privilege—it means you can put your life on hold.

We can't just hear how Zimmerman feels. Nor is it enough for her to acknowledge that the desire to *feel fulfilled* is a luxury. We have to also hear how a theoretical black man might feel, and to get a digression that suggests black men *don't* have midlife crises. Other categories of people who apparently don't have them: anyone with kids, anyone with a need to pay for housing, anyone of color, and anyone gender nonconforming.

All of this anticipates the criticisms the piece would have otherwise gotten (and very well still might get). Not every thirty-two-year-

old woman can just pick up and leave! Yet thanks to that paragraph
and another somewhat self-flagellating one that follows, Zimmerman
can't be typecast as one of those writers who thinks everyone shares
her privileges. Sure, she might still wind up getting accused of privileged obliviousness (when was a female essayist ever *not* so accused?),
but she will at least have some passages to point to in her own
defense. Except in these same passages, she opens herself up to *another* criticism, namely that she's cast doubt on the full humanity of
an array of Others: She assumes members of various marginalized
groups don't care about being happy, and don't ever leave partners
who no longer excite them.

Later in the essay, Zimmerman keeps up the "privilege" motif,
but taps into something far more interesting. Speaking of her own
female friend group, she writes, "We have the privilege to care about
feeling fulfilled, but we don't always have the freedom to try—and
by the time we're old enough to realize what we might want and
believe that we deserve it, it feels too late." And then comes the excellent sentence: "At some point, the privileged man realizes that he
can't keep going forever. At some point, the privileged woman realizes she forgot to start."

Aha! Here's the feminism, but also, in the apolitical sense, here's
what the essay is *about*.

It's perhaps no coincidence that things start getting interesting—
and not bogged down in hand-wringing—once Zimmerman returns
to the personal part of her personal essay. Hers *is* a specific story,
not that of women generally. Its resonances extend beyond her own
life, but not to absolutely everyone on the planet. Her "privilege" digression announces limits on who will or won't relate. Why exclude
potentially receptive audiences? That said, maybe the privilege
digression, in this specific case, was a brilliant literary strategy. It
diverts attention away from the more commonplace accusation a
personal essay like this one might get, namely that it's insensitive to
the feelings of the husband who got dumped, both to dump him and

to write about it. It distracts, in other words, from the more obvious reason a midlife crisis gets cast as self-indulgent.

Whenever one reads a feminist first-person essay these days—and I'm intentionally only writing here about ones that otherwise have a lot going for them—it's only a matter of time until one arrives at the *awareness disclaimer.* That's the place where the writer (probably a cis White Lady,[49] probably straight or bisexual, probably living in Brooklyn, definitely well educated, but not necessarily well-off) interrupts the usually scheduled programming to duly note that the issues she's describing may not apply to a transwoman in Papua New Guinea; to a black or working-class woman; or, more generically, to a woman who isn't quite so privileged.

The awareness disclaimer is everywhere. A sampling: Writing on *Jezebel* about a clever experiment she did, indicating that it's easier to get fiction published as a man, Catherine Nichols included the following nod to the even less fortunate: "My name—Catherine—sounds as white and as relatively authoritative as any distinctly feminine name could, so I can only assume that changing other ethnic and class markers would have even more striking effects."[50] Philosophy professor Carol Hay, writing in *The New York Times Opinionator* blog, described an unpleasant and not entirely unfamiliar-sounding phenomenon, whereby college students, male and female, see their female instructors either as girlfriends or mothers, but not as professors. Hay includes a quote from "Patricia Hill Collins, a philosopher of feminism and race," who "has argued that women of color face even more rigid limitations on their social roles."[51] Does Hay's essay explore those limitations? Not really. But an acknowledgment has taken place!

Writer Nona Willis Aronowitz offers a similarly jarring aside in another otherwise moving and powerful essay about how, at a time in her life when she was caring for a parent and a partner, she found herself drawn to luxury spending: "I recognize that I'm lucky—even though I can't *really* afford this stuff, a well-paid job has made my coping mechanism a short-term setback rather than a financial ca-tastrophe. But retail therapy cuts across class lines,"[52] she explains, with a digression about how one really shouldn't judge poor people for spending beyond their means.

Oh, and there's a Lena Dunham privilege disclaimer, from Dun-ham's speech at an endometriosis fund-raiser. Yes, she suffers from the condition. It could be worse, and she is, let it be clear, *aware*:

> I'm also in a position of extreme privilege. I can create
> my own schedule, I have the financial resources to seek
> medical care outside of my insurance network, and I
> even have insurance in the first place. I can take the time
> I need to recover without worrying about rushing back to
> my minimum-wage job to feed my children.[53]

While more obvious in Dunham's case, perhaps, than others, there's a sense in which the awareness disclaimer isn't so much a display of sensitivity as a preemptive deflection of (likely) accusa-tions. (I'm thinking of the much-quoted line spoken by Dunham's *Girls* character Hannah Horvath: "So any mean thing someone is going to think of to say about me, I've already said to me, about me, probably in the last half hour."[54]) It's a display of self-awareness, but a self-serving one.

However, for a woman to privilege-disclaim, she doesn't need to be especially privileged. Consider this statement, from one telling *New York* magazine piece about the writer's unplanned pregnancy, at nineteen: "As a white, privileged, middle-class stripper, I commit-ted to using my resources to become the best mother and ultimately the best role model I could be."[55] While there's plenty to be said about socioeconomic differences in the experience of sex work, barring some royal connections we don't know about, a pregnant nineteen-year-old stripper is not "privileged." Nor was the author of an essay on *The Billfold* from 2012, "Young, Privileged, and Applying for Food

Stamps," even if she *had* gone to college and spent $1.50 on a coffee.[56] There's a subgenre that hovers between the privilege nonconfession (that is, where a self-evidently not-privileged person refers to their tiniest advantages as "privilege") and the more straightforward White Lady apologetics.

It's no mystery where all these disclaimers come from. White Feminists (or white feminists trying not to be White Feminists?) who fail to affix disclaimers—that is, who, through genuine ignorance or a poor choice of words, speak out about feminism without so much as a nod to intersectional feminism—do get called out for this. In *Tablet*, writer Jamie Kirchick offers the example of the actress Patricia Arquette, whose 2015 backstage Oscars speech asking for members of other marginalized groups to stick up for women may have been intended as progressive, but quickly led to what felt like *the entire Internet* reminding her that some women are black, some women are gay, some women are black and gay.[57] Fellow actress Julie Delpy got the same lesson around the 2016 Oscars, after making still more tone-deaf remarks about women having it tougher than African Americans.[58] These types of comments inspire social-media and think-piece avalanches, the sort an A-list celebrity might bounce back from, but that might go over less well for someone less prominent.

So—either because they're more socially aware than certain celebrities (and thus aware that not all women are rich or white), or because they fear these pile-ons, or both—the best of today's successful white female essayists (and let's throw in Dunham, who's something of a multimedia personal essayist) spell out that they do not think all women are rich and white. They are *aware*. Aware, that is, both of their own nonrepresentativeness, and of the near certainty that critics will call them out on that nonrepresentativeness.

Yet there's also a particularity to the personal-essay form that's at play. In today's literary landscape, an essay will generally need to make some kind of point.[59] It will require a news peg, say, or statistics demonstrating that we're not (horrors) reading just about one person's experience, but are in fact getting some kind of broader, quantitative truth about society. These editorial requirements put personal essayists in a bind. It will seem as if they're claiming to be speaking for everybody, because *no one will print them unless they claim this*. So they make the claim, which—because no, the essay doesn't tell a universal story—demands a disclaimer.

Awareness disclaimers are, at any rate, not unique to the female-confessional genre. At *The Awl*, writer Matt Buchanan regularly affixes a tag to his articles about upscale New York restaurants that reads, "Around Every Single Conversation About Food Culture There Should Be a Huge Set of Brackets in Order to Convey That Almost All of This Is Restricted to the Fairly Privileged."[60] The "brackets" approach contends that if you just add a perma-disclaimer, you somehow negate the schmanciness. As if it's totally fine that restaurant reviews now only have practical use for oligarchs, as long as nonoligarchs are informed that the reviewer is aware of the issue. Awareness disclaimers, then, are baseline irritating and sanctimonious, if understandable from an author or (attuned) editor's perspective.

However, these disclaimers pose specific problems in the feminist personal essay genre. Women speaking their truths on what used to be quaintly known as women's issues must now tack on references to the possibility that other, less privileged women will not relate to their problems. Awareness disclaimers, in this context, are pleas to the reader to *not* take the author's concerns too seriously, because other women, the author insists, have it worse.

Take the disclaimer in Alana Massey's personal essay about writing women-oriented personal essays.[61] She makes a bunch of interesting points about how to subvert the sexism of journalism's pink ghetto, and then suddenly, this statement:

> I must stop momentarily with the admission that the
> reason I was able to write about these topics is not a

matter of my courage and my skill at doing so. I am a young, thin, white, cis gender woman whose inner turmoil is often seen as poetic rather than dangerous. My conclusions about the culpability of men are met with less of the suspicion and vitriol that women without these privileges receive. This advantage cannot be ignored and it must not endure if we are truly committed to unwrapping the white male stranglehold on power in the world.

I suspect this assessment is accurate, but there's still something frustrating about a female, feminist[62] writer insisting that neither "courage" nor "skill" have entered into her success.

What these disclaimers do is dismiss a particular woman's feminist concerns (that is, the woman with these concerns) as unimportant. It's certainly true that feminism shouldn't—doesn't—begin and end with *The Feminine Mystique* plight, or the *Madame Bovary* variant. It isn't *just* about suburban wives who wake up one morning and realize that yoga and lattes (Jess Zimmerman namechecks both) aren't enough. Yet it also isn't *not* about that situation. And the fact that second-wave feminist complaints continue to play out in the twenty-first century is at the very least curious.

These disclaimers amount to a pushback against second-wave feminist bravado, against the feminism that encourages women to speak up proudly about their accomplishments, same as a man would do. The privilege approach asks women to hold back from engaging in unapologetic self-promotion, and to consider—*aloud*—every aspect of their accomplishments that could be attributed to some systemic injustice. It also asks women with personal narratives of challenges they've faced *as women* to qualify those narratives with an acknowledgment that "mere" gender concerns are actually nothing important, and that the *real* struggle lies elsewhere.

The disclaimer, in theory, preempts the charge that the essay ignores the experiences of women who aren't the author. The essay *will* do just that; it will also, disclaimer or no disclaimer, get this criticism. So why provide one? To me, it comes down to two options: Either we say that such concerns are too small compared with, say, police brutality, and simply stop discussing them, or we encourage *self-contained* essays along these lines, while simultaneously promoting writing by a more diverse pool.

THE HAVE-IT-ALL-ERS
ARE ALSO AWARE

WHERE AWARENESS DISCLAIMERIZING really takes off, though, is in the great discussion of women, work, and motherhood. Any topic in this realm, even tangentially, demands *awareness*. Maybe not an extended digression, but a nod. Something. A discussion of the challenges of finding decent maternity clothes isn't complete without an acknowledgment that "[f]or gender non-binary people, finding maternity clothes is tricky on a whole other level, a deep compromise between different kinds of comfort."[63] The (doubtless substantial, I feel compelled to note, thus doing the very thing I criticize) difficulty that population of pregnant individuals faces isn't brought up because the author identifies as gender nonbinary, but precisely because she *doesn't*—it's an it-could-be-worse: a requisite affirmation of the existence of still-greater struggles.

In this arena, privilege in the sense of socioeconomic inequality is, straightforwardly, a big deal. Journalist and novelist Jessica Grose, writing at *The New York Times's* parenting blog, explained that although she and her husband both work, she thinks of the money she earns as specifically destined for childcare. She explains that her attitude toward her family's finances isn't simply (or directly) because she's the woman in a heterosexual couple, but also because of the sort of work she, a writer without a day job (apart from childcare, that is!), does. Work that she explains in terms of what else: "My hours are also more flexible, and I work partly from home. By virtue of this extreme privilege—for which I am very, very grateful—my entire orientation is more domestic."[64] This did not satisfy commenter Tom from the Bronx: "I realize this is a blog, and probably editor-less. But looking through the comments, I'm not seeing anyone else appalled by the piece completing [sic] lacking in self-consciousness about privilege."[65] It could be—stranger things have happened—that this newspaper commenter skipped over the sentence where Grose acknowledged her privilege and labeled it "extreme." Yet it could just as well be that Tom was annoyed not so much by the unexamined privilege as by the *privilege*—that is, by the fact a newspaper frames a relatively well-off married woman's feminist hand-wringing as a serious work-life balance issue.

A larger-scale version of the Jessica Grose-"Tom" conflict played out in response to Princeton professor and public intellectual Anne-Marie Slaughter's *Atlantic* cover story, "Why Women Still Can't Have It All." Slaughter was as up-front as she might have been about the piece's specificity: "I am well aware that the majority of American women face problems far greater than any discussed in this article. I am writing for my demographic—highly educated, well-off women who are privileged enough to have choices in the first place."[66] Nevertheless, *The Atlantic* later published a follow-up interview, "Anne-Marie Slaughter Answers Her Critics,"[67] with an entire section called "On Privilege," in which Slaughter affirmed that she is privileged and aware of it, but privilege is unavoidable if what you're asking is why there aren't more female professional elites.

It *is* a problem that certain topics—in the Grose and Slaughter cases, work-life balance issues—tilt so heavily toward upper-echelon professionals. Given all the topics at stake—paid parental leave, adequate health insurance, class disparities when it comes to two-parent households—it's just plain *true* that privileged families, privileged *women*, have it easier than poorer women. Yet is it really a problem of insufficient privilege awareness? Is the problem that Grose and

Slaughter didn't reflect enough on what makes their experiences unusual? (Which they most assuredly did.) Or is it that the trend for first-person accounts means that we end up reading about the experiences of women at the top of their professions? What would actually work: a return to traditional reporting (minus the personal-essay component), and greater socioeconomic diversity in media. Neither of those developments is forthcoming. It's much more affordable to get an essay from a rich woman, and then to host some reader-generated content wherein commenters debate whether she has properly reckoned with her advantages.

There's a subtle, from-the-right aspect to many of the work-life criticisms. Take Caitlin Flanagan's 2004 *Atlantic* essay, "How Serfdom Saved the Women's Movement." Flanagan wants women of her caste—that is, *wealthy* women; the great swath of partnered women who have professional careers but also work because they want or need the money, and who don't have additional household help for things like changing the sheets, effectively doesn't exist—to "acknowledge that many of the gains of professional-class working women have been leveraged on the backs of poor women." As Flanagan notes—and I can remember 2004 well enough to know this would not have come as a surprise at the time—upper-class two-parent households tend to employ poor, often immigrant women to take care of their children. A feminism that focuses solely on the women newly in the professional workplace, while ignoring those who are taking on those women's household duties, is . . . but wait a moment. Did those duties ever really *belong* to those mothers in the first place?

The should-be-obvious question: What about the fathers? If one sees it as an injustice that, until relatively recently, only men were allowed high-powered careers, isn't the husband-and-father in these scenarios equally responsible for the employment (and labor conditions) of any household help? Flanagan asks that her peers "demand that feminists abandon their current fixation on 'work-life balance'

and on 'ending the mommy wars' and instead devote themselves entirely to the real and heartrending struggle of poor women and
children in this country." An alert reader will wonder whether improving feminism is actually Flanagan's goal. Buried in the piece
are standard-issue gender-essentialist arguments about children
needing their mothers at home with them, and—gratuitously but
tellingly—about women typically falling in love with every man they
sleep with. (Oh really?) It's not for me to say whether Flanagan or
anyone else truly cares about the plight of female domestic workers.
Yet what's clear enough is that *within her essay*, that plight serves a
particular purpose, which is to condemn the desire of wealthy
mothers (including, confusingly, Flanagan herself) to work outside
the home.

Arguments against bourgeois feminism exist on the left as well,
of course, but tend not to be phrased as condemnations of wealthy-
women-but-not-men for existing. In a 2013 *Dissent* magazine article,
Sarah Jaffe makes the case against "trickle-down feminism" and
demands that feminism turn away from stories about CEOs and
focus instead on low-income, female-dominated labor forces.[68] Jaffe
argues for a shift in priorities, noting that greater gender equality at
the top doesn't seem to translate into better labor conditions for the
vast majority of women. In a 2015 *Guardian* piece, author and academic Alison Wolf takes that line of thought further, arguing that
"boardroom quotas" in the UK and elsewhere "are of a piece with
much of the modern feminist media: a combination of elite self-
interest and preoccupation with imagery." Yet Wolf doesn't merely
question mainstream feminism's focus on the relatively well-off. She
dismisses gender equity at the top as *not actually a type of diversity*:
"[W]hy should it be so good for women, or indeed society, to give
seats to women who are mostly middle class and Oxbridge educated
at the expense of middle-class and mostly Oxbridge men?"[69] It's clear
enough why this wouldn't be *optimal* diversity, but have we really

reached the point, when it comes to gender, where elite women are just as privileged as elite men?

And there is—as there always must be—a Hillary Clinton angle. In *Slate*, Michelle Goldberg—yes, the author of the piece on "toxic" online feminism—discusses female midlife invisibility, and explains how her own life experiences lead her toward relating to Clinton.[70] Goldberg acknowledges that hers is a plight felt most strongly by women who were thought cute in the first place, a category with all kinds of racial and socioeconomic components:

> [I]n my own, admittedly very privileged experience—it's only as I approach middle age that I'm aware of what being a woman has cost me. In my twenties and early thirties, I felt that I enjoyed the same professional attention and opportunities as my male colleagues. I didn't realize at the time that being treated as an ingénue and being treated as an up-and-comer are not the same thing, and that only one comes with a continuing skyward trajectory.

I want to be convinced by Goldberg's point about a specific injustice. And I am. Yet it feels wrong to *agree* with her argument, when she's also just instructed the reader that she's "very privileged."

The awareness-disclaimer ritual in women's personal essays and other first-person journalistic writing if anything *reinforces* privilege, with the (in these cases) wealthy or middle-class white woman asserting that they know what a woman from another demographic will or won't identify with, and preempting a woman from one of those demographics, who might otherwise have not called her out, exactly, but told *another* story, one showing that not everyone shares the same experiences. Or that, in some cases, everyone does. (Repeat after me: heartbreak is not a First-World problem.)

One of the Arquette call-outs Jamie Kirchick mentions came from feminist writer Amanda Marcotte, who summed up her grievance with the fellow white woman as follows: "Arquette's political grandstanding played into every ugly stereotype about 'feminism' being about little more than some privileged white women trying to become more privileged."[71] While that should not *be* feminism, in its entirety, it absolutely needs to be a part of it. The word "privileged" doesn't cancel out the "woman" bit. Feminism means that *every* woman should feel entitled to more.

THE AWARENESS DISCLAIMER
MEETS IMPOSTOR SYNDROME

IN A 2015 post on *New APPS*, an academic group blog, Catarina Dutilh Novaes announced her promotion to full professor of philosophy.[72] The post, called "What It Takes to Succeed in Academia," took the form of a privilege self-flagellation. In it Novaes grudgingly admits to having worked hard to get where she was, but takes the opportunity to point out that "[i]t takes an incredible amount of luck and, yes, privilege, for things to work out." Novaes then took the reader on a tour of her myriad advantages, beginning, as such tales so often do, with an aside about struggles overcome. What follows is a bit long, but privilege acknowledgments often are:

> While I am a woman in a male-dominated field, and while I had to overcome hurdles related to coming from the "periphery" of academic action (originally from Brazil, and then developing my career in the Netherlands, which is ok but frankly not Top of the Pops), for the rest I've been extremely privileged. My parents were both academics (my mother still is), so in terms of academic support at home I was particularly well served. For a

number of reasons, I also never had to worry about
economical hardship and financial stability, and thus I
could choose the risk of an academic career without
having to worry whether one day I'd have no food on my
plate. And, last but not least, I am white, not differently
abled, cis, and I fit reasonably well within certain
stereotypical standards of beauty.

Fair enough, one might say. It's easy to imagine how someone
who lacked Novaes's advantages and didn't do well on the academic
job market might resent someone who had those advantages and
landed a good job. The question is what self-flagellation along these
lines accomplishes. For someone other than the self-flagellator, that
is. Is it helpful to hear from a wealthy and beautiful woman that she's
wealthy and beautiful, and also that she can walk, and is white, and
has a biological sex that's in sync with her gender? Does it make those
without the same privileges feel better? Does listing your achievements *and calling them privilege* make the people who didn't win life's
lottery feel better? It's certainly not the same as abandoning the
position.

The blog post in question is an installment—albeit a highbrow
one—in the genre known as #blessed, a humblebrag cultural trend
sufficiently entrenched in our social-media lives as to have received
its own *New York Times* Style section takedown.[73] (I chose Novaes's
post rather than others precisely because I *don't* know the author, and
because it was a public pronouncement; I have seen similar, behind
privacy settings, from acquaintances.) What is frustrating about
these types of post is that they jump in front of whichever envy an
audience might experience. Specifically, they preempt YPIS venting
from those who haven't had it so good. The privileged person is saying that she *knows* she's privileged, and that she doesn't actually think
her good fortune makes her a better person ... and yet is revealing
her goodness through the very act of confessing. The privileged

person who gracefully acknowledges her privilege grates because what's added if not an aura of saintliness? Here's someone with the nerve to be privileged and *likable.*

Yet the most obvious question about the post is: Would a man have written something like it? Do reasonably good-looking cis white male professors whose parents are also academics write blog posts apologizing for having effectively stolen the jobs of the more talented and hardworking? Not generally. They take for granted that they deserve whatever they've achieved professionally, and reflect only upon why, despite being supremely deserving, they haven't been given more.

Which brings us to why the privilege approach is such an odd fit with feminism. A feminism that asks every woman to enumerate her unearned advantages, but that makes no such demand upon men (if only because they're outside this conversation), inevitably reinforces the gender divide. The privilege framework, which defines ever-greater segments of society as "privileged," asks all the many privileged-loosely-defined women to apologize for taking up space, for speaking their mind, which women already do, copiously.

And the privilege-awareness ritual is nothing more than a repetition of the impostor-syndrome thought process. According to the Caltech counseling Web site, impostor syndrome includes "the tendency to attribute success to luck or to other external reasons and not to your own internal abilities. Someone with such a feeling would refer to an achievement by saying, 'I just got lucky this time'..."[74] Whether the women who write these posts actually *experience* pathological self-doubt, only they know for sure; at any rate, it seems misguided to conflate humblebragging with self-sabotage. What concerns me is the newfound veneration *on the left* of that way of presenting female accomplishments. Feminism was, for a time, all about shedding impostor syndrome, but that's going out of fashion. In 2015, on *New York* magazine's women-and-style blog, editor Molly Fischer wrote a piece called "I Hope I Never Get Over My Impostor Syndrome," arguing in favor of self-doubt over being a "blowhard."[75]

The privilege self-critique thus has a way of reinforcing what many women already think—that factors other than their own efforts explain everything that's gone right for them academically or professionally. The hand-wringing that so many women *already do* matches up precisely what the privilege framework demands. It's not that this hand-wringing is based on pure nonsense—of course whiteness, wealth, beauty, and connections impact which women and which men get ahead, but it just doesn't seem as if men are decompensating, to nearly the same degree, over *their* unearned advantages. And why should they? Women *already have the framework* for thinking our successes aren't earned.

A RIGHTEOUS MISOGYNY

LET ME BE clear. The problem is not that women of color have gained platforms and made white women's grievances look relatively minor. Women of color continue to be marginalized, even with all the *awareness* floating around (remember those all-white Oscars?), and white women's grievances *are* relatively minor. So, too, with critiques of "bourgeois" feminism, centered more on class than race. It *is* ridiculous to present the challenges of female Harvard Business School graduates as the be-all and end-all of feminism. If privilege awareness simply meant a nudge toward remembering that wealthy white women aren't the only women, and aren't the most oppressed, then fair enough. That's not how it's worked out.

The problem, rather, is that the very same stance—White Ladies, so entitled!—exists both as a from-the-left check on mainstream feminism, *and* as from-the-right misogyny. The same punch, as it were, can be *both of those things*, depending upon the speaker, depending upon the context. And the context isn't always clear. So we have to make a guess: which of these things is more likely, more often? Absent a specific context, what would we *think* is going on?

For me, what it comes down to is this: the people most vocally riled/threatened/whatever by white women/White Ladies/whatever, and the ones with the most power, are *male sexists* (who aren't especially keen on nonwhite ladies, either), not, say, working-class transwomen of color unconcerned with whether white female CEOs are getting enough quality time with their 2.5 kids. And the White Lady? Not always privileged, not always even white. A rhetorical strategy that can sometimes serve a purpose within the confines of internal activist debates falls apart upon reaching a broader audience. And with the Internet, there aren't so many "confines" to speak of. Thanks to the privilege framework, it's possible—no matter who you are, or why you're doing so—to bash women and be given the benefit of the doubt. Well done, privilege framework. Well played.

5

BIZARRO PRIVILEGE

THE "RIGHT" KIND OF PRIVILEGE

THE MERE WORD "privilege" is one of those terms—like "social justice," "gender studies," or "Clinton presidency"—that reliably draws shudders on the right. Progressive use of the term comes in for regular mockery in conservative publications,[1] enough so that there's now a privilege "beat."[2] Yet mainstream conservatism isn't quite sure where it stands on the concept. On the one hand, commentators have correctly noted that "privilege" is a jargon-and-nonsense gold mine. In principle, the right has the upper hand, because when *it* embraces nepotism and silver spoons and so forth (Trump, Paul, and all those Bushes), it can't be accused of hypocrisy. The thing where a bunch of rich white kids get together to microscopically investigate their own privilege only seems to happen on the left. So it falls on those of us who fall left of center to duck our heads in shame. Therefore, it might seem as if the right could just declare the nonuse of "privilege" as a point in its favor. On the other hand . . . YPIS clearly *works*. It summons emotions and wins arguments. The temptation is just too great to adopt what's clearly an effective silencing technique. (Left-wing students are getting "trigger warnings"? Gosh darn it, conservative students are entitled to some of their own![3])

Which is how we wind up with Tal Fortgang, famed 2014 opponent of privilege checking, publishing a piece in 2015 called "38 Ways College Students Enjoy 'Left-wing Privilege' on Campus" for *The College Fix*, a conservative online student publication.[4] In it, Fortgang explicitly namechecks (and quotes, but doesn't cite) "Peggy McIntosh, the matriarch of privilege's modern construction," and then introduces *his* checklist with what seems like a parody of tone-deaf writing, but is (probably?) not:

> While the marginalization of right-wing thinkers on campus in no way compares to the experience of black Americans throughout history, it might behoove left-wingers on college campuses to think about the various privileges from which they benefit simply by being members of the overwhelmingly dominant group in their academic communities.

The checklist itself mixes fair-enough observations ("I can describe my summer writing job without censoring the name of the publication or its political leanings") with pandering about "'trigger warnings'" and the "'safe space'" concept. The most notable thing about the article, though, is that it exists. It is, however, part of a mini-genre of conservative rhetoric: calling out left hypocrisy (or "trolling" progressives by using their own approach against them). In

2014, the online magazine *The Federalist* ran an item called "People Who Say 'Check Your Privilege' Should Do It," in response to the Fortgang affair.[5] In that article, doctoral student Greg Collins made exactly the point Fortgang himself would a year later:

> To face eye-to-eye with my fellow Millennials who embrace the check-your-privilege gospel: It is a privilege when your views conform with those of more than 90 percent of your professors. It is a privilege when your worldviews are blessed by a proliferation of like-minded commencement speakers and guest lecturers. And it is a privilege when you have university resources, money, and time within fingertips' reach to wield to advance your political cause. Politically homogeneous micro-aggression: The privilege that doth not speak its name.

There is, of course, the even stronger case for checking the privilege of privilege checkers, namely that the people making these accusations tend to be fairly privileged themselves. And one does also find, from conservatives, a certain amount of relatively more straightforward privilege accusation—that is, arguments that someone or some group of people are wrong on account of being advantaged.

The right is thus happy to YPIS Democratic politicians, especially a certain former senator from New York.[6] The actual subhead to a 2015 *Weekly Standard* piece? "The Privilege of Being Hillary Clinton."[7] In it, journalist Noemie Emery explains—shades of Franzen on Wharton—that Clinton's problem is that she's the most privileged person *ever*:

> Many times before, people have run for public office from positions of privilege, having been rich and/or connected, having been famous as athletes or actors, as millionaires funding themselves, or as celebrities whose names were already on everyone's lips. But no one

before Hillary had launched their political career from
the White House as first lady, able to enlist the prestige,
perks, and glitz that surround that position.

Yes, I suppose that's true. Given that same-sex marriage only just
arrived, and that we haven't had any female presidents, she'd sort of
have to be the first.

The strangest candidate, from a "privilege" perspective, though, is
(at the time of this writing) Donald Trump. A symbol, one might think,
of unapologetic privilege—a living cartoon of ostentatious wealth, as
well as born-rich white male New Yorker—his appeal, at least initially,
seemed to be as an example of someone who says a hyped-up version of
what many Americans, at their lowest points, might be thinking. More
id than candidate. The same impulse that makes a hero out of the professor who says outrageous things but declares, *I'm tenured so I do what
I want!* had, it seemed, done the same for the tycoon.

In a *Daily Beast* story from January 2016,[8] national security
expert Tom Nichols—right-leaning, but no fan of the Donald—
attributes Trump's rise to "a new, more virulent political correctness
that terrorizes both liberals and conservatives . . . Any incorrect position, any expression of the constitutional right to a different opinion, or even just a slip of the tongue can lead to public ostracism and
the loss of a job." This new political correctness, he claims, makes
absurd outspokenness an appealing trait:

> These brutish leftist tactics radicalized otherwise more
> centrist people toward Trump not because they care so
> much about gay marriage or guns or refugees any other
> issue, but because they're terrified that they're losing the
> basic right to express themselves.

Journalist Kevin Drum, responding to Nichols from the left, in
Mother Jones,[9] had to (partially) agree:

> [T]he whole "privilege" thing sure does get tiresome
> sometimes. And we do get a little pedantic in our
> insistence that no conversation about anything is
> complete unless it specifically acknowledges the special
> problems of marginalized groups. It can be pretty
> suffocating at times.

While any number of factors may have brought about Trump's moment, the free-speech angle seems central. As even center-left and progressive sorts, one by one, find ourselves on the wrong side of YPIS pile-ons, even those of us who see Trump as a fascist disaster are going to get why a man without the self-censorship button has, in this political climate, made it as far as he has.

That much, then, made sense. Yet now there's *another* version of the Trump-and-"privilege" argument. Writer and political commentator Andrew Sullivan—whose former blog, the *Dish*, I used to work for—spelled out the Trump-and-privilege connection in a *New York* magazine piece[10] that, while highly critical of Trump, sought to understand where his supporters were coming from:

> A struggling white man in the heartland is now told to
> "check his privilege" by students at Ivy League colleges.
> Even if you agree that the privilege exists, it's hard not to
> empathize with the object of this disdain.

Sullivan doesn't appear to be referring to any specific, real-life interaction (where, after all, would the meeting take place?), but rather to the privilege call-out phenomenon. And this dynamic makes sense, to a point. To some extent, the privilege turn is about putting race- and gender-related identity politics ahead of economic inequality. Yet that's not quite it: it's more about a self-awareness, identity, or "feelings" sort of emphasis, including socioeconomic status as a (malleable) set of identity categories. Yes, "white privilege" confuses because it suggests all whites are privileged. Yet "privilege" is used all the time to make socioeconomic points. And as Elizabeth Nolan Brown wisely pointed out, in *Reason*, "both the social-justice left and the so-called 'alt-right' view the world primarily through identity politics." Even beyond the more explicitly racist elements of Trump's fan base, the class-based privilege check is among the more robust.

An earlier version of this take had come from Charles Murray, *The Bell Curve* coauthor and, more recently, the self-appointed mouthpiece of the white working class. In *The Wall Street Journal*, Murray revived his 2012 *Coming Apart: The State of White America, 1960–2010* argument—that elites have walled themselves off, leaving poor white Americans to suffer—and uses that division as an explanation for a resentment candidate's appeal.[11] Clive Crook, who notes that he's the "friend in Washington, D.C." whom Murray had referenced as someone who'd witnessed anti–West Virginian snobbery, reiterates Murray's point in a piece of his own on *Bloomberg View*, but hones in on the snobbery angle: "Trump wages war on political correctness. Political correctness requires more than ordinary courtesy: It's a ritual, like knowing which fork to use, by which superior people recognize each other."[12]

For Crook, as for anyone who's looked around in the past several years, Trump's appeal is his rejection of political correctness. Yet Crook ties the anti-PC allure specifically to a particular regional, racial, and socioeconomic position. As such, he argues, "Supporting Trump is an act of class protest—not just over hard economic times, the effect of immigration on wages or the depredations of Wall Street, but also, and perhaps most of all, over lack of respect."

Have you got that straight? The above passage is a "privilege" argument . . . for Trump. Trump, whose tactic is insulting the marginalized (women, Muslims, Mexicans, immigrants), is to be taken seriously—his fans, to be respected and sympathized with—because what he's actually doing when he expresses hatred for various underdogs is lending support to *other* underdogs. I found the Murray and

Crook pieces via a tweet by the libertarian journalist Julian Sanchez, which summed it all up so beautifully: "So, basically, Trump is how non-campus America responds to microag[g]ressions."[13] Because that's it, isn't it? What is "flyover country" if not a microaggression?

However, it also really *doesn't* make sense. Once the privilege approach is used to support (and not just to explain) resentment racism and xenophobia, it has, it would seem, overstayed its welcome. What the Trump-as-Social-Justice-Warrior angle demonstrates is the readiness with which "privilege" rhetoric can be employed to express just about any sentiment. Including the case for a President Donald Trump.

While the American left—or a branch of it (i.e., Bernie Sanders and his supporters)—puts economic inequality front and center, the right has landed on a cultural, YPIS-infused defense of poor and working-class Americans. The white male ones, at any rate. And the argument goes something as follows: The *real Americans* (white, Christian, small town, not-too-educated) are culturally alienated from a cosmopolitan, un-American elite (consisting of Jewish television producers, the Obamas, and, say, Dan Savage). They're sick of being cast as the one marginalized group it's acceptable to mock. And, on a deeper level, they've been harmed by socially liberal ideals. While it's well and good for some female corporate lawyer to hold off having kids until she's given up her career and married a banker, the evils of non-procreative sex have led to the downfall of the working-class family.

These cultural arguments have been floating around for a while now—Reihan Salam and Ross Douthat's *Grand New Party: How Republicans Can Win the Working Class and Save the American Dream* came out in 2008, which is also when Sarah Palin was going around with her coastal-media-elites stump speech. Charles Murray's "bubble" quiz—the one where, if you don't follow NASCAR or go to country music festivals or whatever, you live in a bubble, aka YPIS—appeared in 2012, to promote his book, *Coming Apart.*[14] Yet in more recent years, they've fused more explicitly with "privilege" rhetoric.

Connor Kilpatrick, one of the main from-the-left critics of the "privilege" approach (see chapter 1), wrote an essay for the socialist magazine *Jacobin* about "another problem with the politics of privilege: the ease with which it's used by conservatives."[15] Discussing "conservative politics," he writes, "a huge part of it is an attack on what they see as a series of unjust and unfair 'privileges' being protected by a liberal state." Kilpatrick turns the hypocrisy charge right back at them, but his isn't a YPIS accusation:

> And yet notice how confident conservatives are that framing issues in terms of "privilege" will always go their way—the diminishment of Medicaid, the defunding of the welfare state—and never towards a solidaristic politics of single-payer. Funny how that works.

His most interesting point, though, is about the overlap between right-wing YPIS and the original:

> Sometimes, the Right will even go across the globe to turn the immiserated American poor into just another privileged class. Whenever they want to dismiss shocking new stats on American poverty, how do they do it? They quickly juxtapose the American poor against the impoverished in less developed countries.

Kilpatrick references the conservative refrain about poor people in America having refrigerators, and then notes, "Ask yourself: is this not, essentially, the same argument as the 'first world problems' meme so beloved by progressives?"

He concludes, going further still, by pointing out that conservatives have employed the privilege framework "for decades now," and suggesting that it's actually the left that's adopted a conservative approach. I'm not sure that's quite right in terms of the chronology, but there's definitely something conservative about YPIS, whatever the ostensible political stance of the person using it. As I argued back in 2012,[16] the framework always somehow winds up in boot-straps territory. It's of course a disaster if you think you're self-made and you're not. Yet if you're accepted as such, you've won. YPIS is about treating *unacknowledged* privilege as the real problem. Owned-up-to privilege (think Mitt Romney) of a premeritocratic, patrician bent is thus spared.

There's been a right-wing populist reappropriation of "privilege" rhetoric, one that in many ways actually overlaps with the original variety. While the emphasis falls more on classism than racism, the gist is the same. While the motives may be a bit more cynical, the diagnosis—that urban elites look down upon small-town nonelites—is fair. At the far right, however, things get trickier. There (and some-times on the center right as well) you see full-on reversals. For example, did you know about "black privilege"? I can't say I did, but someone at the online magazine *American Thinker* thinks it exists ("It's Past Time to Acknowledge Black Privilege"), as does someone at the *National Review* ("White Privilege: Myth & Reality").[17] The depths of the Internet also reveal the belief that "female privilege"—not White Lady, but female, period—needs checking.[18] I'm refer-ring to the famous realm where, whenever society becomes just a smidge more fair, or threatens to, those who used to be at the top of some hierarchy (and maybe still are) start to feel threatened. Yet there are groups that inspire that sort of resentment more than women and black people. Such as . . .

"JEWISH PRIVILEGE"

IN 2011, I had the strange experience[19] of noticing a guy I rec-ognized from college (at least, I think it's him) on an Occupy Wall Street–leaning Tumblr, "We Are the 1 Percent." Subtitle, "We Stand with the 99 Percent." I hadn't known about this man's million-dollar trust fund, but that wasn't the interesting bit in his contribution[20] to that, the most self-flagellating of Tumblrs. As was the style of that moment, the post consisted of a photo of the dude standing behind a big, handwritten sign bearing his social-justice message, the message itself helpfully reproduced in typed text below. It began:

I have always had many advantages. I am:
1) White
2) Male
3) Jewish
4) Son of Wall Street bankers . . .

Items 1, 2, and 4 were pretty self-explanatory. Yet what, I mean *what*, was item 3? Why was he claiming his Jewishness *as privilege?* It seemed—and still strikes me as—obvious that someone could be Jewish *and* white, male, rich, and therefore otherwise privileged. However, that's not what you're saying, if you put "Jewish" on a list like that. You're saying that your Jewishness *is privilege.* Which it isn't! And announcing that it is puts you in not the best company.

In June 2015, the international news agency Jewish Telegraphic Agency (JTA) reported on a "demonstration against 'Jewish privilege' organized by [a] self-described fascist" in a Jewish area of London, England. The fascist in question hoped to "[l]iberate" the area from Jewish oppression.[21] To which one might say, "Oh, look, now even *neo-Nazis* are adopting 'privilege' rhetoric!" Which is, on the one hand, true and noteworthy, and on the other, entirely unsurprising, and not *new* in the least.

While the specific wording about "so-and-so privilege" is *so very now*, the sentiment is as timeless as they come. The belief that Jews are unusually privileged is not a fringe strain or obscure facet of anti-Semitism. It *is* anti-Semitism. It has been for all of modernity, including the days before "anti-Semitism" was coined as a term. And this isn't about Zionism, or not just: From the 1840s French socialists who'd had it with those Rothschilds (for a good time, search Alfred Toussenel's 1847 *Les Juifs, rois de l'époque: histoire de la féodalité financière* (*The Jews, Kings of the Era: History of Financial Feudalism*), readily available online, for instances of *privilège*) to the 1930s German small-business owners who thought Jewish immigrants were stealing their jobs, all the way up to the Nazi-philic trolls of today's Internet, what they all have in common is a belief that Jews have money, power, and influence beyond our numbers, and are using all of it to pull the puppet strings of the world. Anti-Semitism has always been about "liberating" non-Jews from the yoke of "Jewish oppression."

With the notion of "Jewish privilege" so central to anti-Semitism, a Jew who stands accused of "white privilege"—or "privilege"-type—unspecified—may wince, and not out of defensiveness. For reasons stemming from nothing more exciting than the mechanics of headline construction, various articles by Jews attempting to navigate these questions—including one of my own, although I thankfully got a chance to clarify in a subsequent piece—include references to "Jewish privilege," or some variant thereof, when all that's said in the article itself is that "Jewish" doesn't mean *not* privileged.[22] Of course, that said, there are Jews who—out of social-justice zeal—refer to Jews as a privileged group.[23] I don't find the "self-hatred" framework all that useful; when I see remarks around those lines, on social media and such, I think that this is a Jew who hasn't gotten out much. If your perspective is, say, that of someone who grew up in a wealthy and largely Jewish coastal suburb, where well-off Jewish kids were the in crowd, you might imagine Jews to be life's undisputed haves. Yet it's silly and anecdotal (and YPIS-y) to believe this, I realize. People can arrive at ridiculous ideas no matter their life experience.

Attempts at responding to "Jewish privilege" accusations by casting Jews as *not* privileged, however, tend to fall flat.[24] Selectively looking at occasional anti-Semitic hate crimes today—and severe anti-Semitic violence from other times and places—while ignoring the broader context (that is, a country where anyone white or whiteish is ahead of the game) is missing the point. The far better response is to say that anti-Semitism isn't about Jewish underprivilege. Its presence can't be refuted with instances of Jewish success. Spun a certain way, those lists *are* anti-Semitic!

All of this is frustrating, because casual anti-Semitism—the anti-Semitic microaggression, as it were—hasn't gone anywhere. For years, many Jews would avoid speaking out against such incidents, for fear of seeming hysterical. After all, compared with *the Holocaust*, what's a "JAP" or "good-with-money" comment here and there? So it can be tempting, now that calling out polite bigotry has become commonplace, to join in. Yet it never seems to work. The privilege framework offers up a language for our experiences, but forbids us from using it.

Jewish confrontations with "privilege" rhetoric run the gamut, from enthusiastic embrace of the framework to outright rejection. Some American Jews (and I'm thinking of a good percentage of my Facebook feed) are on the far left, and have zero qualms placing Jews (and, boy oh boy, Israel) on the side of all things privilege."[25] While remarks about "Jewish privilege" specifically aren't so common (but I've seen this), it's simply assumed, in progressive circles that Jews are haves. Ashkenazi Jews, for sure, but possibly all plausibly white-looking ones as well. Editor Sigal Samuel reported the following, from a conference for Jews of color:

> [The] preoccupation with privilege was a dominating concern at the conference, for obvious and well-founded reasons. But for some, particularly among the Sephardic and Mizrahi Jews, this preoccupation meant that they

almost self-policed themselves out of attending the conference in the first place.[26]

Yet another example, then, of privilege awareness actually *preventing* marginalized people from speaking up for themselves. After all, there *is* always someone else who has it worse.

Once one leaves the furthest reaches of the social-justice left, however, many Jews aren't prepared to embrace this interpretation.

In 2012, a video appeared by Franchesca Ramsey, called "Shit White Girls Say . . . to Black Girls."[27] The video—the full context of which requires a deep dive into 2012 viral videos—involves Ramsey, an African American woman, wearing a blond wig and imitating the clueless things white women say to their black friends and acquaintances. Mostly, it was straightforward comedy as punch up. Yet featured among the tone-deaf remarks was the following: "Jews were slaves, too. You don't hear us complaining about it all the time." At the time,[28] this struck me as, at the very least, odd. First, and least important: when, in the history of Oppression Olympics, have Jews invoked slavery in ancient Egypt, rather than the Holocaust or, at the very least, pogroms? More to the point: The video gave the impression that Jews exemplified white privilege.

There's a temptation—and I, too, experience it—to just say, that's the *small* picture; the *big* picture here is anti-black discrimination. Shouldn't we just overlook a bit of casual anti-Semitism if it's in the service of anti-racism? (The video not only went super viral, but got a favorable write-up[29] from a Jewish woman of color, who used it as a prompt for discussing racism she's faced within the Jewish community.)

The video was somewhat controversial, but the controversy it started was over whether it constituted (as NPR put it[30]) "reverse discrimination." Which is striking, because it puts a specific dig at *Jews* under the heading of reverse racism, and therefore not actually racism. According to the privilege framework, anti-Semitism is a plight of haves. If Jews are white, anti-Semitism can't be racism. If Jews are "privileged," then any Jewish complaints about oppression are rooted in the desire of haves not to give up their unearned advantages. And yet . . . there *is* anti-Semitism! The question is one of how to discuss it.

Here's what I blogged in 2011:

> We're now living in an age of dividing the marginalized from the privileged . . . While "marginalized" as defined in America these days is not entirely about class, the fact that Jews are understood to be a group of well-off white people means Jewish-specific concerns are understood as by definition First World Problems.[31]

While I couldn't say the same of every blog post that I wrote years ago, in this case, I still think I was onto something. In March 2015, I expanded on the topic—and on a post I'd written for the *Dish* in 2014[32]—in *The New Republic*:

> [T]he privilege framework—the now-default one used for addressing marginalization—fails to be of much use when challenging anti-Semitism. If anything, it can make matters worse. This is in part because anti-Semites have hijacked the framework: A glimpse at the #JewishPrivilege hashtag on Twitter reveals white supremacists embracing a warped version of privilege theory, according to which non-Jewish white people are marginalized by Jews. Theirs is a form of bigotry that presents itself as an anti-oppression movement.[33]

About a week after that piece appeared, writer John-Paul Pagano had an essay in *Tablet* magazine that made a similar point.[34] (Knowing the timescale on these articles, I have every reason to think we came upon the same thought independently.) Here's Pagano:

> The "prejudice plus power" idea erases real anti-Semitism—a construct with its own history of horrific effects, which is often lumped in with racism, but is actually something else. To borrow from comedy parlance, most racism "punches down"—an incumbent group constructs and subordinates an underclass. The stereotypes that make up such racism diminish their victims. For example blacks, to the white racist, are inferior, criminal, stupid, lazy, and lusty. Anti-Semitism is often the opposite, envisioning the Jew as a preternatural creature—as evil, brilliant, controlling, connected, rich, and powerful beyond measure. Anti-Semitism is a conspiracy theory. As such, Anti-Semitism often "punches up."

Variants of this point appear all over the place. Here's Cathy Young, a journalist skeptical of the "SJW" approach, in June 2015, in *The Observer*: "[S]ince Jews in Western society today are seen as more privileged than not, 'social justice' discourse sheepishly sidesteps anti-Semitism—surely one of the most pernicious forms of bigotry in Western history."[35] Or see the (accurate-for-the-article) headline of a February 2015 *Tablet* essay by Jamie Kirchick: "Rock, Paper, Scissors of PC Victimology: Muslim > Gay, Black > Female, and Everybody > the Jews."[36] And finally (but there's more out there, rest assured), editor and commentator David Frum, in his April 2015 *Atlantic* analysis of Garry Trudeau's comments on the *Charlie Hebdo* massacre, faulted Trudeau for overreliance on "privilege," and, more broadly, on putting "exposing privilege" before exposing the truth: "There are many dogs in any fight, and the task of identifying which one is the underdog is not so easy." Yup. Frum went on to connect the privilege quest with the "surge of violent anti-Semitism," much of it from Muslims, in Europe, noting, "The concept of the 'underdog' becomes unstable and uncertain in these conditions."[37]

Indeed.

As delightful as it's been to see a theory I've long held enter the mainstream, the truth it hones in on is an upsetting one. The more "privilege" takes hold, the more it's the case that complaints about anti-Semitism read as not only relatively trivial, but altogether reactionary. An exception can only be made in the admittedly not all that rare cases when the ideology comes unambiguously from the right, as when journalist Julia Ioffe received all manner of anti-Semitic (and explicitly pro-Nazi) harassment after she'd written a less-than-hagiographic profile of Melania Trump.[38] That, of course, counts. Yet, strangely, the fact that Jews suffer online abuse from white supremacists (and I have personal experience of this) doesn't call to question, in progressive circles, whether Jews are full beneficiaries of white privilege.

The Jews-and-privilege debate plays out, with the expected fanfare, on college campuses in the United States and Britain.[39] Things got especially heated at Oberlin, when it was revealed that a professor there was posting anti-Semitic conspiracy theories to Facebook.[40]

Columnist Roger Cohen summed up these controversies clearly and calmly in a *New York Times* column:

> The zeitgeist on campuses these days, on both sides of the Atlantic, is one of identity and liberation politics. Jews, of course, are a minority, but through a fashionable cultural prism they are seen as the minority that isn't—that is to say white, privileged and identified with an "imperialist-colonialist" state, Israel. They are the anti-victims in a prevalent culture of victimhood; Jews, it seems, are the sole historical victim whose claim is dubious.[41]

Indeed, in part because support for Israel has become a right-wing cause, anti-Jewish oppression isn't something the left these days is especially interested in fighting. And just as the fact of anti-Semitism in the Labour Party has *also* been exploited by that party's critics,[42] so, too, have conservative critics of academia hopped on each of these stories, perhaps, at times, overstating the case.[43] Yet if I'm reluctant to attribute left anti-Semitism to the fact that the US (Christian) right is so rah-rah Israel (or to the fact that Jews on the right seem more than pleased to agree that Israel is a "white" country, and that Jewish values are Western ones), it's because progressive ambivalence in this area has a storied tradition from long before the state of Israel's founding in 1948. Throughout the nineteenth century, French socialists dabbled in anti-Semitism; it was only with the Dreyfus Affair, at the turn of the century, that the French left began to accept that even "bourgeois" Jews could be oppressed. And it wasn't just France! The use of the expression, "the socialism of fools," to describe anti-Semitism, stems from nineteenth-century Germany.[44] While plenty of anti-Semitism comes from the right (and yes, I'm thinking of Ted Cruz's "New York values" dog whistle), the left has never quite known what to do with anti-Jewish oppression that frames itself as revolution.

In twenty-first-century America, causes otherwise liberal Jews might otherwise support (and often enough, *do* support) get classified as inherently anti-Israel, with varying degrees of anti-Semitic subtext. (Must I go through the ritual? *Not all criticism of Israel is anti-Semitism.*) From #BlackLivesMatter[45] to activism against campus sexual assault,[46] just about every righteous cause gets linked to the Israeli-Palestinian conflict. Insisting upon an anti-Zionist stance winds up alienating even many progressive Jews, as writer Mark Joseph Stern shows, in a *Slate* piece about anti-Semitism within LGBTQ activism.[47] Specifically, he discusses the concept of "pinkwashing," which, as he explains "presumes that the Israeli government has no interest in promoting LGBTQ rights except to help mask its oppression of other groups. This presumption is totally unique to Israel."

My interest here is not to digress into commentary on intractable international conflicts. Rather, it's to point out why the privilege framework is *worse than useless* as a tool for understanding anti-Semitism. It forces us to speak only of cases where Jews were hated for being impoverished, rag-wearing, pious shtetl dwellers. Think *Fiddler on the Roof.* And this sort of anti-Semitism was sanitized for a Broadway audience, because actual anti-Semitism has never, ever, been about this. Even in times and places where the typical Jew *was* observant and poor, modern anti-Semitism is about the fear of Jews who assimilate a little *too* well, and who are, of course, dripping with cash.

And so, attempts at describing anti-Semitism *in* privilege-framework terminology—that is, of discussing issues of representation, "microaggressions," and so forth—place Jews, no matter their political affiliations, on the right. If Jews are "privileged," goes the thinking, then a Jew who feels oppressed is in the same boat as any other white person with that racist, entitled delusion.

FORTGANG'S COMPLAINT

WHAT EXISTS FOR some Jews is a kind of whiteness dysmorphia: We who nearly always read as white to the outside world—with all the benefits that entails—will imagine ourselves to be racial Others. Which we *are*, in our minds, thanks to our exposure to decades' worth of popular culture where nebbishy Jewish men lust after *shiksas*, while nebbish-ette Jewish women sit at home on Saturday nights, Rhoda Morgenstern–style, waiting for Mr. Nebbish (or better yet, *Dr.* Nebbish) to call. (Which he won't, because he's out with a strapping blonde.) From *The Mary Tyler Moore Show* to the Fockers franchise, from Woody Allen to Philip Roth and back again, Jewish difference and exclusion is *felt.* And all of this *counts*, even if the "privilege" framework has no place for it. Yet it doesn't count quite as much as being viewed as nonwhite to the outside world as well.

Which is, I think, what was going on in the notorious Tal Fortgang essay from 2014. Given the title, "Checking My Privilege: Character As the Basis of Privilege," in the *Princeton Tory*, the student journal where it first appeared, and republished as "Why I'll Never Apologize for My White Male Privilege" in *Time* magazine, the piece is neither as obnoxious as that second headline suggests, nor as subtle as the first does.[48] Fortgang opens by stating that he's had his own privilege checked "several times this year." His first impulse, it seems, was a reasonable one:

> That's the problem with calling someone out for the
> "privilege" which you assume has defined their narrative.
> You don't know what their struggles have been, what
> they may have gone through to be where they are.

True! Then . . . less true: "You don't know whose father died defending your freedom. You don't know whose mother escaped oppression." He's completely right that these things aren't known, but not that they'd have any relevance here. If your family suffered for you to have an obstacle-free (or obstacle-lite) existence, *you are privileged*. A cutoff has to be put somewhere. That, or you wind up being like one of those politicians who digs and digs and lo and behold, finds some distant ancestor who bore some working-class semblance. And then we suddenly hear all about that farmer or coal miner or whatever in all of their speeches. If you're not running for office, *don't do this*. Even if you are, maybe give it a pass?

Fortgang, then a Princeton freshman, had the misfortune (or privilege?) to express, in a viral essay, something awfully close to the thoughts I had, as a kid, when the (white) teacher told the (all or nearly all white) class to feel bad about what "we" had done to the slaves. I remember thinking that the phrasing, the all-inclusive "we," was ridiculous. *My* family, as I'd been learning since infancy, hadn't been in America at all prior to the Civil War, and was in fact busy being pogrommed in the old country. While obviously some of them did, not all of my ancestors made it out of Europe in time to escape the Holocaust. How on earth was *I* responsible for victimization that happened when my ancestors themselves were victims? It was only much later—I'm going to say, postcollege—that I even *heard* about white privilege, meaning that, no matter who your family is, if, upon arrival in America, your family landed on the "white" side of things, you'd wind up benefiting from the racist system already in place.

Ultimately, I think the truth falls between the two extremes. My point here is simply that I don't find it all that strange that Fortgang would, as a Jewish college freshman hearing about white privilege for the first time, balk. Having read the essay many times at this point, it's still not clear to me whether his objection is to being accused of a form of privilege (white privilege) that he, *as a Jew*, does not possess, or whether his point was that no one—not even a *Mayflower* descendent—has systemic advantages from being white. Was his family history to be interpreted as a striving-immigrant tale, shared by most white (and many nonwhite) Americans? Or was the concentration-camp part of the story meant to indicate that he, as the not-so-distant descendent of people rounded up on the basis of insufficient whiteness, couldn't be white-privileged? Was his issue that "white privilege" isn't real, or that he, personally, didn't have it? When he writes, "I do not accuse those who 'check' me and my perspective of overt racism, although the phrase, which assumes that simply because I belong to a certain ethnic group I should be judged collectively with it, toes that line," it's clear from the context (that is, the top of the essay, where he hasn't yet addressed the Jewish angle) that the "ethnic group" he's referring to is *white people*, not Jews.

One could chalk this tension up to the ambiguity of identity (or to the fact that *this essay is a freshman composition*), but it can't be both of these things. If Fortgang's objection is to Jews—as a marginalized minority—being accused of white privilege, *because* they're marginalized, then he'd have to buy into the white-privilege framework. Right?

Fortgang's tough-to-untangle musings on whiteness and Jewish identity are quite a bit less interesting than the analysis they prompted in the more intellectually oriented wing of the Jewish parochial press. *Tablet* ran two diametrically opposed takes in the aftermath of Fortgang-gate. The first, from writer Liel Leibovitz, defended the essay—and essayist—from critics on the left:

> To assume that he, the grandson of a poor Jewish immigrant, stands shoulder-to-shoulder in the same privilege bracket as the grandson of, say, a well-heeled patrician just because both are white men whose parents can afford a good college is to assume that neither is able to transcend the happenstance of his birth and that both, despite having grown up in such radically different traditions, arrive at a conversation with precisely the same point of view, shaped exclusively by their skin, their cocks, and their cash.

If he'd left it there, fine, but he did not. He instead swung over, Fortgang-style, to the usual conservative talking points, noting, somewhat gratuitously I'd say, that "nearly three-quarters of all black Americans are born to unwed mothers."[49] His point seemed to be that if you care about privilege, you should be offering patronizing advice to black people.

In any event, fellow *Tablet* writer Marjorie Ingall wasn't having it. In her rebuttal,[50] Ingall offered an array of data points about life being just plain harder for women and people of color. And since Fortgang's gender was never up for debate, she honed in on the *other* bit. Here's Ingall, addressing Leibovitz:

> What you're really asking, skeptically, is when Jews
> became white folks. But by and large, in America, we are.
> Our median net worth is three times that of the average
> American's. Our circumcised dudes disproportionately
> win Oscars and Nobel Prizes. We're CEOs and elected
> officials. When Fortgang's grandfather fled Poland in
> the 1930s, the picture was pretty different.

Ingall emphasizes that she doesn't think anti-Semitism is kaput, only that white-male privilege is something that a Jew can have. Which—much as I reject that framework—I'd mostly have to agree. As for whether disproportionate Jewish achievement points to an end of anti-Semitism, that's another story. There I'd have to go with *no*. In 1930s Europe—to pick up on Ingall's argument—anti-Semites didn't hate Jews for being oppressed refugees, at least not initially. They hated Jews for overachieving, which is to say, for *any* achievement, because any Jewish success was seen as usurping non-Jewish dominance.

Meanwhile, at the *Forward*, Sarah Seltzer offered an analysis remarkably similar to Leibovitz's, but landing in a very different place:

> I wish I could tell Fortgang that yes, his family's history
> in the Holocaust has created residual trauma, echoing
> through the generations, that is deserving of sympathy
> and creates a disadvantage, for sure. And yes, the work
> that his family put into raising their own up is admirable.
> But at the same time, here he stands! He remains a white
> male Princeton student, which puts him pretty close to
> the top of the heap.

She adds, in the piece, that Fortgang "is not exactly as privileged as his WASPy classmate, Biffy St. Snoot, but [he is] up there."[51] There seemed to be general agreement, among Jews responding to the episode, that the Holocaust in some way matters for assessing Jews' relationship to "white privilege." What's emerged, then, is a split over how much it matters, and in what way.

A further awkwardness in the Jews-and-whiteness conversation: There's an ostensibly anti-anti-Semitic mantra that involves insisting that there's no such thing as "looking Jewish." In its most progressive variant, this denial manifests itself as a reminder that there are Jews of color, Jews of possible color (for example, Sigal Samuel on her Mizrahi identity[52]), and, just generally, Jews who don't read as white. More commonly—at least, until *very* recently—rejection of the "looking Jewish" concept meant emphasizing that Jews are just as white as the next white person, and would involve those tiresome lists of famous blond Jews—born Jewish as well as converts to Judaism. (Did you know that Scarlett Johansson? . . .) On the one hand, there are a lot of blond Jews around, *and* there's intracommunal discrimination against Jews who look either whiter or less white (*especially* less white) than, I don't know, Sarah Silverman. On the other, it remains the case that "looking Jewish" is a term recognized in the culture. Jews who happen to meet the physical description—whether or not more Jews do than non-Jews (which is dubious, once you're bringing *everyone* who counts as white in the contemporary United States into the mix)—experience discrimination on that count. It's possible that something has happened between performer Vanessa Hidary's 2010 video, sharing an all-too-familiar story of someone telling her, as a compliment, that she didn't look Jewish, and *Broad City*, with its celebration of young Jewish (and stereotypically Jewish-looking) women as comedic heartthrobs.[53] The point being, insistence on Jews' "whiteness"—and, moreover, on it being anti-Semitic as well as exclusionary to suggest that a "Jewish" appearance exists—makes it just about impossible to respond to anti-Jewish appearance-based racism. A Jewish woman who feels bad about her hair, nose, whatever, is, according to "privilege" understandings, a white woman who needs to get over herself.

The privilege framework always fails when two underdogs face off. Take the parallel questions of gay male misogyny and homophobia among straight women. Both exist—but is the answer to decide who's more privileged, a gay man or a straight woman, and declare one of the two bigotries inherently impossible? According to the rules of "privilege," though, that's the only way.

Are Jews white? (The "white" ones, that is.) This question is one I've thought (and read[54]) about for years, and I don't have a satisfactory answer, beyond a tentative *yes, but.* The whole scholarly and journalistic question of Jews' newfound whiteness—the narratives of assimilation and upward mobility—ignores the fact that Jews were actually pretty much *always* white. Even in Nazi Germany! Why do we think Jews were forced to wear the yellow star? Jews—in Europe, and in white settings in North America—are at most a quasi-visible minority. That's been true even at moments rife with racialized theories about "The Jew," and it's no less so in calmer moments. I have ample anecdotal evidence from France (where I've lived and speak the language) and Flemish Belgium (where I *try* to communicate, but as my in-laws can attest, not so much) that I read as white *even there*, even in places *known for anti-Semitism.* And in the States, where to begin? I don't get followed around stores or pulled over while driving or hassled by cops. My Canada experience is, at this point, limited, but in Toronto, where the reigning xenophobia is (going by the casual racism I've overheard) anti-Asian, there is no doubt whatsoever that in Toronto, I'm white. And then there's the fact that I, a Jew, and a firm believer in speaking frankly and unapologetically about the existence of such a thing as looking Jewish, can't always tell who's who.

Yet whether American Jews are white is, in a sense, the wrong question. What's clear is that—with the exception of the very few who are—Jews are not black. And the major form of racism in the contemporary United States is anti-black. It doesn't take being the world's greatest anti-racist ally, or the closest reader of Ta-Nehisi

Coates, to have picked up on which group bears the brunt of American racism, if you yourself don't happen to be black, that is. Even if your historical knowledge is limited to something-something slavery, something-something Jim Crow, you may have noticed how, for example, the seat next to a black man (however dressed) on a commuter train will remain empty while the rest fill up. You may have seen cops hassling black teenagers, and have found yourself in countless situations where the servers can be distinguished from the served on the basis of skin color alone.

Unless your head is deeply buried *somewhere*, you'll have noticed that all Americans who aren't black wind up benefiting from that fact. All-things-equal benefiting, that is; there are of course individual nonblack Americans who are, for systemic or idiosyncratic reasons, screwed. George Zimmerman, arguably the face of anti-black racism in America today, is a half-Peruvian man whose appearance is sufficiently nonwhite that, had the story gone otherwise, one could easily imagine a man resembling him being the victim of a racist attack by a white person. The man referred to by *The Daily Beast* headline, "White Cop Convicted of Serial Rape of Black Women"[55] is half white and half Japanese. (More on *that* complicated question in a moment.)

For some Jews, the fact that America treats us as white is proof that America is a less racist place than Europe. That American Jewish whiteness more or less hinges on anti-black racism creates an additional barrier for us to really *getting* how central racism is to American life. If you grow up learning about how oppressed—how *racially* oppressed—you'd be if you lived anywhere else in the world (except Israel, which poses its own problems), you're going to think of America as a place that's transcended old-world xenophobia, rather than as one that exported it and invented new varieties. David Brooks gets at this in a column called "Listening to Ta-Nehisi Coates While White," the headline being, here, quite instructive.[56] He writes, as if to Coates:

> [T]he disturbing challenge of your book is your rejection
> of the American dream. My ancestors chose to come
> here. For them, America was the antidote to the crushing
> restrictiveness of European life, to the pogroms. For
> them, the American dream was an uplifting spiritual
> creed that offered dignity, the chance to rise.

Brooks then notes, "Your ancestors came in chains." Yes, that's about the size of it. In America, Jews' difference, Jews' oppression, can get worked into an immigrant narrative, one with a happy ending, and one that in no way precludes Jewish whiteness.

A new round of Jews-and-whiteness debate emerged around the question of Democratic candidate Bernie Sanders. Jewish, yes, but Jewish *enough?* More specifically, some Jews wondered whether Sanders's insistence upon his own whiteness was a denial of his Jewishness. In a JTA blog post, journalist Ron Kampeas expressed discomfort with Bernie Sanders's "discussing his white privilege" in the run-up to the Nevada primary.[57] While Sanders was explaining that he, unlike Obama, benefited from having white ancestors (and again invoked his Polish heritage), in order to make a point about discrimination against African Americans, he was also, Kampeas argues, deflecting potential anti-Semitism:

> The Jews of Sanders' father's generation—and to a
> degree of Sanders' (he's 74)—were not as inclined as
> are tribe members today to reveal their background. At a
> time when bigotry was much more prevalent, they used
> their whiteness to "pass" as members of the majority.

What's interesting, for our purposes, about this story is the place of "privilege" in all of it. What we're looking at, with Sanders, is a case where admitting to privilege may *also* be an escape. In one sense, Sanders is just echoing where he stands in the culture. References to him as the *white male* opposition to Clinton abound.[58] There's a certain reassurance, for Jews, in checking our own "white privilege." There's the same masochistic element as there is for all white people, but there's also a sense of relief, of freedom, in insisting that *you are the "have."* And that remains the case, even if you're *apologizing* for your unearned advantages. Whether we choose to, in the manner of David Brooks, believe earnestly in the American dream, or go the Sanders route and self-flagellate for whiteness, it amounts to the same: both routes are about protesting (too much?) that American Jews aren't marginalized.

The assimilation question is always a tough one, though, because it presumes an authentic, *Jewier,* identity that someone is taking pains to hide. However, though, what if this is just who Sanders is? In a *New Republic* piece on Sanders's Jewishness, Mark Oppenheimer (a former editor of mine) admits that Sanders—unlike Joe Lieberman—can't possibly be hiding religious particularity (yarmulkes and such) because he's not observant. Oppenheimer nevertheless wishes Sanders would open up about *something*: "He could discuss how he left ritual observance behind, decided not to go to synagogue, married out of the faith."[59] He could, I guess, but there's not much to say about the faith one *isn't* practicing. I also don't go to synagogue (despite Hebrew school as a kid) and my husband isn't Jewish. And there isn't some closeted part of me that's religious, and has a Jewish husband. (I'm now picturing a character played by Ben Stiller jumping out of the closet, literally, and yelling, "Surprise!") There's a bit more to be said about whether Sanders is hiding his cultural particularity, but he's been living in *Vermont,* after all, not on the Upper West Side of Manhattan. Oppenheimer's most persuasive when he moves beyond Sanders specifically and looks at what it says, more generally, that it takes a Sanders-type Jew to break down barriers:

> The real test of Americans' tolerance, of our embrace of minority cultures, is whether minorities can win office

while being unapologetic, proud, visible, and obvious about their minority identities. And on that count, I don't think the United States is even close.

That assessment seems right. And what it tells us is that a candidate who speaks out about his own white privilege is preferable, to the electorate, to one whose whiteness is in doubt. Again, the interesting angle here is not whether inside of democratic socialist Bernie Sanders there's a Hasid just screaming to get out. No, it's that owning one's white privilege can so readily function as a way of *using* the same. That dynamic holds true whether you're Bernie Sanders or not, and, indeed, whether you're Jewish or not. It's built into the very ambiguity of the expression, to *own* one's privilege.

THE NEW JEWS?

I started to wonder about the "privilege" these two minority groups experience, and how the numbers shape the perception of us in the media and ultimately in the admissions office. What does "privilege" mean for a Jewish American? What does it mean for an Asian American? What does privilege mean to someone who must toe the line between these two cultures, desperately trying to come out "just American"? I didn't find a simple answer to that immense question, but I did realize that even as a double minority, I enjoy a lot of privilege.[60]

The above excerpt is from Samantha Yi's article in the *Forward* called "Checking My Privilege as a Korean Jew." As a 2015 graduate of Northwestern, Yi's essay is, on one level, another installment in the checking-my-privilege genre. A format that (see chapter 1) serves as reliable "content" in the new-media landscape, given that everyone with an Internet connection and some modicum of privilege seems able to churn one out. As is so often the case with such essays, a story that might have been compelling and specific (I mean, a Korean-Jewish American who grew up feeling like "a mini Barbra Streisand"!) gets funneled into these limiting parameters, and winds up being about the tired question of whether or not the author a) is privileged, and b) has properly checked the privilege in question. My interest in how privilege-aware strangers on the Internet qualify themselves is, as I think you'll have picked up on by this point, quite limited. However, there's a bit more to it in this case. Specifically, Yi's in a unique position to weigh in on where Asian and Jewish Americans fit in the "privilege" framework. That she doesn't have an answer tells us more, I think, than if she did. The answer is: It's complicated.

In a certain sense, if the privilege approach screws over Jews, it really does a number on Asians and Asian Americans, those other so-called model minorities. The framework's ability to label marginalized people "white," and therefore white-privileged, has its issues when it comes to white-looking Jews. Things get that much trickier when the "white" person in question isn't "white" by any definition. Can you be white-privileged but not white? In a relative sense, of course you can (i.e., discrimination against dark-skinned black people), but is that *white privilege,* exactly, if you could still be hated, *racially* hated, for your nonwhiteness?

In a *Daily Beast* item called "Cop Used Whiteness as His Weapon to Rape Black Women"—and tagged, simply, "privilege"—editor Goldie Taylor wrestles with the fact that the white-privileged cop in question was, while plenty evil, not actually all that white: "Technically, [Daniel] Holtzclaw is biracial: born to a white veteran police officer and a Japanese mother—but, make no mistake, Holtzclaw claimed to be white."[61] That he did, Taylor notes, by referring to his "white cock" during the assaults: "He wanted [his victims] to know that he was white. He wanted them to know that they were black and therefore powerless." As the tag would suggest, Taylor accepts Holtzclaw's self-proclaimed whiteness at face value:

> In his estimation, he was everything they were not: middle class, white, and male. Based on his own words, Holtzclaw embraced some of the most unfortunate aspects of that privilege. Despite his mixed racial heritage, he bought into and used that sense of suprem- acy to sexually violate his victims and the oath he swore to serve and protect them.

Neither Taylor nor I have been granted special insights into this man's psyche, but it at least seems possible that all the insistence upon his own whiteness stemmed from insecurities around *not* being white.

As Hua Hsu observed, in reference to the Isla Vista killer— another half-white and half-Asian criminal whose horrific acts were attributed to white privilege—it's more complicated: "Maybe white- ness does explain something, but in an indirect, unconscious, aspi- rational way. Perhaps, in this reading, he was not a benefactor of 'white privilege and entitlement' but someone vexed by its seeming elusiveness."[62] It seems just as possible that the same thing would have been going on with Holtzclaw. And, as Hsu points out, ques- tioning the "whiteness" of a racist criminal doesn't have to mean denying the relationship between the crime and a racist society.

Except under the privilege framework, it does. It's either-or: A person of color can't be racist, ergo a racist can't be a person of color. Yet even more importantly, the privilege approach puts all the em- phasis on identifying the least-privileged party, while remaining hazy on who's who at the *other* end of the spectrum. That haziness encour- ages scapegoating. As long as a have-not has been correctly identi- fied, it hardly matters which relative have is taking the fall. To suggest that it does is to cast yourself as Team Privileged (that is, as someone whose sympathies are in the wrong place), and quite possibly to have derailed the conversation.

Consider the case of Peter Liang, the New York police officer found guilty of manslaughter in the death of Akai Gurley, an unarmed black man, *The New York Times* reported that many-but-not-all in the city's Asian and Asian American community felt that "the officer, who is Chinese-American, [was] a scapegoat who was targeted at a time when there is a roiling national debate about the policing of black neighborhoods."[63] It was an understandable reaction, especially given that the tragic death occurred from a ricocheted bullet.

Outside of certain fraught contexts, where such expressions could be read as detracting from still-more-pressing anti-racist battles, it's generally understood on the left that Asians *don't* read as white, and, as such, face discrimination. Cultural-appropriation scandals—Oberlin's Asian-fusion dining-hall cuisine, a protest of a Boston museum's kimono exhibit—regularly involve Asians and Asian Americans in the "victim" position. And, on a more positive note, it's greeted as progress whenever there's any kind of nonstereo-typical representation of Asians on TV. Particularly when—as on *Crazy Ex-Girlfriend* or *Master of None*—an East-Asian American man gets cast as the heartthrob. There's a sense in which the privilege framework, as understood on the so-called SJW left, gets the Asian American experience right. Rather than—as has happened with Jews—simply taking the "model minority" cliché at face value, the progressive left has, for the most part, accepted Asians under the "of color" umbrella.

The Asian American experience of racism think piece is an established, and not particularly challenged (at least, not from the left), part of the new-media landscape.[64] Editor Nicole Chung wrote a massively popular personal essay for feminist humor Web site *The Toast*, in which she describes how hurt she feels when she receives variants of you-all-look-alike. The incident that sparks the discussion involves someone telling her, at a party, that she resembles an (attractive) Asian American actress.[65] It's exactly the sort of "racial microaggression" (her words) that could easily seem like nothing, except to the person experiencing it. And it's incredibly difficult, not to picture an equivalent article being written by a Jewish woman, but to imagine such a piece winding up in a *progressive* outlet, rather than a right-leaning one. Which is, in a certain sense, fair. Unlike Jews, who often have a choice between passing as just white (oh Bernie Sanders, you with your "Polish" ancestors) and announcing our difference, Asians are a visible minority (well, many different ones).

For the social-justice left, for the most part, the fact that Asian Americans are visibly nonwhite is enough. I mean, if you search, you can find a contingent of Asian Americans on the far left who understand themselves as Asian-privileged (as versus simply Asian as well as, in some other way, privileged), much like my Jewish trustafarian-Tumblr classmate above.[66] The notion that something like "Asian privilege" exists gets regularly shot down on the left, however.[67] The left seems to understand—and rightly so—that "Asian privilege" is a bigoted concept.[68]

Where Asians fall in the US "privilege" framework more broadly—that is, beyond social-justice, social media, and progressive think pieces—often winds up depending on where powerful white people want to place them. If the goal is patting oneself on the back for "diversity," Asians count as "diverse." Meanwhile, if the goal is complaining that white kids are no longer quite as privileged as they used to be in, say, education, that oh-so-nefarious Asian advantage gets to be condemned.

There isn't space (or need) here to fully rehash the whole Asians-as-the-new-Jews conversation, but a bit of background is in order. In the early twentieth century, Harvard and other elite universities tried to keep out Jews, who would otherwise have been overrepresented in the student body, by rejiggering admissions requirements toward "character," defined as . . . basically, as not being Jewish. Today's so-called model minority, Asian Americans, are similarly overrepresented at elite schools and universities, and may also face a more difficult time getting admitted.[69] Affirmative action, which is in principle about raising the number of under-represented minority students, also contributes to a holistic, balance-seeking approach that winds up doing a favor for society's famously favored: white people.

There are instances of white people benefiting from diversity efforts in this way playing out all around, as Kate Robinson alluded to in *Jacobin*, writing that privilege theory tends "to encourage a type of politics in which various marginalized groups are held responsible for the oppression of others, such as the construction of Asian Americans as enablers of white supremacy."[70] That's a side note in her piece, so she doesn't give examples. I, meanwhile, will stick with the one I know best: New York City schools. Major media outlets—*The New York Times*, *Slate*, *The Atlantic*—regularly run news stories and analysis of the diversity crisis at New York City's "specialized" magnet high schools.[71] While I know why *I* read these stories—I went to Stuyvesant—I'm never entirely sure why a more general audience would care. Unlike the Ivy League stories that also appear in these publications, the question of what a bunch of immigrant high school students from Queens are up to isn't exactly a *glamorous* one. Its interest, I think, lies elsewhere.

Before getting at why I think this, a word on the numbers: Going by the census, New York City, in 2010, was 33.3 percent (non-Latino) white, 25 percent black, 12.7 percent Asian, and 28.6 percent Latino. Including whites who identify as Latino or Hispanic brings the city's white population up to only 44 percent.[72] Thus the outrage when TV shows set in the city are all white—that's not what the city looks like. New York City's private, or "independent," schools, meanwhile, are an impressive 63.5 percent "European American," which presumably means white; they can't all be new arrivals from, say, Switzerland. The amount these schools pat themselves on the back for not being 100 percent European American is quite something.

They tout statistics on the number of "students of color," a category that most certainly includes Asians.[73] (A Riverdale brochure illustrates its 33-percent-of-color stat with a photo of a white boy and an East Asian boy working on some kind of project together, as if such a scenario were something to write home about.[74]) And they have to, because they need all the statistical "color" they can get.

Yet in the very same city, at the very same time, a public high school whose student body is 80 percent of color can be the target of tremendous diversity criticism . . . because 73 percent of those students are Asian.[75] Stuyvesant High School, which is, again, *20 percent white*, gets taken to task for not catering to students of color . . . but "of color," differently defined.

It's *accepted* that private schools will be rich and white. That's a given. As is the notion that as long as they aren't waving Confederate flags, as long as they're giving their handful of black students prominent places in promotional materials, and making a big, big deal about the fact that not every last student is white, they get to pass themselves off as bastions not of privilege in the bad sense, but of noblesse oblige.

However, jump down a rung or ten, to where the city's middle classes broadly defined are fighting it out, and suddenly it's a problem that . . . well, what *is* the problem, exactly? It sounds most sympathetic to say—and it's correct—that there aren't enough black and Latino kids at the most selective public high schools. But is that the complaint? Or is it that there's this enormous, newish building *in Tribeca* offering an excellent (well, prestigious, at any rate) free education, and not a whole lot of white kids are benefiting. Complaining about that, however, is socially unacceptable. So the complaint gets phrased as, what about black and Latino kids? It is an important intervention, but one that can be both a fair point and a cover for a more sinister one.

The hypocrisy here is even that much more outrageous when one looks at the whole "cost-of-tutoring" angle: The private schools charge tens of thousands of dollars a year in tuition, but are to be praised for giving the occasional scholarship. That some families pay a few hundred dollars for a prep course to help their kids get into a more competitive public school is, meanwhile, evidence of a system that favors the rich.

Ah, but private services are different from public ones! To which I'd say, that they are, but we're talking about YPIS outrage, not legal distinctions. If you see it as a travesty that education all too often fails to counteract inequality, isn't it a problem that there even *are* private schools? Somehow . . . no. That's just how it is. No one would dare to dream that the really, really, *really* rich would be sending their kids to any public school, even one filled with fancy Chinese and Korean immigrants whose parents could, at one point, spare literally *hundreds* of dollars for tutoring.

For the city's rich, white, but diversely brochured private schools to get called out for *their* privilege, they need to do something outrageous. It can't just be that the kids attending these schools will sometimes-but-not-always get dropped off by a car and a driver, while their public school counterparts are taking the subway. Yes, as personal finance writer Helaine Olen has shown, coastal prep schools are pricier and more exclusive than ever.[76] Yet that's unsurprising. No, for the schools to bring about real rage, it has to be *bigger* than that.

Appropriately, the most rage I've noticed directed at private schools in recent years has stemmed from a *New York Times* story called, "At New York Private Schools, Challenging White Privilege from the Inside."[77] In it, Kyle Spencer reports on a seemingly well-funded effort, on the part of these schools, to alert the white-privileged to their white privilege:

> In the past, private school diversity initiatives were often focused on minority students, helping them adjust to the majority white culture they found themselves in, and sometimes exploring their backgrounds in annual

assemblies and occasional weekend festivals. Now
these same schools are asking white students and
faculty members to examine their own race and to dig
deeply into how their presence affects life for everyone
in their school communities, with a special emphasis on
the meaning and repercussions of what has come to be
called white privilege.

It's a brilliantly written piece, because Spencer never outright says that there's something absurd and hypocritical about the endeavor. In *Salon*, Corey Robin expressed what was, I think, almost the inevitable response: "You'd think that if the parents and teachers of these masters of the universe were truly concerned about racial and class privilege they'd simply abolish private schools."[78] The closest Spencer gets to overt criticism along those lines is to note, "It may seem paradoxical that students at elite institutions would decide to tackle the elitism they seem to cherish." Yes, it certainly might. A cringe-inducing opening anecdote describes some students at Friends Seminary gazing into the navels of their nonoppression and complaining of the bigotry they face for being "ditsy" and "privileged." Lingering in the background (and oh, in the comments) is the fact that the students at these schools are benefiting from something a bit more than just *white* privilege. What about how they live in New York and are really, really rich?

Yet the hypocrisy angle may have been overstated. What jumped out,[79] to me, about the efforts was that they're being sold not as earnest anti-racism, but as training for the modern world. Writes Spencer: "Educators charged with preparing students for life inside these schools, in college and beyond, maintain that anti-racist thinking is a 21st-century skill and that social competency requires a sophisticated understanding of how race works in America." As cynical and bleak as that may sound, it is, from the perspective of someone shelling out tens of thousands a year for *the best*, the sort of thing that ought to be included. We *do* live in a society where a seemingly racist faux pas can lead to someone's downfall. (Or, perhaps, to their Republican presidential nomination.) Knowing what "white privilege" is, and how to avoid letting yours show, absolutely is a "skill" these days. The rich-getting-richer aspect of elite privilege-awareness education put me off, and I wasn't alone. As Conor Friedersdorf put it, in *The Atlantic*, "These educationally privileged students will become exquisitely adept at invoking privilege to signal moral sophistication and guard their status among similarly acculturated peers."[80] Coming at the question from well to Friedersdorf's left, Robin arrived at the same: "Global society, 21st-century skills: These are buzzwords for the international capitalism the students of these schools are being trained to lead. Far from being educated to dismantle privilege, they're being schooled to perpetuate and preside over it."

Freddie deBoer also, not surprisingly, jumped on this story as well, with a blog post[81] that's, if anything, harsher on the schools: "In these contexts, the obsessive focus on conversations, awareness, and knowing becomes inevitable. Solutions must, like causes, remain vague, indistinct, and resistant to material evaluation." Where I'd split with him on this, though, is his insistence that once, back in some unspecified Golden Age, the privilege framework worked:

> Perhaps no form of subtle social control better exemplifies privilege's ability to dominate through soft power than the way in which privilege theory itself becomes a commodity, monetized and peddled to the privileged as easily as consumer electronics or expensive clothes.

In deBoer's interpretation, a righteous anti-oppression theory got corrupted once the rich and powerful came up with ways to use it to serve their own ends. But was it ever otherwise? I keep coming back to the fact that Peggy McIntosh taught at Brearley. It's hard for me to look at the prep-school privilege workshop story as a case of an otherwise subversive theory getting corrupted. Even beyond that, though, there's little reason to think the privilege framework ever *wasn't* superficial, or that it ever wasn't about rich people patting themselves on the back or ritualistically absolving themselves of well-deserved guilt. What these workshops, in all their big-picture absurdity, point to isn't so much the hypocrisy of any individuals, or the perversion of an otherwise sound approach, as a problem intrinsic to the privilege framework. From its origins, it's always been about self-awareness, and the enemy is always the person who's said the wrong thing. The and-now-what of privilege checking has never been articulated.

Privilege-awareness education—which has become enough of a trend that it has its own scholarly detractors[82]—shifts the paradigm. It used to be that sensitivity meant being discreet about which students are on scholarship, or, at public schools, about which qualify for a free lunch. (My homeroom teacher was a master of lack of discretion where that was involved.) That approach wasn't perfect. It often left socioeconomically disadvantaged students feeling invisible, while allowing socioeconomically blessed kids to blithely go around thinking everyone shared their advantages. Today, the idea is to put the privileged students on the spot, and to make them reflect on what it means that they *don't* face these obstacles. Of course, there's no way to alert privileged students to their privilege that doesn't also highlight the disadvantage of the others. And there's no way to alert posh students to their poshness that doesn't make them, on some level, that much more pleased with themselves.

IN PRIVILEGE'S NO-MAN'S-LAND

OSTENSIBLY, THE POINT of privilege checking, of YPIS, is to achieve justice. *Social* justice, if I may use the term. So it seems relevant that the lens has been adopted, with such enthusiasm, in the service of maintaining the status quo. While the right has always borrowed rhetoric from the left to serve its own purposes—like when the absence of conservatives in academia gets cast as a need for "ideological diversity"—something new has gone on with "privilege." The term isn't only used to articulate how conservatives are the real victims, although that does, as we've seen, happen. It's also used as a way of casting discrimination of all kinds as a form of anti-oppression. There's always going to be some selective understanding of the truth, according to which the hated ticks more "privilege" boxes than the hater.

On this much, the privilege framework is accurate: Society has hierarchies, and some categories of people are—all things equal—luckier than others. Those who deny that "privilege" exists in those broad, sweeping areas where you'd need your head rather deep in the sand not to have noticed—that is, who deny that the rich have it better than the poor, white people better than black people—need not so much a *privilege* check as an introduction to reality. The trouble is that those hierarchies don't explain all injustice, and that they don't always correspond to the hierarchies that "count" according to the privilege framework. Privilege at best describes an all-things-equal advantage, and doesn't account for the individuals doing worse than their identity categories would predict. However, if the privilege-checking consensus is that your group doesn't count, that its plight isn't real, you're screwed. And you're screwed not just because you don't get to use "privilege" rhetoric to articulate your situation. You also lose because, according to the privilege framework, if you complain about oppression *but are actually privileged*, you are, in fact, the worst.

The "privilege" approach, according to which anyone deemed "privileged" is fair game and by definition impossible to victimize, backfires, in a serious way, when the target is chosen wrong. Once the righteous "punch" becomes the highest form of argument, there's absolutely nothing to stop punches in every which direction from getting the benefit of the doubt.

When it comes to intermediaries, the issue isn't just that the privilege lens treats all who don't have it the absolute worst as privileged. Rather, it's that intermediaries so often become the *face* of "privilege," functioning as scapegoats for society's most powerful. It's not that there are people who, all things equal, have it worse than Asians or Jews—*which there are*—but that Asians and Jews end up being cast as the ultimate haves. Which lets the ultimate haves (in this case, white gentiles) off the hook.

This intermediary-bashing dynamic is also what's going on with the White Lady construct we met in the previous chapter. There as here, someone who's almost the most privileged winds up *embodying* "privilege"—and getting taken to task for societal injustices—in a way that the very most privileged somehow do not. Yet we also see this play out in garden-variety YPIS, where someone who drops a biographical detail indicating that he or she is . . . middle class—and not a starving refugee—gets declared, for a fifteen-minute increment, the face of privilege. Because that's who generally comes in for these pile-ons on comment threads or in Facebook debates. That's who's available. It's the nobody in a thread who makes a casual reference to shopping at Banana Republic (ooh, fancy, it's as if he doesn't know that *some* people can't afford *Kmart!!!*), not the head of a bank or corporation.

And I don't see this as a coincidence. Rather, it's one of the great appeals of privilege theory *for the most privileged*. If a group that isn't *quite* at the top gets to function as a stand-in for the one that is, then the hierarchy doesn't have to shift. No revolution is needed. The have-nots and the have-not-quite-as-much contingents will just fight things out among themselves.

CONCLUSION

AFTER PRIVILEGE

AN *ONION* PIECE from 2014, "White Male Privilege Squandered on Job at Best Buy," seems, from the headline, like it could go either way.[1] Is it hilarious that a man who had everything in his favor ended up where he did? Or is the joke that we're now calling Best Buy employees—well, ones with certain, altogether common demographic traits—"privileged"? The item's brilliance lies in the fact that this ambiguity is maintained through to the end: "At press time, the man born into the world's most affluent and privileged socioeconomic group was spending his 15-minute break silently consuming a sleeve of Donettes purchased out of a vending machine." If we read it as critical of the concept—and, perhaps wishfully, I do—it would seem that *class* might be the unstated element, and the post is a takedown of an expression—"white male privilege"—that evokes a person who has still other unearned advantages. Yet whatever a white man's reasons for ending up in a job like that (and of course, plenty do, including some with college degrees and from relatively well-off backgrounds, especially post-2008), at a certain point, where someone has landed tells you more about how "privileged" they are than where a likely inaccurate calculation of their unearned advantages would place them. (Does intelligence count? Does drive?) Privilege theory would have it that Best Buy dude is privileged. Common sense might offer a different interpretation.

The question rarely asked about "privilege," which is also really the only one worth asking, goes as follows: Has it helped? Has the introduction of this framework brought about a more just society?

It's only once the framework gets examined from *that* angle that the flaws become self-evident. The privilege approach is, practically speaking, about raising awareness of the minutiae of injustice. While gaps remain, huge swaths of awareness have certainly been raised. And? Let's set aside (briefly) the question of whether we'd think this would lead anywhere. Has it done so?

Jia Tolentino gets at the flaws of the awareness fixation in a brilliant December 2015 *Jezebel* post about the relationship between "offense" and online journalism:

> Contemporary life means being hyper-aware and worse off than ever; we are increasingly shut out of the mechanisms of representational democracy and simultaneously being forced to know more and more and more. We know many rape kits are backlogged in all the big cities, how many black teenagers have been shot by the police this year, how shamelessly the NRA pulls its levers, how corporate campaign finance ensures that the wealth gap is here to stay. And we can't change any of it—or at the very least,

not very easily, not when it's so much easier to sit around
and get very precisely insightful online.[2]

Tolentino's point was especially striking given the context. Left-
and youth-leaning media generally, and *Jezebel* especially, has devoted itself to awareness-raising and witty-but-sensitive online
observations for years. What does it say that members of the media
are themselves (*ourselves*) tiring of this? We have, in the one corner,
journalists producing intricate articles parsing exactly what was the
teensiest bit racist or sexist in the (out-of-context) speech of whichever actress or male scientist, and, in the other, fairly blatant, out-
there online abuse getting directed at (among others) these same
journalists. It can seem—whether or not there's any truth to this
impression—that there are some forest-for-the-trees issues at play.
The blame lies not just with the privilege framework in the abstract,
but also with a media landscape that—for reasons that have as much
to do with what readers want as with production costs—favors the
churning out of "privilege" content (celebrity gaffes, navel-gazing
from the ordinary-but-privileged) over, say, war reporting. (If the two
pay the same, which is to say, nothing or not much . . . ?[3])

Honing in on YPIS specifically, Berkeley senior Efe Atli offers
the following damning critique, in a *Daily Cal* op-ed ("Checking
privilege serves to reinforce it") from January 2016:

> The number[s] don't lie. Three decades of checking
> privilege directly correlate with an astronomical rise in
> income inequality. The more inequality we have, the
> more privilege gets checked by more privileged people,
> and the more the privileged feel pleasure (and power) in
> being aware of their privilege and so, grow in power.[4]

That seems about right, although it hasn't been quite "Three decades of checking privilege"—more like, at the time of Atli's writing,

eight years. Still, the culture was already neck-deep in privilege awareness when the 2016 all-white Oscars lineup rolled around. The term "microaggression" had entered the lexicon when Donald Trump started winning primaries with a platform based almost exclusively on hurling the macro variety. It goes without saying that privilege awareness didn't bring about a revolution on the ground. (While quite prepared to call out Hillary Clinton for bourgeois feminism, Bernie Sanders's supporters tend to lean anti-"privilege," and to view Clinton as the embodiment of style-over-substance liberalism.) Yet even when it comes to pop culture, to the more superficial concerns, *even there,* not much has changed since the early 2000s, at least not for the better.

There's a limit, though, to what we can conclude from the apparent inefficacy of the "privilege" approach. Is leftist infighting (and I'm including hyperbolic criticism coming from the center left) distracting progressives from the real issues? Probably, if not necessarily in terms of individual commitment, then at least as far as media coverage is concerned. And can we root Trump's popularity (especially because, as journalist Matt Taibbi has written, so much of it is *private* popularity[5]) in widespread fears of saying the wrong thing on social media and getting fired? Here's a guy whose *thing* is saying outrageous things publicly—maybe that's only appealing in a climate where saying a slightly wrong thing (or a thing that was intentionally misinterpreted as offensive, to get clicks) is such a social crime?[6]

Maybe. Or maybe not—there was plenty of outspoken racism, sexism, and xenophobia before the privilege turn. The causation case is there, but is tougher to demonstrate than—as Atli subtly mentions—the correlation one. Yet correlation alone should be reason enough for concern. Even setting aside the many ways "privilege" seems to have backfired, we have to consider its failure to bring about a kinder society, let alone a more just one. If "privilege" hasn't worked—and it hasn't—then it's time to stop assuming that people who reject the framework necessarily do so for defensive or reactionary reasons. It's time, more to the point, to step away from the question of individual motivation altogether, and to approach questions of injustice from more productive angles.

I've never quite sorted out by what mechanism awareness of privilege is meant to inspire a desire to shed oneself of it. Back in the good old days, when elites knew *exactly* who they were, were they eager to redistribute their wealth? No—if you'll excuse my historical oversimplification—they were not. While there's certainly something irritating about the elites of today who mistakenly think they're scrappy or "normal," what happens differently when unearned advantage is out in the open? Children of politicians are presumably aware of the unearned advantages that their name-recognition inspires, yet Bushes and Kennedys (not to mention Windsors!) don't seem too worried about it, and even get to claim that actually, it was *harder* for them, what with all the expectations. What's to make the average schmo turn down a job gotten through connections? Where's the gorgeous person who, however much he or she disapproves of beauty standards in the abstract, would like to be uglier, or for society to make no distinctions on the basis of appearance?

The privilege framework promises a neat, as-the-world-should-be relationship between background and character, which results in the surely-you've-never framing of so many privilege accusations. For example, rather than tell someone that he's being an asshole to the waitress, you have to make a pronouncement about how he's surely never worked in food service. It is an interesting way the world *might* work, but I've seen little evidence, out in the world, that it does. And there's research backing this up: Northeastern University psychology professor David DeSteno presented his and some other studies in *The New York Times*, concluding, "Living through hardship doesn't either warm hearts or harden them; it does both."[7] Research, in this case, lines up with common sense: Life experience has some impact on empathy, but not a direct and simple one. It's not always—as the privilege framework would have it—that insensitivity stems from a lack of personal experience with things that don't involve falling ass-backward into good luck.

"Privilege" is best understood not as a real trait, but as a construction. Anyone can be "privileged" if it suits someone else's argument. There's no wealth or income threshold for "privileged." It doesn't require membership in the One Percent, or even the top 50 percent. And anyone can, with proper rhetorical flourish, play the role of the implicitly underprivileged. To call out another person's white privilege, you yourself can be white. And to call out class privilege, you don't need to demonstrate that you yourself *aren't* a J.Crew-wearing Whole Foods shopper. The trick is simply to announce that this *other* person is those things, and to do so in a tone that *suggests* that you go around in a potato sack and subsist on lentils (or better yet—because lentils suggest cultural capital—McDonald's). YPIS is about constructing an underdog *stance*. It's about making as if you're craning your neck to look (and punch) up, regardless of where you're actually situated.

"Privileged" is part of a family of terms used for euphemistically describing the not-destitute (or the "middle class," or—for a double whammy of socialism and Francophilia—the "bourgeoisie"). Like the others, "privileged" is ambiguous and can refer to everyone from unambiguous elites to people who simply have *some* advantages—a college diploma, say, or a childhood spent in a two-parent household. However, "middle class" and "bourgeois" allow, at least rhetorically, for the existence of an upper class, an aristocracy. They're not just word-variance synonyms for "rich"; whereas there's nothing *above* privilege, no implied higher rung. Referring to everyone who isn't desperately poor as "privileged" may be inaccurate as well as off-putting. Yet it's a shortcut to always seeming self-aware.

From its inception, proponents of the privilege framework have warned against leaving it at that. Awareness, they remind in unison, isn't enough. Critics of the framework, who insist that it's all talk and no action, aren't always being fair to proponents, who do—at least if we're talking about scholars and activists, and not fourteen-year-olds on Tumblr—acknowledge this. Yet it's never entirely clear, not merely *how* progress would follow from privilege awareness, but *why* it would, and, moreover, why the reverse wouldn't be the case. Why, precisely, would rendering all hierarchies transparent lead to these hierarchies' disappearance? Why, indeed, wouldn't it just lead to those at the bottom of each despairing, while encouraging those at the top to view their unearned advantages as that much more precious? This implicit, but implausible, step *after* the awareness epiphany is, at its essence, my issue with "privilege." Constantly reminding everyone of where they fall . . . why *would* such candor lead to empathy? Why wouldn't a society where systemic injustices are front and center in everyone's mind at all times only serve make interactions between men and women, blacks and whites, rich and poor, that much more fraught, inhibiting the development of everyday social and professional bonds?

THE CRUELTY OF "PRIVILEGE"

BUILT INTO "PRIVILEGE" is the idea that the normal state of affairs is for things to be going *terribly*. This assumption emerged as a necessary corrective to the idea that it's "normal" to be rich, white, able-bodied, and so forth, but has wound up—as tends to happen with "privilege"—as overcorrection. It can seem as if the desired goal is for everyone to be oppressed, rather than for all to be free from oppression. Is it a problem that white killers are captured alive by police? That white drug addicts appear in the media as real people with a medical condition? Or is the problem that black killers and drug addicts, respectively, don't get that treatment? It seems right to use "privilege" if your point is that some people do indeed have it too easy. That is, after all, what "privilege" implies, which is why it's such an odd fit for cases where the point being made is that the world is just for some and unjust for others. Calling justice "privilege" is certainly a way of highlighting that not all experience it. The problem is that it also implies that no one should.

The biggest glitch in the privilege framework is the it-could-be-worse component. Whether we're talking about progressives casting doubt on "bourgeois feminism" or conservatives wondering what black Princeton students could possibly have to complain about, this supposedly hypersensitive way of looking at the world somehow manages to be incredibly dismissive of any plight that isn't quite as bad as another.

As anyone with a Facebook account and some earnest acquaintances has probably noticed, "privilege" has turned every conversation about tragedy into one about how other tragedies are worse. You know the routine. One person posts something sad, and another responds that actually, something else is much sadder, and so it goes until most of the thread participants have retreated to cat-photo Instagram. Yet where this really took off was in the aftermath of the deadly November 2015 Paris attacks. Sure, those were sad, but isn't it *even sadder* that white tragedies (involving the deaths of plenty of nonwhite people, too), get more attention than others? Isn't *that* the real story, and shouldn't your friends with those Eiffel Tower photos feel bad?

What played out on my social-media accounts (that is, the wave of "here's a photo of me on vacation in Paris," followed by "what about Beirut???") was, it soon emerged, representative of something greater. On Twitter, *Guardian* writer Jamiles Lartey offered a spot-on rebuttal to the "tragedy hipsters" who responded by shaming those who'd posted messages of grief about the attacks.[8] Shaming them, that is, for not caring enough about other, more obscure (if still reported-on) global tragedies, particularly another (less lethal) ISIS attack that occurred around the same time in Beirut. I'd reacted to that social-media tendency toward dismissal of Paris grief along about the same lines as Lartey, asking that those grieving (because yes, that's what some of those Paris posts were about) be given a moment to do so before getting chastised for implicit racism.

Once the "What abouts?" started, it was tough to question them without seeming defensive and—horrors—lacking in *awareness*. However, Lartey's inclusion of caveats, as well as a privilege disclaimer ("Obviously there are salient asymmetries in power and privilege which govern this response, but it nonetheless feels dismissive & insensitive"), helped his case, as did his after-the-fact point about how it's not one-upmanship if you're *Lebanese* and posting about Beirut. It also may have helped that Lartey is black, left leaning, and therefore not easy to dismiss as being motivated by defensive pro-white-people impulses. Through a combination of his arguments and his place in the culture, he got the point across: "We (the left)," he wrote, "need to be cautious that the reparative weighting of the suffering of marginalized people doesn't cross into minimization."

Yet the privilege lens makes such "minimization" inevitable. Every situation gets instantaneously analyzed in terms of privilege. To mention any form of suffering that doesn't result from a clear-cut lack of privilege is to come across as bratty, oblivious, first-world-problems-ish. Fine, if the problem is, say, that it's just so hard to decide between Ibiza and Saint-Tropez for your next vacation, but people who are privileged—privileged on paper, privileged along one or more axes—do deal with personal tragedies that are anything but frivolous. A defender of "privilege" might say that I'm missing the point—that of course you could be privileged and unlucky (for example, see Parul Sehgal's *New York Times* article on that time when Joan Didion got YPISed for a book about her daughter's very untimely death[9]). And that's where "privilege" *really* loses me. It's a nifty rhetorical point—systemic injustice doesn't map up with individual circumstances, and that people who don't *get* privilege don't *get* this—but in the world of actual people, flagging the privilege of those dealing with something dreadful is a deraiting of the cruelest sort.

It's bad enough that "privilege" has brought about pseudoconcepts like "Asian privilege," "female privilege," and so forth. In a category all of its own, though, we'd have to put something like "rape privilege." What's that, you might wonder? Well, it depends who's YPIS-ing. There was the time when conservative commentator George Will wrote, in reference to one claim of sexual assault, that US colleges "make victimhood a coveted status that confers privileges," and claimed that the "privileges" of victimhood extended to female college students' accusations of rape. How was it that he described college students, again? Oh, that's right: as "especially privileged young adults."[10]

Although an even better example might be the headline given to a *New York Times* op-ed by public-affairs professor Callie Marie Rennison: "Privilege, Among Rape Victims."[11] The headline belied what Rennison was saying:

> Women at the margins are the ones who bear the brunt of the harshest realities, including sexual violence, and they do so with the least resources. Am I saying that we should ignore sexual violence against the wealthy and educated? Of course not. Nor is it wrong to pay special attention to college-age women: The one risk factor that remains consistent whether women are advantaged or disadvantaged is age, and women ages 16 to 20 are sexually victimized at the highest rates.

That sounds reasonable. Yet "Privilege, Among Rape Victims" posits a privileged rape-victim caste, or, worse, some sort of epidemic of "privilege" among rape victims, with some sexual-assault survivors lording it (whatever "it" might be, in this context) over the rest. Social disparities, racial disparities, and more will obviously extend even to categories like "rape victim." But there's something tasteless and vile, really, about using "privilege" to describe that situation.

For me, the biggest indictment of "privilege" is the frequency with which it's used to refer to some of life's least fortunate. Actually, "life's least fortunate" doesn't quite cover it; the dead can, as we shall soon see, be YPISed. It might seem that there'd be some sort of "life privilege" that trumps all other forms. Not so! In 2012, *Jezebel* published a post[12] by Katie J.M. Baker called "How to Feel When an Impossibly Promising 22-Year-Old Passes Away," in reference to Marina Keegan. How promising was Keegan? "She was a 22-year-old recent Yale graduate about to start a job as an editorial assistant at *The New Yorker* in a few weeks—before then, her plan was to revise the musical she had written, set to run at the New York International Fringe Festival later this summer." And! "Keegan had already contributed to *NPR* and the *New York Times*." And! "She was also president of the Yale College Democrats and involved with Occupy Wall Street." Consider that the past tense here was not because Keegan had graduated, but because she had *died in a car crash*. Dead is dead, one might think. Since that *Jezebel* post, Keegan became a *New York Times* bestselling author. *Posthumously*.[13]

Yet Baker (or whoever wrote her headline) had committed the crucial sin of telling the *Jezebel* readership "how to feel." What if you aren't particularly sad that this young woman has died, hmm? Some commenters were not sad, thank you very much, and resented being told that they should be.

The comment thread devolved into a discussion of "privilege": how much of the stuff Keegan had (well, *had* had), and whether it's really a good idea to be talking about how sad it is that a twenty-two-year-old died when there are other, sadder situations, like the existence of living twenty-two-year-olds who don't have jobs at *The New Yorker*. A contingent in the comments took a fair point—the media values some lives more than others—and chose a *wildly inappropriate* context for making it. Yet that was the mood of the moment, of the threads on that site and of progressive online media more generally. Where there was privilege, it had to be checked. The possibility that some truth greater than "privilege" might exist—that the story might not be *about* privilege—was simply not fathomable. So off the commenters went:

> [F]or every Keegan who dies too young there is a POC from a poor background who worked just as hard under worse circumstances with extra pressures. So while I don't think we need to undermine Keegan's work, there is nothing wrong with asking why we are so drawn to her accomplishments that are markers of privilege, and not others.[14]

There is something wrong with checking the privilege of a specific person *who is dead*. The time to parse whether "Yale" and "*The New Yorker*" fall more into the unearned-advantages category than the achievement category *has passed* once the person has. The (fictional) "POC" who had it worse than Keegan (and, apart from the slight, if evocative, biographical sketch, with little knowledge of how easy, exactly, she had it) is nevertheless *alive*. Doesn't a person—yes, even one of color!—who's still with us have more unearned advantages than someone who's not? In the land of YPIS, categories must be analyzed according to the rigid, sanctimonious framework. And the framework has no place for the category of "dead."

And on it went:

> She was young, wealthy, talented, well educated, and white. She was given more chances than most people ever get, and while my heart is saddened by the fact that she could potentially have made good contributions to the world, I can't help but feel our time would not be best spent mourning what could have been but rather working to help those with a fraction of her gifts reach THEIR potential.[15]

And these comments—the ones that admitted that a twenty-two-year-old dying is awful—were among the more reasonable. Some were far more cold: "She's White, pretty, and a graduate from an Ivy League college. That's enough to get coverage for something that happens to millions (you know, death) on Earth everyday."[16]

It's hard to know, here, where to start. The commenter appears to think that dying at twenty-two is the most normal thing in the world outside of rarified circles. Why take that tack? Tellingly, some of these commenters use the present tense, as if privilege were a force so strong as to extend beyond the grave.

Another, however, reached peak YPIS:

> Her life is of value, simply because she lived it, but also because she tried to leave her mark on the world. But her life is not of more value because she bears certain markers of privilege, and the fact that her death has received so much attention when younger and less privileged men and women of color are largely ignored in the media, and often subjected to character assassination even when they do manage to garner such attention, a far more savage defamation than questioning the priorities of the media in covering the story in the first place, is not unworthy of note.[17]

So far, about the same as the others. Then, here it comes:

> And for the record, the ability to dismiss privilege (putting the word in all caps doesn't lessen its salience, but it certainly conveys your contempt) as intangible and (cough) imaginary tells a lot about the position from which you are castigating others. Must be a nice view from up there above the fray.

This comment is the most YPIS of all, because it's no longer just the dead girl who's privileged, but anyone who's spoken out against YPISing a young woman who is, after all, *dead*.

What was going on, exactly? Were these commenters so overcome with righteous concern for the alive-but-oppressed that they simply *had* to say something? Or was the response—or some part of it, at any rate—jealousy? It's not socially acceptable to complain that a dead girl has all the luck, so maybe that discomfort was what was being channeled? The psychology here is, of course, unknowable. However, I'd put my money on a third possibility. It had, in that climate, simply become so ingrained that *YPIS is the only possible response* that commenters YPISed the dead young woman almost reflexively. The story seemed as if it fit a Missing White Girl–type narrative, so that's the narrative these commenters went with.[18] In doing so, they backed themselves into a corner of cruelty and absurdity.

Some other *Jezebel* commenters, thank goodness, were at hand in the thread to point out the problem with a "privilege" take in this context:

"Bollocks to privilege," wrote one, adding, "When someone dies before their time it's a tragedy, colour/race/religion/wealth be damned."[19]

Regular *Jezebel* commenter LaComtesse summarized the mini-controversy quite well:

What I got from this article: A promising young woman, who had already contributed her young, female voice to a lot of issues that Jezebel readers care about has died. This is understandably very sad. What I got from these comments: I am not allowed to be touched by anyone's death because death is not a unique experience. I am particularly not allowed to be touched by the death of someone who had even a teeny bit of that dreaded P-word: privilege.[20]

Another commenter, though, got straight to the point: "God, I hope I never read the word, 'privilege' ever again."[21]

That is my sentiment as well. The Keegan thread was the moment it crystallized for me that YPIS is nothing short of a disaster.[22] What's changed in my view of YPIS, since 2012, is that "privilege" itself harms more than it helps. Its role as an aide in online bullying exceeds its utility as a theoretical framework. The underlying (and legitimate) point the YPIS-hurlers ostensibly cared about—injustices in media coverage—got damaged in the process.

The "privilege" framing, with its focus on unearned advantage rather than unjust *disadvantage*, doesn't fit with situations where even the "privileged" person is still quite screwed. It's true and tragic that the typical American woman lacks Angelina Jolie's access to medical care.[23] Yet "privilege" suggests there's something spa-like about the preventative removal of potentially cancerous body parts.[24] There isn't, even under the "best" of circumstances. And yes, one probably could attribute some of the disproportionate attention the Paris attacks received to racism and xenophobia. But is watching your city get *attacked by ISIS* ever "privilege"? Even if people worldwide are sending messages of support? That a situation is terrible but could be *even worse* doesn't mean that it makes sense to speak of it as a *good* situation. Much as "white privilege" serves to confuse and to summon defensiveness in white people who aren't otherwise privileged, so it goes with "privilege" in the context of tragedy. It cuts against common sense—but more importantly, basic decency—to classify these types of situations in this way.

All of which brings us back to a main flaw of "surely you've never" approach to deciding who has the authority to speak about which topics. From the outside, it's not clear who's been dealt which hand. A framework centered on "grit," and on obstacles overcome, requires obstacles to be out in the open. I suppose there's a "privilege" of sorts in having only invisible obstacles, but it doesn't take long to think of individual cases where an invisible challenge would be greater than a visible one.

Progressive writer Matt Bruenig has a great blog post[25] on what he calls "identitarian deference" (ID)—that is, the tendency, on the left, to declare the person without a given form of privilege the winner of any argument related to that identity group—and its implicit sharing requirement:

> ID works the most smoothly for identities that are readily apparent. Most of the time, you can tell what someone's gender and race is just by looking at them. But when the identity is less apparent, or indeed totally invisible, the only way to establish yourself as belonging to a particular identity is by revealing all sorts of private details about your life.[26]

This winds up placing anyone with obstacles, but not quite the right ones, in a bind. The dangers of sharing are generally going to be greater than the ones in keeping quiet. Share, and you reveal idiosyncratic challenges that make you seem like what would be called, in college-admissions lingo, a "liability." Refuse to share, though, and you've tacitly nodded along to the world's assessment of you as someone who's had it easy. Suffering that falls through the cracks of the privilege framework gets dismissed. I'm thinking of a line from a satirical but not especially clever *Medium* post, "It's Not Easy Being a White, Heterosexual Male": "You've got problems with the system? Tell me about it. I have to stand in line at the DMV, too, you know."[27] But that post also recalls the proverbial white Best Buy employee. The privilege framework doesn't know where to place the person who should, going by the crudest identity rubric, be at the top of life's hierarchy, but for whatever reason hasn't wound up there.

That brushing-off is its own insult, as one sees in a post by another white male progressive writer, Freddie deBoer, responding to an accusation he'd fielded on Twitter from someone insinuating that he had never faced "trauma."[28] Not content to play the role of privileged-by-assumption, deBoer goes on to tell the story of his own tragic childhood, then writes, "Understand: I have never experienced trauma, according to the theories of the time. Not in the way that politics recognizes. Not in a way that they regard as legitimate."

Yes, one could point out that tragedy *also* strikes people who aren't white men. One could even go further and note that we have, historically, heard a disproportionate amount, in literature and media, about the travails (including really serious ones) of people who happen to be white and male. Yet what does that add? Who's helped? Privilege ought to be about all-things-equal advantage. All things, however, are not equal. Some people who fit every last privilege-checklist category wind up facing tremendously bad luck. Enough so that they're actually worse off than a great many people who lack their systemic privileges. However technically true it may be that A is more privileged than B, if A nevertheless has it worse on the whole, why are we drumming on about A's privilege in the first place? Why not have that all-things-equal conversation, but leave A out of it? The cruelty of a framework that treats certain types of suffering as, in effect, logically impossible exceeds any social-justice benefits (doubtful at best) that come from privilege-checking people while they're down. Or dead.

FROM TREND TO ZEITGEIST

IN 2007, THE New York Times (specifically, food writer Melissa Clark) discovered kale salad. "Tuscan kale does not have to be cooked to be edible," read the caption, exhibiting such blissful ignorance of the near-decade of raw-kale veneration that would follow.[29] All along, though, we've known, or rather, we *should* have known, that kale would have its moment on menus and in lifestyle pagers, only to join the lineup of yuppie clichés gone by. When a trend is at its height, it can have a way of feeling eternal.

There were times, while writing this book, that I wondered if what I was offering was a microhistory of that time when everyone was caught up with "privilege," either from the vantage point of a new micro-era, one with its own preoccupations, or, at the very least, from the perspective of someone who understands that the moment will pass. As of 2016, I think there's more to it. I can't predict whether "privilege" will be with us forever; my inclination is to doubt that any concept possibly could. Yet it's become clear that "privilege" isn't a blip. Yes, certain privilege motifs, particular rhetorical turns of phrase, have already become passé. The "X Shows Y's Privilege" think-piece template, while surprisingly persistent,[30] sounds stale.

However, that moving on hasn't happened. In February 2016, a *New York* magazine piece on the concept of "white privilege" went viral.[31] The submission page of *Pacific Standard* magazine includes an explicit awareness requirement. Under "What we're not looking for," they've included, "Pitches that do not consider or reflect upon anything outside the affluent white, male experience."[32] This item is, in effect, inviting rich white men to pitch I've-examined-my-privilege essays. (These men aren't going to *not* pitch.) Or, worse, to pitch thoughtful articles that go beyond their personal experience, but that must, because of privilege, include digressions where their privileged white selves come under the microscope. There's also a hint of the patronizing toward writers who *aren't* rich white men, as if anything they'd produce (except, I suppose, a hagiography of a rich white guy) would arrive with a certain level of thoughtfulness.

It's perhaps not so surprising that "privilege" lives on, because it's more than a buzzword. More, even, than a theoretical framework. It's a generally accepted worldview. The "clear and executable moral theory" David Frum attributes to cartoonist Garry Trudeau— "1. Identify the bearer of privilege. 2. Hold the privilege-bearer responsible."[33]—remains the lens through which everyone interprets everything, and I exaggerate only slightly.

The temptations of YPIS are great. So great that the accusation's detractors on the left wind up making them. Once it's *your* cause on the line, *your* pet issue, it's easy to drum up a privilege argument that makes your case.

The best case for "privilege" is a circular one: It's the concept that's used these days to address injustice, so you can't, practically speaking, announce that it's counterproductive and leave it at that. As long as journalists, activists, and scholars who are otherwise doing good work opt for "privilege," it's clumsy as well as dismissive, *in that moment*, to hold forth on why you're not a fan of the term. Insofar as "privilege" is used as a form of protest, as a way for people in marginalized groups to express grievances (whether or not those in nonmarginalized groups are convinced that the grievances "count"), it is best to just set aside the fact that your interlocutor has used "privilege" and to listen. Anything else can rightly be called derailing.

Yet the point I've just made is a tepid defense of the framework at best. That there are moments when questioning the efficacy of "privilege" would be inappropriate doesn't mean the term *is* effective. Yes, "privilege" refers to various important phenomena—but is it important (or necessary, or helpful) to use "privilege" to speak of them? And yes, sanctimoniousness is better than rabid bigotry, but it hardly follows that we can't do better than that. The concept's well-intentioned users are vastly overshadowed, if not in number than in influence, by a sea of narcissistic self-righteousness and privilege denial. In principle, having some sort of basic step that everyone agrees to, and that's the starting point for all of us finding ways to make the world a better place, has a certain idealistic appeal. In practice, "privilege" just seems to breed resentment. Those accused of certain specific types of "privilege" hear this word, "privilege," that would seem to imply that they've had it easy, which is, in effect, an invitation for them to tell you exactly how far that is from the mark. A 2015 study showed that white people prompted to ponder "white privilege" wind up exaggerating their own disadvantages in other areas.[34] Is this defensiveness evidence that white people should be further educated in their privilege, or maybe that an entirely different angle is needed? Do we really need more workshops where white people tell other white people to acknowledge their privilege, when such endeavors result so predictably in resistance?[35] So it goes, too, with other forms of privilege. Tell a man he has "male privilege." Tends to go well. And the swapping out of "rich" for "privileged" as a way of discussing wealth is the quickest way to get your rich interlocutor to summon the one biographical detail that makes him seem plausibly scrappy, to have you know that he and his parents summered in one of the *lesser* Hamptons.

That "privilege" so reliably prompts the accused to list his or her disadvantages can, I suppose, be interpreted as an aha of sorts in favor of privilege as a concept. It's just *that powerful*! However, it's also clear evidence that this approach tends to accomplish the precise opposite of what it's meant to do. If the idea is to inspire people to reveal and then renounce their advantages, it fails, mainly because the framework is confusing. And if the idea is to promote engagement, to bring allies onboard, and so on? There, too, it's a dubious proposition. YPIS from haves reads as sanctimony. And YPIS from have-nots tends to inspire, at best, self-flagellation and other forms of navel-gazing. At best, the privileged recipient of a well-earned YPIS becomes that much more preoccupied with his or her own psyche. Rather than looking outward, he or she will try to sort out (and it won't always be self-evident!) how he or she has inadvertently offended (and admitting to ignorance will be interpreted as willful disregard). A widespread increase in self-awareness sounds like a good thing. Yet the privilege framework has made self-awareness—or, more accurately, self-presentation—at the center of all struggles, of all conversations. It produces—daily, with every

Twitter/think-piece controversy—winners and losers, the individuals who *get it* and those who do not.

BEYOND "PRIVILEGE"

THIS BOOK IS an argument against using the concept of privilege to understand and fight against injustice. Still, in the course of writing, I've often been struck by how much my sympathies lie with many of the *people* who use the term, and how off-putting I find so many of the arguments floating around against it. What I don't want this book to be is a contrarian anti-"privilege" take, one amounting to a mockery of those who use a particular term. It's all too easy to take ideas for granted once they've taken root, and to forget what life was like earlier. In many cases (not all), the privilege turn is more a matter of overshooting the mark than fully getting things wrong. Awareness overload is an overreaction to the apathy that preceded it.

But if not "privilege," then what? To suggest an alternate term, though, is to presume that the only problem with "privilege" is the word itself. If you're wondering what to hurl instead of a YPIS, my advice would be to simply refrain from hurling, period. Telling someone that his or her cluelessness is showing isn't any real improvement. While individuals' naïveté may betray larger societal injustices, unsolicited education in the form of a call-out isn't productive, whether the word "privilege" is used or not.

That said, shouldn't there be some way of describing and addressing inequalities of all kinds? Would chucking the "privilege" framework mean a return to an overly simplistic view of life's unfairness? Would it mean backtracking to the bad old days, when things like the Puerto Rican Day Parade *Seinfeld* episode could happen? Or *has* overt bigotry actually decreased following the "privilege" turn in pop culture?

If we do move away from "privilege," there are ways to keep the good and lose the bad. Some suggestions follow:

- Less awareness. Or, rather, we should hang onto awareness in the *numbers* sense. By all means, be aware if your company is favoring white men, or if the university you're in charge of is only admitting billionaires' kids. Be aware if you're a reporter and your news publication is featuring only elites and their travails. Be aware, as a person—as a citizen, if you prefer—of what's going on in the world, in your locale. However, that's a different, and fully external, sort of awareness. It's not about looking into our own navels and contemplating *why* we may act in ways that support discrimination. Indeed, given that members of marginalized groups often internalize bigotry against them, the whole surely-you-think-X-because-of-who-you-are assumption is flawed.

- A return to the anti-prejudice framework of yore, but with intersectionality this time around. There's no reason that an –ism approach (racism, sexism, anti-Semitism) can't be used to describe forms of bigotry that weren't much discussed until recently. (Yes, "transphobia" sounds jargony and I'm sure the *National Review* finds the very thought hilarious, but anti-trans discrimination is a real concern.) Nor is there any reason one would need to present society in terms of privilege in order to acknowledge the unique struggles of those facing more than one form of systemic discrimination. Speaking of prejudice rather than privilege doesn't fix the call-out issue, but it's a way of addressing injustice that doesn't end up inaccurately categorizing huge swaths of humanity under the haves umbrella. It avoids the inevitable confusion when someone white *and wealthy* apologizes for what is ultimately not *just* white privilege.

■ A returned focus on capital-capital, and (partially) away from cultural capital, in discussions of class. Less "socio," more "economic." That doesn't mean focusing less on race and gender, but it does mean giving some of the more amorphous cultural stuff a rest. As it stands, we've been sliding toward an ever-broader definition of what it means to be culturally privileged. How "privileged" is a college graduate with enormous loans and no job prospects? YPIS encourages the calling-out of people whose cherry-picked consumer choices would seem as if they could be extrapolated into dare I say *holistic* assessments of their financial situation. The markers also shift too quickly—cultural hints that someone's *loaded* (specific brands, styles, etc.) will generally only mean something for approximately five minutes if at all. That someone has an iPhone in one hand, a latte in the other, tells us . . . what, exactly, at this point? We need a common-sense definition of "elite," one that doesn't lump in everyone who's ever had cold-pressed green juice or worn expensive yoga pants.

■ A shift back toward the macro, away from the micro, where aggressions are concerned. That doesn't mean mirroring the problems of "privilege" and responding to specific, but relatively minor, complaints by pointing out that things could be worse. Rather, it means looking into editorial strategies and social-media approaches that don't involve digging for digging's sake. The emphasis on micro gives the false impression that the macro problems are done. That racism these days consists merely of pop stars culturally appropriating, or of Princeton students finding building names problematic. Even when (as with the building names) those speaking out are right about the merits, the disproportionate coverage these issues tend to get makes it seem as if the Left, as a whole, has its priorities wrong.

■ Enough with the gaffe story already. The aspect of "PC" I fully support is where it's no longer acceptable to be casually bigoted in polite society. Yet the fifty aggregated think pieces that appear every time a celebrity says something that could be interpreted as problematic (a quote that will reliably, with context, appear less so if at all) haven't actually moved things forward. All that they've done is turn the person-accused-of-bigotry into a sympathetic figure. What remains is a glazed-over reading public, prepared to believe, one minute, that Meryl Streep is a super-duper racist who thinks everyone's African and so diversity doesn't matter, only to await the next round of information letting us know that, oh, wait a moment, she didn't actually say that, so maybe she's not pile-on worthy after all.[36] (How any actual Africans benefited from the "Africans" controversy, and the conversation it launched, is unclear.) I don't blame the writers, though, and unfortunately don't know how to break the cycle of pop-culture journalism's celebrity-outrage coverage. But let's start writing and assigning something else, even if (and here's where this suggestion is probably hopeless) that means a slower pace of new content.

■ A complete and utter (and here I will, for once, get word police-y) halt on use of "violence" to describe things that are not, in fact, violence. Shootings, sexual assaults: violence. Cultural appropriation? Tweets of questionable tone? Not violence. This rhetoric, and its cousins ("rape culture" for discussions of billboards of women in lingerie, "white supremacy" for casual racism in the you-all-look-alike vein), is not only jargony and confusing, but also sets things up so that detractors will have an easier time dismissing relatively minor concerns as irrelevant.

- Rethink the concept of the "ally." Scrap it, or better yet, restrict it to the people who are full-time dedicating themselves to a cause that doesn't line up with their identity. (Unless it's Rachel Dolezal. If you're posing as a member of the group you're trying to help, you're in your own special category.) What we can do without is the category of a "woke" layperson. The *default* should be human decency. Not some sort of hyperawareness where everyone is magically in on what might offend everyone else. Just don't be overtly racist, sexist, or otherwise discriminatory. It's that simple.

- Keep social justice as a means to an end, not the end in itself. While the "I don't see color"-type approach clearly fails, so, too, has the hyperawareness reaction. The goal needs to be recognizing the humanity of all, which means remembering that life isn't just about structural oppression and the feelings it inspires. Too much awareness from haves winds up becoming exhausting for have-nots, who would like their hurt to be acknowledged, but who would also like to be seen as just *people,* people who experience joy and heartbreak and annoyance that the café Wi-Fi is down. Relatedly, let the privilege lens be a lens for reading books or watching TV shows, not the only one. Don't expect entertainment by-and-about women, gay people, people of color, etc., to be overtly political.

- Understand that the haves want to remain in power, and that their enlightenment is not, in fact, the road to justice. Yes, one microaggression is avoided when a prep-school senior remembers not to mention his family's estate in Saint-Tropez. Yet his choice to cultivate sensitivity doesn't in any way change the social structure that allows his family to have a second (or tenth) home while his interlocutor can barely make rent on a first. Ostentatious self-awareness has become a way of signaling status in its own right. I don't mean that insensitivity is the real social justice (ahem, Trump), but it needs to be understood, *generally* understood, that gaffe elimination can only accomplish so much, and in no way implies any further steps in any particular direction. Attempts to encourage a more just society shouldn't depend on those with power becoming flawlessly sensitive to the concerns of those without.

Impeccable, unimpeachable self-awareness is *not* part of the human condition. Everyone's oblivious to life beyond his or her own experiences, and that's *normal*. This obliviousness needs to be the assumption and the starting point. We should be suspicious of the people who claim to have transcended such limitations, not condemnatory of those who've failed to do so. Awareness isn't a necessary first step, but a futile, and often dangerous, diversion.

AFTERWORD

IN MAY 2016, I turned in a revised manuscript for *The Perils of "Privilege."* It's a mere two months later, as I finish going through copyedits. Not a long time, under normal circumstances, but the past couple months have been anything but. As I write this Afterword, Donald Trump has recently accepted the Republican nomination for the US presidency; when this book appears, there may be a President Trump. Even if (as I hope) Hillary Clinton is elected, the success of her opponent's hate-filled message revealed that much of the electorate endorses that hate, or at least finds it tolerable. Nativist ideas long limited to the extreme right have suddenly become mainstream in America and beyond. The June 2016 "Brexit"—the United Kingdom's startling vote to leave the European Union—marked the abrupt beginning of a new era.

There's a sense in which Trumpism can be interpreted as a reaction to the "privilege" framework. Absent any further context, one might guess that the constant drumbeat against "political correctness" at the 2016 Republican National Convention was merely white working-class frustration. Frustration, that is, at an elite culture in which "white" has, all too often, become a euphemism for "privileged."

Alas, I think that would be *way* too generous an interpretation. In the 2016 presidential campaign, "white working class" has emerged as a dog whistle. It now refers not just to the plights of those who actually meet that description (such as: layoffs, income inequality, and cultural elitism—all of which also impact the *non-white* working class, as well as working-class women, who don't seem to register in this narrative), but also to racist, sexist resentment experienced by many white American men across the socioeconomic spectrum.

What if Trump's appeal isn't (just) that he gives the impression of caring about overlooked communities in Appalachia, but that he confers victimhood status to great swaths of the population that aren't actually *victims* of anything?

Trumpism isn't about weaving poor and working-class white men back into discussions of socioeconomic inequality. It's about declaring whiteness and maleness *forms of marginalization*. The problem with the "privilege" approach, remember, isn't that it offers an incorrect assessment of who falls where. The approach's messiness surfaces when its use is imagined to extend *beyond* description. The way to counter "privilege" isn't to maintain the framework, while using it to offer up a plainly inaccurate description of the social structure. Yet that's precisely what Trump fans have done.

Frustratingly, the relativism inherent to the "privilege" approach makes the left wary of speaking out against Trumpist bigotry. To denounce sexism and white supremacy—not inadvertent microaggressions on Tumblr, but overt declarations from a major party's presidential nominee—now comes across as snobbish and condescending. It's no longer socially acceptable to criticize racism or sexism without affixing a point-weakening disclaimer about the legitimate cultural and economic resentments of Trump's white male supporters. Trumpism subverts "political correctness," such that it's now politically incorrect to reject Donald Trump. It's thus more urgent than ever for those concerned about systemic injustice to find alternatives to the "privilege" approach. Addressing unconscious bigotry—never the most effective strategy—is altogether hopeless against the *conscious* variety. And it's the conscious one we're now up against.

—Toronto
July 29, 2016

ACKNOWLEDGMENTS

THIS BOOK WOULD not have happened without the following two brilliant people: William Callahan, my agent at Inkwell
Management, who realized before I did that there was a book in me;
and George Witte, my editor at St. Martin's Press, who had a clear
vision how that book could actually happen, and whose feedback
improved the manuscript—as well as my writing—immeasurably. I
would also like to thank Sara Thwaite of St. Martin's for helping
guide me through the process; Heather G. Florence for her counsel;
and St. Martin's as a whole for taking on this project.

I'd like to thank everyone who agreed to speak with me about
the concept of privilege, especially Jena Barchas-Lichtenstein, Jessica
Leigh Blau, Isaac Butler, Eric Glatt, and Sara Naomi Lewkowicz. I'm
also grateful to those who provided leads and encouragement in that
area, in particular Brenda Fine, Kathryn Kleppinger, Laura Oppenheimer, and Jeremy Barnett Reff.

Several editors at *The Atlantic* and *The New Republic* helped me
with pieces that led, in one way or another, to this book. I'd particularly like to mention Eleanor Barkhorn, David A. Graham, and Ryan
Kearney. Delightful conversations on *Bloggingheads.tv* with Aryeh
Cohen-Wade, Conor Friedersdorf, and Autumn Whitefield-Madrano
also influenced my thinking on privilege and more. So, too, did
many back-and-forths over the years with commenters at my blog,
What Would Phoebe Do.

Conversations with friends and colleagues—about the idea of
privilege and about writing generally—also played a huge role in

making this book happen. I'd like to mention Valérie Desmarais, Clémentine Gallot, Paul Gowder, Jason Guriel, Rachel Hills, Rita Koganzon, Jacob T. Levy, Mark Oppenheimer, Anya Paretskaya, Amy Braverman Puma, and Tracy Walsh. I would also like to thank my parents for their love and encouragement.

Thank you, Jo, for bringing calm (and pasta) on those nights when I—in a display of petulance and, no doubt, copious unchecked privilege—wondered how, exactly, I was going to teach full time and write a book. Thank you for that and so much more.

And I must acknowledge Bisou, a fluffy, strong-willed miniature poodle, who knows more about privilege than any human ever will.

NOTES

EPIGRAPH

1. www.youtube.com/watch?v=Xe1a1wHxTyo
2. www.thestranger.com/blogs/slog/2011/01/25/6472065/cisgender-able
   -bodied-thin-privileged-class-privileged-white-male-body/comments/59

INTRODUCTION: THE "PRIVILEGE" TURN

1. www.newstatesman.com/politics/2015/05/we-have-distinguish
   -between-outrage-and-justified-rage-marginalised
2. My theories as to why Dunham, why 2012, are found in chapter 3.
3. www.bustle.com/articles/157129-what-lena-dunham-and-everybody
   -else-gets-totally-wrong-about-donald-trump
4. theprincetontory.com/main/checking-my-privilege-character-as-the
   -basis-of-privilege/; I first wrote about the piece, but not the Jewish

angle, here: www.theatlantic.com/politics/archive/2014/05/check-your
-check-your-privilege/361898/

5. time.com/85933/why-ill-never-apologize-for-my-white-male
   -privilege/

6. www.nytimes.com/2014/05/03/nyregion/at-princeton-privilege
   -is-a-commonplace-b-misunderstood-or-c-frowned-upon.html; www
   .washingtonpost.com/blogs/compost/wp/2014/05/08/never-check-a
   -privilege-princeton-writer-tal-fortgang-are-you-mad/; www.theguardian
   .com/commentisfree/2014/may/07/princeton-white-privilege-tal
   -fortgang-idiot

7. www.theatlantic.com/politics/archive/2014/05/check-your-check
   -your-privilege/361898/

8. More on the Fortgang episode and its significance is in chapter 5.

9. www.thecollegefix.com/post/23072/

10. mic.com/articles/14277/bill-clinton-dnc-speech-the-35-most
    -memorable-quotes#.cRdarlHR7

11. www.newyorker.com/news/hendrik-hertzberg/we-built-it

12. www.washingtonpost.com/wp-dyn/content/article/2010/10/22
    /AR2010102202873.html

13. www.pbs.org/newshour/rundown/white-educated-and-wealthy
    -congratulations-you-live-in-a-bubble/

14. www.pbs.org/newshour/making-sense/do-you-live-in-a-bubble-a
    -quiz-2/

15. www.nytimes.com/2012/07/13/opinion/brooks-why-our-elites-stink
    .html

16. twitter.com/irin/status/615914262318288896

17. twitter.com/kvxll/status/628633990472331264

18. opinionator.blogs.nytimes.com/2014/11/05/what-white-privilege
    -really-means/

19. news.harvard.edu/gazette/story/2012/12/using-privilege-helpfully/

20. Michael S. Kimmel and Abby L. Ferber, eds., *Privilege: A Reader* (Boulder, CO: Westview Press, 2003), 147–60.

21. Ibid., 148.

22. Ibid., 150–53.

23. Ibid., 148.

24. www.newyorker.com/books/page-turner/the-origins-of-privilege

25. Kimmel and Ferber, *Privilege*, 9.
26. Ibid., 149.
27. lithub.com/men-explain-lolita-to-me/
28. www.nytimes.com/2015/07/19/magazine/how-privilege-became-a
    -provocation.html
29. twitter.com/jbouie/status/578221648840646657
30. jamellebouie.net/post/56331188547/what-does-it-mean-to-be
    -privileged
31. twitter.com/jbouie/status/578221648840646657
32. www.theguardian.com/commentisfree/2013/may/31/louise-mensch
    -privilege-internet
33. blog.shrub.com/check-my-what/; www.theguardian.com/society/2013
    /jun/05/check-your-privilege-means
34. portland.indymedia.org/en/2002/08/18010.shtml
35. www.amazon.com/The-Sharks-Jens-Bjorneboe/dp/1870041208
36. whatwouldphoebedo.blogspot.com/2004/11/university-of-chicagoan
    -empire.html
37. www.nytimes.com/2015/12/30/business/economy/for-the-wealthiest
    -private-tax-system-saves-them-billions.html
38. jezebel.com/a-lot-of-white-millennials-get-significant-financial
    -1745456844
39. www.newyorker.com/books/page-turner/the-origins-of-privilege
40. www.nytimes.com/2015/07/19/magazine/how-privilege-became-a
    -provocation.html
41. www.salon.com/2014/05/05/we_dont_need_your_apology
    _princeton_kid/
42. www.nytimes.com/2015/02/15/magazine/how-one-stupid-tweet
    -ruined-justine-saccos-life.html
43. jezebel.com/an-open-letter-to-affirmative-action-reject-abigail-fis
    -570774253
44. whatwouldphoebedo.blogspot.com/2013/06/a-fisher-in-barrel.html
45. www.buzzfeed.com/dayshavedewi/what-is-privilege#.uiWP2rjXE
46. www.buzzfeed.com/nathanwpyle/this-teacher-taught-his-class-a
    -powerful-lesson-about-privil#.xkxKom6jB
47. boingboing.net/2015/05/22/on-a-plate.html; thewireless.co.nz/articles
    /the-pencilsword-on-a-plate

48. whatever.scalzi.com/2012/05/15/straight-white-male-the-lowest-difficulty-setting-there-is/

49. twitter.com/LOLGOP/status/615517648655417344

50. xkcd.com/386/

51. jezebel.com/documentary-on-white-privledge-isn-t-that-just-the-h-1716572668

52. twitter.com/jbouie/status/578221648840646657

53. www.nytco.com/alessandra-stanley-moves-to-new-beat-covering-inequality-in-america/

54. publiceditor.blogs.nytimes.com/2015/06/25/is-greater-focus-on-the-superrich-right-for-the-times/

55. publiceditor.blogs.nytimes.com/2014/09/22/an-article-on-shonda-rhimes-rightly-causes-a-furor

56. www.nytimes.com/2015/05/17/opinion/sunday/poor-little-rich-women.html

57. www.nytimes.com/2015/06/08/business/media/publisher-to-put-asterisk-on-primates-of-park-avenue.html

58. www.nytimes.com/2015/06/08/arts/television/review-in-odd-mom-out-competition-among-manhattans-wealthy.html

59. www.theawl.com/2014/11/the-history-of-the-new-york-times-styles-section

60. www.nytimes.com/2007/12/09/realestate/09cov.html?pagewanted=all; whatwouldphoebedo.blogspot.com/2007/12/definitive-first-world-problem.html

61. sites.middlebury.edu/tedx/tedxmiddlebury-2010/tedxmiddlebury-2011-embracing-risk/speakers/peggy-mcintosh/

I. THE ONLINE YPIS WARS

1. www.washingtonpost.com/posteverything/wp/2015/07/09/i-tried-to-escape-my-privilege-with-low-wage-work-instead-i-came-face-to-face-with-it/

2. *Gawker* had about the same take as that commenter: gawker.com/guy-challenges-his-privilege-by-working-in-a-falafel-sh-1717050466.

3. time.com/97369/louie-so-did-fat-lady/

4. www.xojane.com/issues/white-privilege-ferguson; www.bustle.com/articles/97064-why-white-people-dont-like-admitting-that-white

-privilege-exists-according-to-science; entitledmag.com/dehumanisation
/coming-terms-privilege/; www.huffingtonpost.ca/posterella/my-privilege
-is-a-problem_b_6142064.html

5. thoughtcatalog.com/maghen-nicole/2014/09/confronting-my
-privilege/

6. thoughtcatalog.com/jodi-sagorin/2014/08/with-great-privilege
-comes-great-responsibility/

7. thoughtcatalog.com/chelsea-fagan/2014/09/the-uncomfortable
-privilege-of-being-catcalled/

8. As Hamilton Nolan put it, in 2013, in his introduction to *Gawker's*
satirical "Privilege Tournament" (gawker.com/the-privilege-tourna
ment-1377171054): "These days, teary privilege confessionals pour
forth from the lips of college students in equal proportion to the fiery
critiques of our grossly unjust world that pour forth from the unprivi-
leged masses."

9. thoughtcatalog.com/kate-menendez/2013/09/being-privileged-is-not
-a-choice-so-stop-hating-me-for-it/

10. gawker.com/brave-privileged-person-speaks-out-against-anti-privile
-1372207675

11. jezebel.com/5745172/in-defense-of-the-gay-white-male; www.advocate
.com/politics/commentary/2011/01/20/im-white-cisgender-gay-man

12. www.xojane.com/it-happened-to-me/it-happened-to-me-there-are-no
-black-people-in-my-yoga-classes-and-im-uncomfortable-with-it

13. In the piece itself, that is; the "privilege" subtext was apparent to readers
more tuned into the vocabulary: www.xojane.com/issues/i-assigned
-that-yoga-class-piece-and-heres-why.

14. superselected.com/it-happened-to-me-the-5-best-responses-to-that
-silly-yoga-essay/

15. www.theatlantic.com/technology/archive/2011/11/whats-wrong
-with-firstworldproblems/248829/

16. www.nytimes.com/2015/12/06/magazine/white-debt.html

17. www.thedailybeast.com/articles/2015/07/27/antiracism-our-flawed
-new-religion.html

18. www.washingtonpost.com/posteverything/wp/2016/01/28/when
-white-people-admit-white-privilege-theyre-really-just-congratulating
-themselves/

19. www.nytimes.com/2015/12/06/magazine/white-debt.html#permid
    =16832799
20. www.nytimes.com/2015/12/06/magazine/white-debt.html?hp
    &action=click&pgtype=Homepage&clickSource=story-heading
    &module=mini-moth&region=top-stories-below&WT.nav=top
    -stories-below&_r=0#permid=16826821
21. www.theguardian.com/commentisfree/2014/dec/05/criming-while
    -white-people-privilege
22. www.slate.com/blogs/outward/2014/12/26/do_butch_lesbians
    _have_cisgender_privilege.html
23. www.huffingtonpost.com/gina-crosleycorcoran/explaining-white
    -privilege-to-a-broke-white-person_b_5269255.html
24. dailycaller.com/2015/03/01/rubio-i-come-from-extraordinary
    -privilege/
25. planettransgender.com/does-a-butch-woman-have-cis-privilege
    -absolutely/
26. blog.shrub.com/check-my-what/; www.scn.org/friends/ally.html.
27. www.buzzfeed.com/regajha/how-privileged-are-you#.yw5dloQ47
28. www.spectator.co.uk/columnists/hugo-rifkind/8925681/check-my
    -privilege-i-have-thanks-youre-still-wrong/
29. www.spectator.co.uk/columnists/hugo-rifkind/8925681/check-my
    -privilege-i-have-thanks-youre-still-wrong/#comment-920916068
30. www.chow.com/food-news/8443/walmart-presents-feasting-on-the
    -cheap/
31. bitchmagazine.org/post/why-i-was-never-a-riot-grrl#comment
    -69100
32. bookriot.com/2013/05/13/a-librarians-response-to-whats-a-library/
33. itheedread.jezebel.com/job-applicant-insecure-confused-brides-are
    -like-victi-1686998865
34. www.theguardian.com/society/quiz/2013/jun/05/check-your
    -privilege-quiz
35. jezebel.com/check-your-vertebrate-privilege-cephalopods-are-people
    -1417648693
36. www.clickhole.com/article/cartoon-does-bad-job-explaining-what
    -privilege-2683
37. gawker.com/the-privilege-tournament-1377171054

38. gawker.com/we-have-found-the-least-privileged-group-in-america-1440678724

39. magazine.good.is/articles/hustlin-we-re-the-privileged-poor-why-aren-t-we-talking-about-it

40. userpages.umbc.edu/~korenman/wmst/privilege1.html

41. socialistworker.org/2012/03/22/barrier-fighting-oppression

42. prospect.org/article/moving-past-acknowledging-privilege

43. www.blackgirldangerous.org/2014/02/4-ways-push-back-privilege/

44. www.newstatesman.com/politics/2012/12/problem-privilege-checking

45. www.jacobinmag.com/2016/02/socialism-liberalism-social-justice-activism-tumblr-fandom/

46. www.jacobinmag.com/2015/04/1-99-percent-class-inequality/

47. whatwouldphoebedo.blogspot.com/2012/02/can-you-name-this-nascar-champion.html

48. www.npr.org/2016/03/01/468185698/understanding-the-clintons-popularity-with-black-voters

49. medium.com/@karpmj/four-thoughts-about-new-york-s-democratic-primary-55624188bd24#.mgwg7dgpd

50. twitter.com/hillaryclinton/status/699710951562596355

51. twitter.com/BenjaminNorton/status/699747409824456704

52. medium.com/@tonybrasunas/please-recognize-your-privilege-if-you-can-afford-eight-years-of-hillary-clinton-and-the-status-quo-fc1b9dc62bcd#.60plkrpiq

53. twitter.com/ckilpatrick/status/658678836540887040

54. twitter.com/ckilpatrick/status/727940662381969408

55. twitter.com/freddiedeboer/status/659926099418218496

56. twitter.com/HillaryClinton/status/715217490368827396

57. qz.com/644985/privilege-is-what-allows-sanders-supporters-to-say-theyll-never-vote-for-clinton/

58. www.theguardian.com/commentisfree/2016/mar/07/democratic-vote-hillary-clinton-election-2016-bernie-sanders

59. www.theatlantic.com/politics/archive/2016/03/susan-sarandon-bernie-sanders/475875/

60. www.dailykos.com/story/2016/3/28/1507426/-Susan-Sarandon-A-Privileged-Fool

61. www.thestranger.com/slog/2016/03/31/23890388/bernie-or-hillary
    -or-both
62. www.nytimes.com/2016/03/31/opinion/campaign-stops/bernie-or
    -bust-is-bonkers.html
63. www.slate.com/blogs/xx_factor/2016/03/29/susan_sarandon_is
    _perfect_spokeswoman_for_neverhillary.html
64. twitter.com/tweetertation/status/710223652525047809
65. twitter.com/chrislhayes/status/715947922127515648
66. fivethirtyeight.com/features/the-mythology-of-trumps-working-class
    -support/
67. www.jacobinmag.com/2016/02/bernie-sanders-democratic
    -presidential-primary-young-people-millenials/
68. www.newyorker.com/culture/cultural-comment/should-millennials
    -get-over-bernie-sanders
69. www.forbes.com/sites/avidan/2014/08/25/what-do-you-call-a-17
    -year-old-ad-campaign-priceless/#32670a89466a
70. www.tabletmag.com/jewish-news-and-politics/188090/straight-outta
    -chappaqua
71. twitter.com/JillFilipovic/status/727514849912061953; twitter.com
    /JillFilipovic/status/727514309190778880; twitter.com/JillFilipovic
    /status/727513726828433408)
72. www.theguardian.com/society/2013/jun/05/check-your-privilege
    -means
73. www.newstatesman.com/politics/2012/12/problem-privilege
    -checking
74. www.slate.com/articles/life/culturebox/2014/12/the_year_of_outrage
    _2014_everything_you_were_angry_about_on_social_media.html
75. www.xojane.com/issues/i-dont-feel-bad-for-not-tipping-you
76. twitter.com/BFriedmanDC/status/725158208579461121
77. twitter.com/soledadobrien/status/725163948572467200
78. twitter.com/AjaMuch/status/725168075650256896
79. twitter.com/BFriedmanDC/status/725168655676395521
80. tigerbeatdown.com/2011/10/17/come-one-come-all-bloggers-bear-it
    -all-out-feminist-and-social-justice-blogging-as-performance-and
    -bloodshed/#comment-44652
81. whatwouldphoebedo.blogspot.com/2008/10/for-need-based

-economy.html; whatwouldphoebedo.blogspot.com/2008/10/pity
-unpaid-intern.html

82. whatwouldphoebedo.blogspot.com/2010/10/scrappiness-one-upman
ship.html

83. whatwouldphoebedo.blogspot.com/2011/02/sanctibullying.html;
whatwouldphoebedo.blogspot.com/2011/02/alternative-to-sancti
bullying.html

84. offbeatempire.com/2012/10/liberal-bullying; www.theguardian.com
/commentisfree/2012/oct/18/online-bullying-ugly-sport-liberal
-commenters

85. offbeatbride.com/2015/07/tattooed-brides-california-wedding

86. tigerbeatdown.com/2011/10/17/come-one-come-all-bloggers-bear-it
-all-out-feminist-and-social-justice-blogging-as-performance-and
-bloodshed/

87. briarpatchmagazine.com/articles/view/a-note-on-call-out-culture

88. melissafong.wordpress.com/2014/02/08/check-your-privilege-meme
-and-why-it-is-ineffective/

89. www.theatlantic.com/daily-dish/archive/2011/02/gender-confe
rences-mean-always-having-to-say-youre-sorry/176353/

90. See the following exchange: www.feministe.us/blog/archives/2014/02
/27/checking-privilege-take-452-this-time-its-illustrated/#comment
-811940; and here, see the remarks about "jargon" and "ability": pyro-
maniacharlot.wordpress.com/2012/04/03/the-unicorn-ally/.

91. See Sharon Smith: socialistworker.org/2015/04/13/why-checking-your
-privilege-isnt-enough; socialistworker.org/2014/11/18/the-politics-of
-privilege-checking.

92. www.slate.com/blogs/outward/2014/12/26/do_butch_lesbians
_have_cisgender_privilege.html

93. westandwiththe99percent.tumblr.com/

94. twitter.com/jbouie/status/572489849460146177

95. www.nytimes.com/2008/03/18/us/politics/18text-obama.html
?pagewanted=all&_r=0

96. twitter.com/jbouie/status/578221648840646657; leftfootforward.org
/2013/01/comment-on-feminism-and-the-suzanne-moore-contro
versy/

97. nymag.com/thecut/2014/07/new-privilege-loudly-denouncing

-privilege.html. A similar point was made the previous day, in a post on an academic blog (doctorcleveland.blogspot.com/2014/07/snobs-vs-ivy-league-or-question-of-bill.html): "There is nothing a snobbish Ivy Leaguer likes better than putting down the Ivy League. It's an easy way to signal that you are above your own Ivy League school and the privilege it confers—all a big humbug that your superior perspective sees right through—while holding on to every last scrap of that privilege. It allows you to position yourself as not only 1. better than people who didn't get into Harvard, Princeton, or Yale, but 2. the benevolent champion of those little people who didn't get in and also 3. better than everyone else who *did* get into your school and who, unlike you, need to take the place seriously."

98. See Laura Kipnis on "studies" disciplines: laurakipnis.com/wp-content/uploads/2010/08/Shame-review-Harpers.pdf.

99. nymag.com/daily/intelligencer/2015/01/not-a-very-pc-thing-to-say.html

100. www.slate.com/articles/life/culturebox/2014/12/the_year_of_outrage_2014_everything_you_were_angry_about_on_social_media.html

101. chronicle.com/article/Sexual-Paranoia-Strikes/190351/; chronicle.com/article/My-Title-IX-Inquisition/230489/

102. www.newscientist.com/article/dn27699-what-nobel-winner-tim-hunts-sexist-outburst-actually-tells-us/#.VX-MEBNViko; www.theguardian.com/uk-news/2015/jun/23/stop-defending-tim-hunt-brian-cox-richard-dawkins

103. See Kevin Drum's article on the Tim Hunt episode: www.motherjones.com/kevin-drum/2015/06/are-we-really-control-our-own-outrage-case-social-media-and-tim-hunt.

104. www.theatlantic.com/magazine/archive/2015/07/there-will-be-no-debate/395252/

105. www.dailykos.com/story/2014/05/21/1300741/-Why-we-should-stop-using-the-term-white-privilege#

106. nymag.com/daily/intelligencer/2015/02/political-correctness-good-for-the-left.html

107. nymag.com/daily/intelligencer/2015/01/secret-confessions-of-the-anti-anti-pc-crowd.html

108. www.theguardian.com/commentisfree/2013/may/30/reality-based -feminism-louise-mensch; www.iop.harvard.edu/%E2%80%9Cpriv ilism%E2%80%9D-when-privilege-becomes-insult

109. www.dailymail.co.uk/news/article-2047664/Occupy-Wall-Street -Children-1-good-time-protests.html

110. hexaneandheels.tumblr.com/post/69147969788/average-intelligence -privilege

111. www.eastportlandblog.com/2011/04/05/monogamous-privilege -checklist-by-cory-davis/

112. observer.com/2015/06/hysterical-activism/

2. LONELY AT AMHERST

1. www.yale.edu/life-yale 2/15/16

2. www.theatlantic.com/magazine/archive/2015/09/the-coddling-of -the-american-mind/399356/

3. nymag.com/thecut/2014/09/emma-sulkowicz-campus-sexual -assault-activism.html

4. www.nytimes.com/2015/11/23/nyregion/at-princeton-addressing-a -racist-legacy-and-seeking-to-remove-woodrow-wilsons-name.html

5. www.cnn.com/2015/11/09/us/missouri-protest-timeline/

6. www.theatlantic.com/notes/all/2015/08/debating-the-new-campus -pc/402113/; www.theatlantic.com/magazine/archive/2015/09/greg -lukianoffs-story/399359/;www.theatlantic.com/politics/archive /2015/12/campus-protests/419505/; and more.

7. www.theatlantic.com/education/archive/2016/01/campus-protest -roundup/417570/

8. www.nytimes.com/2015/11/22/opinion/sunday/debates-on-campus .html

9. whatwouldphoebedo.blogspot.ca/2008/11/thats-nice-or-thats -patronizing.html; whatwouldphoebedo.blogspot.ca/2008/04/more -from-pallor-studies-department.html

10. www.newyorker.com/culture/cultural-comment/the-year-of-the -imaginary-college-student

11. medium.com/@aaronzlewis/what-s-really-going-on-at-yale -6bdbbeeb57a6

12. www.newyorker.com/culture/cultural-comment/yales-unsafe-spaces

13. www.newyorker.com/news/news-desk/a-new-family-feeling-on
-campus
14. www.theatlantic.com/education/archive/2013/12/the-false-promise
-of-holistic-college-admissions/282432/
15. www.nytimes.com/video/us/100000002769674/frustrating-black
-hair-remark-at-harvard.html
16. www.nytimes.com/2015/09/13/magazine/why-we-should-fear
-university-inc.html
17. www.nytimes.com/2015/10/06/opinion/david-brooks-the-big
-university.html
18. www.theatlantic.com/politics/archive/2015/11/brown-universitys
-100-million-plan-to-be-more-inclusive/416886/; www.the-american
-interest.com/2015/11/25/ivy-league-presidents-try-appeasement/
19. www.brown.edu/about/administration/institutional-diversity/sites
/brown.edu.about.administration.institutional-diversity/files/up
loads/Plan%20for%20Diversity%20and%20Inclusion%20with%20
Letter%2011.19.15.pdf
20. www.forbes.com/sites/karinagness/2015/12/30/ten-most-ridiculous
-college-protests-of-2015/
21. whatwouldphoebedo.blogspot.ca/2008/03/how-to-write
-conservative-article-about.html
22. www.weeklystandard.com/article/lower-education/554092
23. www.thedailybeast.com/articles/2011/03/03/the-story-behind
-northwestern-universitys-live-sex-class.html
24. www.theawl.com/2011/03/that-northwestern-human-sexuality-class
-was-the-best-course-i-ever-took
25. whatwouldphoebedo.blogspot.ca/2011/03/already-dreading-search
-engine-traffic.html
26. chronicle.com/article/Sexual-Paranoia/190351/; www.nationalreview
.com/article/419163/laura-kipniss-incredible-ordeal-and-beginning
-end-pc-david-french; www.nationalreview.com/article/429960/political
-correctness-college-campuses-princeton-woodrow-wilson
27. www.nationalreview.com/corner/427740/campus-virus-jay-nordlinger
28. www.thenation.com/article/laura-kipnis-melodrama/
29. newrepublic.com/article/121353/college-safe-spaces-hypersensitivity
-are-not-all-students-fault

30. On broader disparities between hook-up myths and facts, see Rachel Hills's *The Sex Myth: The Gap Between Our Fantasies and Reality* (New York: Simon & Schuster, 2015).

31. ncac.org/resource/ncac-report-whats-all-this-about-trigger-warnings

32. www.pewresearch.org/fact-tank/2015/11/20/40-of-millennials-ok-with-limiting-speech-offensive-to-minorities/

33. chronicle.com/article/Today-s-Freshman-Class-Is/235273

34. observer.com/2015/09/wesleyan-students-petition-against-free-speech/

35. jezebel.com/wesleyan-student-government-retaliates-for-dumb-op-ed-b-1737277336

36. www.economist.com/news/united-states/21689603-statement-heart-debate-over-academic-freedom-hard-say

37. www.amherst.edu/amherst-story/president/statements/node/620480

38. A sampling of "privilege walk" activities hosted or promoted by US colleges and universities: ginsberg.umich.edu/content/privilege-walk-activity; www.life.arizona.edu/docs/social-justice/privilege-walk-race.pdf?sfvrsn=2; faculty.wagner.edu/seeing-white/privilege-walk/; www.suffolk.edu/magazine/235.php#.Vf8noZ1Viko; newsroom.ucla.edu/stories/students-reach-mutual-understanding-201561; www.indiana.edu/~vpue/walk/walk.html; www.albany.edu/ssw/efc/pdf/Module%205_1_Privilege%20Walk%20Activity.pdf.

39. www.thedailybeast.com/articles/2015/03/15/the-privilege-of-checking-white-privilege.html

40. www.imdb.com/title/tt4197092/

41. www.nytimes.com/2016/01/17/magazine/the-trials-of-alice-goffman.html

42. chronicle.com/article/Time-for-a-Teaching-Intensive/230605/; and the comment he's referring to: chronicle.com/article/Time-for-a-Teaching-Intensive/230605/#comment-2058717483

43. www.facebook.com/michael.berube.169/posts/713427995450398?pnref=story

44. www.princeton.edu/~joha/Johannes_Haushofer_CV_of_Failures.pdf

45. www.theguardian.com/commentisfree/2016/may/01/only-successful-people-can-afford-cv-of-failure

46. www.thedailybeast.com/articles/2016/01/24/the-wild-world-of
-oppression-studies.html; nces.ed.gov/fastfacts/display.asp?id=61

47. tressiemc.com/2016/01/06/when-your-curriculum-has-been-tumbl
rized/

48. college.usatoday.com/2015/05/13/viewpoint-colleges-must-force
-students-to-check-their-privilege/

49. www.latimes.com/opinion/op-ed/la-oe-daum-mattress-girl-meets
-boko-haram-survivors-20150526-column.html

50. www.theatlantic.com/politics/archive/2015/11/the-new-intolerance
-of-student-activism-at-yale/414810/; www.weeklystandard.com/how
-babies-are-made/article/1061807

51. bloggingheads.tv/videos/29603

52. www.theatlantic.com/education/archive/2014/05/how-to-improve
-privilege-training-at-harvard/370927/

53. www.nytimes.com/2015/11/29/us/with-diversity-comes-intensity-in
-amherst-free-speech-debate.html

54. "The campus protests remind us that any system that requires exceptional fortitude from certain categories of people is an unjust
one. The jargon that tried to name this injustice and serve as a tool
in the struggle against it—white privilege, microaggression, safe
space, etc.—caught on so fast because it named something that people
recognized right away from their own lives. Like any new language
that seeks to politicize everyday life, the terms were awkward,
heavy-handed, and formulaic, but they gave confidence to people de-
siring redress for the subtle incursions on their dignity that they
suspected were holding them back." harpers.org/archive/2016/03
/we-out-here/2/.

55. newrepublic.com/article/123912/whos-afraid-of-yale-student
-privilege

56. www.nytimes.com/2015/12/06/magazine/the-profound-emptiness
-of-resilience.html

57. medium.com/@aaronzlewis/what-s-really-going-on-at-yale-6bdbbeeb
57a6#.105qhkrz7

58. newrepublic.com/article/121540/privilege-checking-debate-often-over
looks-income-inequality

59. thenewinquiry.com/blogs/zunguzungu/against-students-stories/

60. www.newyorker.com/culture/cultural-comment/the-year-of-the
-imaginary-college-student

61. www.theatlantic.com/education/archive/2013/12/when-teachers-talk
-about-their-students-on-facebook/282241/

62. I'm thinking both of the Laura Kipnis episode, and of the controversy
over the "Dear Student" series in *Vitae* (chroniclevitae.com/news/964
-dear-student-my-name-is-not-hey; www.jessestommel.com/blog/files
/dear-chronicle.html).

63. www.washingtonpost.com/news/grade-point/wp/2015/11/30/college
-president-rejects-safe-spaces-writing-this-is-not-a-day-care-this-is-a
-university

64. gawker.com/this-personal-essay-will-get-you-into-columbia-4782
17730; www.ivygateblog.com/2013/04/columbia-class-of-2017-post-their
-application-essays-say-the-darndest-things/

65. gawker.com/i-kind-of-want-to-chastise-you-for-having-a-laugh-at-th
-478484528

66. Think Tal Fortgang (www.thecollegefix.com/post/23072/) or Suzy
Lee Weiss (www.nationalreview.com/phi-beta-cons/420733/student
-describes-sexual-war-zone-campus-nathan-harden; www.post-gazette
.com/opinion/Op-Ed/2015/03/08/I-was-recruited-by-the-thought
-police/stories/201503080008).

67. Conor Friedersdorf, at least, seems to get that criticism of student sensitivities shouldn't be rounded up to denunciation of students themselves: "The purpose of writing about [Yale students'] missteps now is
not to condemn these students. Their young lives are tremendously
impressive by any reasonable measure. They are unfortunate to live in
an era in which the normal mistakes of youth are unusually visible. To
keep the focus where it belongs I won't be naming any of them here."
www.theatlantic.com/politics/archive/2015/11/the-new-intolerance
-of-student-activism-at-yale/414810/.

68. www.washingtonpost.com/blogs/compost/wp/2015/11/06/ben
-carson-west-point-and-the-frantic-quest-for-adversity/

69. www.theatlantic.com/education/archive/2016/02/whats-wrong-with
-college-admissions/462063/

70. www.theatlantic.com/education/archive/2013/12/the-false-promise
-of-holistic-college-admissions/282432/

71. thechoice.blogs.nytimes.com/2010/09/07/essay-as-memoir/
72. www.nytimes.com/2014/06/15/opinion/sunday/frank-bruni-over
sharing-in-admissions-essays.html
73. www.nacacnet.org/events/2012/session-archives/Documents
/2011%20Documents/SpecialCircumstance.pdf
74. myusf.usfca.edu/student-life/intercultural-center/check-your
-privilege
75. www.nytco.com/social-responsibility/college-scholarship-program/
76. www.nytimes.com/2016/04/14/nyregion/beating-tragedy-and-odds
-10-earn-new-york-times-college-scholarships.html
77. www.lacycrawford.com/checking-whose-privilege/
78. www.theprospect.net/top-3-college-admissions-essay-mistakes-i-love
-you-princeton-i-mean-um-yale-5242
79. magoosh.com/hs/college-admissions/2014/common-mistakes-that
-will-kill-your-college-essay/
80. collegeapps.about.com/od/essays/tp/supplemental-essay-mistakes
.htm
81. theneuroticparent.com/2015/04/why-your-brilliant-child-didnt-get
-into-the-ivies-2.html
82. www.huffingtonpost.com/gianna-sengupta/7-cliche-college-applicat
_b_5993986.html; funnyhamlet.wordpress.com/2010/08/16/the-crabby
-counselor-returns/
83. blog.campusexplorer.com/2012/08/30/3-ways-to-make-your-college
-essay-stand-out/; www.nytimes.com/2014/05/10/your-money/four
-stand-out-college-essays-about-money.html; thechoice.blogs.nytimes
.com/2010/10/11/essay/; www.wsj.com/articles/SB10001424127887
324108204579024823824933690
84. learning.blogs.nytimes.com/2010/10/14/going-beyond-cliche-how-to
-write-a-great-college-essay/
85. humanitariansoftinder.com/
86. www.newyorker.com/magazine/2014/10/20/college-application
-essay
87. www.essayhell.com/2013/08/dont-let-your-privilege-show.html
88. www.standard.co.uk/showbiz/starinterviews/it-costs-me-a-lot-of
-money-to-look-this-cheap-6696737.html
89. www.nytimes.com/2011/06/01/opinion/l01elite.html

90. qz.com/457284/white-people-please-stop-blaming-people-of-color -for-your-mediocre-grades/; jezebel.com/an-open-letter-to-affirmative -action-reject-abigail-fis-570774253
91. www.wsj.com/articles/SB100014241278873240007045783903400 64578654
92. www.theprospect.net/the-suzy-lee-weiss-mindset-how-not-to -approach-college-admissions-1146
93. www.huffingtonpost.com/yingying-shang/an-open-letter-to-suzy-lee -weiss_b_3041458.html
94. dailyprincetonian.com/opinion/2013/04/an-open-letter-to-suzy-lee -weiss/
95. features.thecrimson.com/2014/freshman-survey/admissions/
96. www.insidehighered.com/news/2012/06/01/wesleyan-shifts-away -need-blind-policy-citing-financial-and-ethical-concerns
97. www.coalitionforcollegeaccess.org/; accessed 2/18/16.
98. www.nytimes.com/2015/10/18/opinion/sunday/an-admissions -surprise-from-the-ivy-league.html
99. chronicle.com/article/Researchers-Goal-An/233625
100. www.nytimes.com/2016/02/07/opinion/sunday/real-compassion-in -college-admissions.html
101. www.nytimes.com/2014/03/09/magazine/the-story-behind-the-sat -overhaul.html
102. www.theatlantic.com/education/archive/2015/01/new-sat-new -problems/384596/
103. www.princetonreview.com/college/sat-changes
104. www.forbes.com/sites/nataliesportelli/2014/08/04/alternative -applications-rewrite-the-rules-of-college-admissions/
105. blogs.wsj.com/economics/2014/10/07/sat-scores-and-income -inequality-how-wealthier-kids-rank-higher/
106. www.washingtonpost.com/news/morning-mix/wp/2015/07/28/how -the-sat-came-to-rule-college-admissions/
107. qz.com/467338/george-washington-universitys-new-test-free-policy -isnt-as-diversity-friendly-as-it-seems/
108. www.the-american-interest.com/2015/09/06/the-end-of-the-sat/
109. dailycaller.com/2015/07/29/fancypants-rich-kids-school-that -waitlisted-poor-kids-for-being-poor-dumps-sat-act/

110. www.bloomberg.com/news/articles/2014-10-03/wesleyan-temple -among-colleges-scrapping-admission-tests
111. www.insidehighered.com/news/2012/06/01/wesleyan-shifts-away -need-blind-policy-citing-financial-and-ethical-concerns
112. www.forbes.com/sites/noodleeducation/2015/07/30/when-colleges -go-test-optional-who-benefits/
113. www.nytimes.com/interactive/2014/04/13/education/edlife/you -cant-always-get-what-you-want.html
114. news.brynmawr.edu/2014/07/21/bryn-mawr-adopts-test-optional -admissions-policy/
115. pitweb.pitzer.edu/admission/test-optional-policy/
116. www.bates.edu/admission/optional-testing/
117. www.washingtonpost.com/blogs/answer-sheet/wp/2015/07/27/a -list-of-180-ranked-schools-that-dont-require-act-or-sat-scores-for -admissions/
118. www.nytimes.com/2013/09/29/nyregion/didnt-ace-sat-just-design -microbe-transplant-research.html
119. www.theatlantic.com/education/archive/2013/09/no-grades-no-sat -scores-just-essays-bards-misguided-new-admissions-plan/280110/
120. www.bard.edu/financialaid/
121. www.bard.edu/financialaid/procedures/package/
122. www.nytimes.com/2013/09/29/nyregion/sample-topics-for-appli cants-research-papers.html
123. www.slate.com/articles/life/education/2014/06/the_bard_admis sions_exam_four_essays_no_common_application.2.html
124. www.imdb.com/title/tt0642903/
125. www.nytimes.com/2015/09/06/magazine/can-i-lie-to-my-father -about-being-gay-so-he-will-pay-for-my-college-education.html

3. THE "PROBLEMATIC FAVE"

1. www.clickhole.com/splitpic/if-george-clooney-ever-says-something -racist-use-s-4320
2. On the history of the phrase, see: www.buzzfeed.com/charliewarzel /meet-the-man-behind-twitters-most-infamous-phrase#.uaWlLr6zE.
3. www.newstatesman.com/culture/film/2015/09/your-fave-problema tic-why-are-we-so-bad-talking-about-diversity-pop-culture

4. www.theatlantic.com/entertainment/archive/2014/05/cultural
-appropriation-in-fashion-stop-talking-about-it/370826/; www.nytimes
.com/2015/10/15/fashion/should-fashion-be-politically-correct
.html

5. www.theawl.com/2014/11/serial-and-white-reporter-privilege

6. www.theguardian.com/film/2015/nov/23/trans-rights-activists
-lpetition-zoolander-2-boycott

7. maisonneuve.org/article/2015/06/10/jerry-rigged/

8. www.nytimes.com/2013/12/13/business/media/snl-to-add-black
-female-cast-member-in-january.html?_r=0

9. time.com/97369/louie-so-did-fat-lady/

10. www.upworthy.com/sometimes-it-takes-a-white-dude-to-get-real
-about-racism

11. fredrikdeboer.com/2015/09/07/whats-happening-and-why-and-why
-does-it-matter/

12. observer.com/2014/11/no-privilege-needed-in-defense-of-serial/

13. www.slate.com/articles/life/culturebox/2014/12/the_year_of
_outrage_2014_everything_you_were_angry_about_on_social
_media.html#part-4

14. www.washingtonpost.com/news/act-four/wp/2015/09/14/why-our
-conversations-about-art-and-politics-are-so-unproductive/

15. www.washingtonpost.com/posteverything/wp/2015/07/06/dont
-believe-her-defenders-amy-schumers-jokes-are-racist/

16. theinterrobang.com/washington-post-writer-who-accused-amy
-schumer-of-racism-never-saw-her-standup-or-tv-show/

17. www.dallasobserver.com/music/thank-you-ryan-adams-for-mans
plaining-taylor-swift-to-the-world-7619007

18. www.bostonglobe.com/arts/music/2015/09/21/ryan-adams-turns
-taylor-swift-into-mellow-gold/3LaScG0qUt4CrUJlj4qCEL/story
.html

19. www.salon.com/2015/05/22/taylor_swift_is_not_an_underdog_the
_real_story_about_her_1_percent_upbringing_that_the_new_york
_times_wont_tell_you/

20. www.theatlantic.com/entertainment/archive/2016/03/marie -and-the
-privilege-of-clutter/475266/

21. twitter.com/freddiedeboer/status/714896976546934785

22. www.theatlantic.com/entertainment/archive/2016/03/marie-kondo
    -and-the-privilege-of-clutter/475266/#comment-2588539474

23. www.huffingtonpost.com/entry/university-of-ottawa-yoga_56536
    246e4b0d4093a589bd3

24. jezebel.com/yoga-class-for-disabled-students-cancelled-because-of-c
    -1744166920

25. www.nytimes.com/roomfordebate/2015/08/04/whose-culture-is-it
    -anyhow

26. www.bostonglobe.com/arts/2015/07/18/counter-protesters-join
    -kimono-fray-mfa/ZgVWiT3yIZSlQgxCghAOFM/story.html

27. www.japantimes.co.jp/culture/2015/07/18/books/underneath
    -orientalist-kimono/#.VhqSUI9Viko ; www.japantimes.co.jp/opinion
    /2015/08/04/commentary/japan-commentary/kimono-cultural
    -appropriation/#.VhqTxo9Viko

28. www.washingtonpost.com/news/wonk/wp/2015/11/12/what-a
    -creepy-bloomingdales-ad-tells-us-about-americas-understanding-of
    -rape/

29. reason.com/archives/2015/11/18/bloomingdales-holiday-catalog

30. fusion.net/story/252567/stay-woke/

31. jezebel.com/world-weeps-in-gratitude-for-woke-hungarian-who-did-7
    -t-1751448258

32. Amanda Hess offered a similar assessment as that of Charles
    Pulliam-Moore, in a *New York Times Magazine* essay (www.nytimes.com
    /2016/04/24/magazine/earning-the-woke-badge.html): "[T]hose who
    try to signal their wokeness by saying 'woke' have revealed themselves
    to be very unwoke indeed. Now black cultural critics have retooled 'woke'
    yet again, adding a third layer that claps back at the appropriators. 'Woke'
    now works as a dig against those who claim to be culturally aware and
    yet are, sadly, lacking in self-awareness."

33. www.nytimes.com/2015/02/15/magazine/how-one-stupid-tweet
    -ruined-justine-saccos-life.html; also discussed in Ronson's *So You've
    Been Publicly Shamed.*

34. I'm thinking specifically of two *Jezebel* posts from early 2016: Kara
    Brown, on slavery movies (jezebel.com/im-so-damn-tired-of-slave
    -movies-1755250873), and Jia Tolentino, on people's vows to avoid
    reading books by white men (jezebel.com/damn-youre-not-reading-any

-books-by-white-men-this-yea-1751094468), as well as a great *New York* magazine blog post, by Allison P. Davis: "Macklemore Is All My Woke Ex-Boyfriends" (nymag.com/thecut/2016/01/macklemore-is-all -of-my-woke-ex-boyfriends.html).

35. www.nytimes.com/2016/02/28/fashion/skiing-race-matters-workplace -cursing.html

36. www.nytimes.com/2016/02/28/fashion/lupita-nyongo-and-trevor -noah-table-for-three.html

37. www.newyorker.com/culture/cultural-comment/the-trouble-with -white-people

38. www.rawstory.com/2013/05/the-real-problem-with-check-your -privilege-its-too-generous/

39. www.salon.com/2013/08/01/why_privilege_is_so_hard_to_give _up/

40. www.newyorker.com/magazine/2016/03/07/broad-citys-slapstick -anarchists (see also Freddie de Boer in the *Washington Post,* on Macklemore and the white privilege self-check: www.washingtonpost.com /posteverything/wp/2016/01/28/when-white-people-admit-white -privilege-theyre-really-just-congratulating-themselves/).

41. www.theguardian.com/us-news/2016/jan/10/white-man-pathology -bernie-sanders-donald-trump

42. www.theguardian.com/music/2016/jan/22/macklemore-white -privilege-stephen-colbert-mark-ruffalo

43. www.brainpickings.org/2014/10/08/some-thoughts-on-privilege/; whatwouldphoebedo.blogspot.ca/2011/08/joys-of-international-travel .html

44. www.slate.com/articles/life/roiphe/2011/12/what_s_wrong_with _angry_commenters_.html

45. www.thecrimson.com/article/1993/10/7/katie-roiphe-and-her -neverending-polemic/

46. jezebel.com/5825809/tavis-says-her-new-magazine-will-be-subversive ?comment=41402039#comments; the-toast.net/2015/08/05/interview -with-tavi-gevinson/#IDComment989050483

47. intothegloss.com/2014/11/quincy-davis-surfer/

48. variety.com/2008/scene/markets-festivals/producer-bill-finnegan -dies-at-80-1117996662/

49. www.harpersbazaar.com/culture/features/a2341/chloe-sevigny
    -natasha-lyonne-interview-0614/
50. medium.com/@jonahweiner/you-should-be-left-with-a-fucking-mess
    -of-unanswered-questions-94dd8352395c; Louis C.K. offers a similar
    response in a Boston Public Radio interview: www.wbur.org/npr
    /95567572.
51. www.newyorker.com/magazine/2015/06/01/off-diamond-head
    -finnegan
52. www.nytimes.com/2010/05/27/movies/27sex.html
53. www.nytimes.com/2012/12/21/movies/this-is-40-from-judd-apatow
    -and-starring-paul-rudd.html
54. A sliver of the Dunham-as-privileged conversation: www.newstatesman
    .com/laurie-penny/2012/10/lena-dunham-caitlin-moran-and-problem
    -unexamined-privilege; www.buzzfeed.com/rachaelmaddux/stop
    -blaming-lena-dunhams-success-on-nepotism-7bve#.lpVlpE4Pj; www
    .vulture.com/2013/02/dont-call-lena-dunham-brave.html; www.nytimes
    .com/2015/09/17/magazine/constance-wu-is-making-her-way-in
    -hollywood.html.
55. www.npr.org/2012/05/07/152183865/lena-dunham-addresses
    -criticism-aimed-at-girls
56. www.washingtonpost.com/news/act-four/wp/2014/11/06/what-lena
    -dunham-has-that-the-rest-of-us-deserve/
57. www.theguardian.com/tv-and-radio/tvandradioblog/2012/apr/18
    /girls-sex-and-the-city-television
58. nymag.com/arts/tv/features/girls-lena-dunham-2012-4/index1.html
59. www.sfgate.com/news/article/Girls-review-HBO-s-groundbreaking
    -sitcom-3475778.php
60. www.newyorker.com/culture/culture-desk/white-girls
61. gawker.com/lena-dunham-does-that-thing-that-lena-dunham-does
    -513784615
62. www.newyorker.com/magazine/2010/11/15/downtowns-daughter
63. www.thedailybeast.com/articles/2014/11/04/will-white-feminists
    -finally-dump-lena-dunham.html
64. www.people.com/article/lena-dunham-apologizes-comparing-gawker
    -abusive-husband; radaronline.com/exclusives/2015/01/lena-dunham
    -apologizes-bill-cosby-holocaust/

65. www.vulture.com/2015/03/broad-city-ilana-glazer-abbi-jacobson
    .html
66. www.slate.com/blogs/browbeat/2015/03/19/broad_city_finale
    _review_the_way_the_show_handles_class_dynamics_is_the.html
67. www.slate.com/articles/podcasts/doublex_gabfest/2015/04/alison
    _bechdel_s_fun_home_on_broadway_instagram_envy_and_the
    _third_season.html
68. deadline.com/2015/09/emmys-2015-creative-arts-winners-live-blog
    -1201523192/
69. www.vox.com/2015/6/26/8853001/amy-schumer-feminism-video
    -princess
70. www.peabodyawards.com/award-profile/inside-amy-schumer
71. www.nytimes.com/2015/11/15/arts/television/aziz-ansari-on-acting
    -race-and-hollywood.html?_r=0
72. www.vulture.com/2015/11/master-of-none-and-interracial-dating-on
    -tv.html
73. www.vulture.com/2015/06/amy-schumers-not-a-racist-but-she-is-a
    -comic.html
74. www.theguardian.com/tv-and-radio/2015/jun/28/amy-schumer
    -comedys-viral-queen
75. www.huffingtonpost.com/lauren-duca/mindy-kaling-elle_b
    _4561454.html
76. www.npr.org/2014/10/16/356390794/comedian-mindy-kaling-on
    -refusing-to-be-an-outsider-and-sexism-on-set
77. www.theatlantic.com/entertainment/archive/2015/05/how-comedi
    ans-became-public-intellectuals/394277/
78. time.com/4292506/unbreakable-kimmy-schmidt-season-2-review/
79. www.themarysue.com/tina-fey-cops-out/; www.net-a-porter.com/maga
    zine/330/19
80. www.theguardian.com/tv-and-radio/2016/apr/19/unbreakable
    -kimmy-schmidt-pc-culture-tina-fey-south-park
81. www.vulture.com/2016/04/unbreakable-kimmy-schmidt-recap
    -season-2-episode-3.html
82. www.newstatesman.com/2015/08/heres-why-people-are-boycotting
    -stonewall-movie; deadline.com/2015/10/suffragette-movie-protesters
    -london-film-festival-premiere-1201568993/

83. www.vanityfair.com/hollywood/2015/09/stonewall-review-roland
    -emmerich

84. www.advocate.com/commentary/2015/9/25/defense-stonewall

85. www.alternet.org/speakeasy/geri-silver/lena-dunham-privileged-yes
    -you-should-still-watch-girls

86. www.newstatesman.com/politics/feminism/2015/10/what-did
    -suffragette-movement-britain-really-look

87. www.buzzfeed.com/krystieyandoli/people-are-upset-about-meryl
    -streeps-id-rather-be-a-rebel-th#.ge1ZgkvpW

88. www.timeout.com/london/film/meryl-streep-and-the-stars-of
    -suffragette-on-feminism-family-and-fame

89. www.thestranger.com/film/feature/2015/11/04/23117815/why-our
    -reviewer-refuses-to-write-a-review-of-suffragette

90. www.theglobeandmail.com/arts/books-and-media/the-people-v
    -jonathan-franzen/article26141645/

4. PRIVILEGED IMPOSTORS

1. feministing.com/2009/02/05/day_in_the_life_of_a_feminist/

2. feministing.com/2009/02/12/feminism_and_privilege_draft/

3. See, for example, this 2008 *Feministe* post on the importance of
   checking one's privilege: www.feministe.us/blog/archives/2008/09/12
   /shall-we-talk-about-privilege/.

4. nymag.com/thecut/2014/01/qa-the-woman-debunking-myths-about
   -sex-work.html www.thenation.com/article/why-do-so-many-leftists
   -want-sex-work-be-new-normal/; www.nytimes.com/2016/05/08/maga
   zine/should-prostitution-be-a-crime.html

5. www.newyorker.com/magazine/2014/08/04/woman-2

6. www.theatlantic.com/politics/archive/2014/11/would-an-anti
   -catcalling-law-afflict-the-weak-or-the-powerful/382439/; time.com
   /3556523/street-harassment-isnt-about-sexism-its-about-privilege/

7. prospect.org/article/moving-past-acknowledging-privilege

8. www.thenation.com/article/feminisms-toxic-twitter-wars/

9. Michelle Goldberg links to Katherine Cross's blog post: quinnae.com
   /2014/01/03/words-words-words-on-toxicity-and-abuse-in-online
   -activism/

10. therumpus.net/2012/05/peculiar-benefits/
11. See Rebecca Cooper-Reilly's tweet about "white women who loudly decry 'white feminism' on social media" (twitter.com/boodleoops/status /686963306159058944).
12. Ibid.
13. www.theguardian.com/commentisfree/2014/nov/18/feminism -rosetta-scientist-shirt-dapper-laughs-julien-blanc-inequality
14. www.theguardian.com/commentisfree/2013/apr/18/are-you-too -white-rich-straight-to-be-feminist
15. thenewinquiry.com/essays/can-the-white-girl-twerk/ (see also: thenew inquiry.com/features/the-white-women-of-empire/).
16. See my *New Republic* piece on the White Male Writer™ phenomenon (newrepublic.com/article/123088/white-male-writers-no-longer -default-not-terribly-interesting).
17. Yes, a thing (www.washingtonpost.com/news/answer-sheet/wp/2015 /11/24/teacher-a-student-told-me-i-couldnt-understand-because-i-was -a-white-lady-heres-what-i-did-then/). A *Mad TV* sketch also parodied this phenomenon (www.youtube.com/watch?v=JaewfHk9KiA).
18. jezebel.com/damn-youre-not-reading-any-books-by-white-men -this-yea-1751094468; jezebel.com/world-weeps-in-gratitude-for-woke -hungarian-who-did-7-t-1751448258; fusion.net/story/252567/stay -woke/
19. www.autostraddle.com/femme-privilege-does-exist-a-little-153400/
20. www.youtube.com/watch?v=qMRDLCR8vAE
21. freebeacon.com/politics/jezebel-writer-hillary-clinton-advocate-well -off-white-women/
22. www.theguardian.com/us-news/2016/jan/18/hillary-clinton-bernie -sanders-black-voters-south-carolina
23. mattbruenig.com/2015/10/27/an-emerging-feminist-age-divide/
24. www.nytimes.com/2015/12/13/us/politics/moms-and-daughters -debate-gender-factor-in-hillary-clintons-bid.html; www.theguardian .com/us-news/commentisfree/2016/jan/24/hillary-clinton-young -women-voters-jill-abramson
25. nymag.com/thecut/2015/11/bernie-sanders-bros-are-coming-for-the -hillary-clinton-bots.html

26. Ibid.
27. www.thenation.com/article/why-im-supporting-hillary-clinton-with -joy-and-without-apologies/
28. www.politico.com/magazine/story/2016/02/hillary-clinton-2016 -young-women-gender-213620
29. jezebel.com/fathers-and-childless-women-in-academia-are-3x-more -lik-1758704068
30. www.nytimes.com/2016/01/31/opinion/campaign-stops/why-dont -boomer-women-like-hillary-clinton.html
31. twitter.com/stevesalaita/status/662748374932680704
32. gawker.com/there-are-only-two-issues-1744172647
33. www.newrepublic.com/article/122110/i-dont-want-be-excuse-racist -violence-charleston;
34. everydayfeminism.com/2015/06/navigating-whiteness-feminism/
35. www.returnofkings.com/8167/why-modern-feminism-is-white -womans-privilege
36. book.babewalker.com/; www.buzzfeed.com/annehelenpetersen/coke -and-dicks-and-privilege
37. reason.com/blog/2015/12/08/dont-want-to-bomb-syria-misogynist
38. www.damemagazine.com/2014/12/15/white-women-please-dont -expect-me-wipe-away-your-tears
39. gawker.com/sandra-bland-and-why-we-can-no-longer-look-away -1720634864
40. www.salon.com/2016/01/26/white_women_of_publishing_new_survey _shows_a_lack_of_diversity_behind_the_scenes_in_book_world/
41. www.nytimes.com/2015/12/06/magazine/white-debt.html#permid =16837753
42. gawker.com/dude-yes-i-totally-hear-you-why-is-this-what-the-he -888544134; gawker.com/this-right-here-is-why-i-will-never-work-retail -again-886881453
43. www.msnbc.com/rachel-maddow-show/when-the-right-goes-after -clinton-the-left; www.nytimes.com/2015/05/17/us/politics/the-right -aims-at-democrats-on-social-media-to-hit-clinton.html
44. www.nationalreview.com/article/391348/pathetic-privilege-kevin-d -williamson
45. www.newyorker.com/magazine/2012/02/13/a-rooting-interest

46. www.nytimes.com/times-insider/2015/06/03/primates-of-park -avenue-reporters-notebook/
47. www.huffingtonpost.com/wednesday-martin/new-misogyny-women -one-percent_b_7506088.html
48. penguinrandomhouse.ca/hazlitt/feature/midlife-crisis-any-other-name
49. That's not to say transwomen never painstakingly acknowledge their privilege. Jennifer Finney Boylan devoted a *New York Times* column, "Trans Deaths, White Privilege," to acknowledging her own, relative to that of poor transwomen of color (www.nytimes.com/2015/08/22 /opinion/trans-deaths-white-privilege.html).
50. jezebel.com/homme-de-plume-what-i-learned-sending-my-novel-out -und-1720637627
51. opinionator.blogs.nytimes.com/2016/01/25/girlfriend-mother -professor
52. thebillfold.com/i-ll-take-care-of-you-557aef2f4411#.ud2pk1lkj
53. nymag.com/thecut/2016/04/lena-dunham-endometriosis-blossom -ball.html
54. www.theguardian.com/commentisfree/2014/sep/29/lena-dunham -tell-all-book-not-that-kind-of-girl
55. nymag.com/thecut/2016/03/unplanned-pregnancy.html
56. thebillfold.com/young-privileged-and-applying-for-food-stamps -a078b267d321#.wbpeou5m5
57. www.tabletmag.com/jewish-news-and-politics/189030/victimhood -olympics
58. www.thewrap.com/julie-delpy-hollywood-dumps-women-sometimes -wish-african-american/
59. Thus my call for more fiction (thenewinquiry.com/essays/true -stories/).
60. www.theawl.com/tag/around-every-single-conversation-about-food -culture-there-should-be-a-huge-set-of-brackets-in-order-to-convey -that-almost-all-of-this-is-restricted-to-the-fairly-privileged
61. medium.com/matter/the-monetized-man-d0cc3fe2b159#.8wd prxt5b
62. twitter.com/alanamassey/status/669160456909664256
63. jezebel.com/my-maternity-clothes-struggle-1755152190

64. parenting.blogs.nytimes.com/2013/04/16/why-do-i-think-my-salary
    -pays-for-child-care/
65. parenting.blogs.nytimes.com/2013/04/16/why-do-i-think-my-salary
    -pays-for-child-care/#permid=93
66. www.theatlantic.com/magazine/archive/2012/07/why-women-still
    -cant-have-it-all/309020/
67. www.theatlantic.com/politics/archive/2012/07/anne-marie-slaughter
    -answers-her-critics/259274/
68. www.dissentmagazine.org/article/trickle-down-feminism. A footnote
    specifies that Sarah Jaffe didn't coin the phrase.
69. www.theguardian.com/commentisfree/2015/jan/21/feminists
    -obsessed-elite-metropolitan-lives-low-paid-females
70. www.slate.com/blogs/xx_factor/2016/01/06/the_head_of_the_dnc
    _says_young_women_are_complacent_she_s_not_totally_wrong.html
71. www.slate.com/blogs/xx_factor/2015/02/23/patricia_arquette_on
    _pay_equality_insulting_to_feminism.html
72. www.newappsblog.com/2015/10/what-it-takes-to-succeed-in
    -academia.html
73. www.nytimes.com/2014/05/04/fashion/blessed-becomes-popular
    -word-hashtag-social-media.html
74. counseling.caltech.edu/general/InfoandResources/Impostor
75. nymag.com/thecut/2015/11/i-hope-i-never-get-over-my-impostor
    -syndrome.html

5. BIZARRO PRIVILEGE

1. A sampling: www.nationalreview.com/article/417198/people-now
   -whining-extroverts-have-social-privilege-katherine-timpf; www
   .mediaite.com/tv/the-pending-implosion-of-the-check-your-privilege
   -movement/; www.nationalreview.com/article/431192/university-check
   -size-privilege; www.weeklystandard.com/article/beyond-pale/724717;
   www.theamericanconservative.com/dreher/privilege-grad-school
   -mehra-eric-garner/.
2. www.nationalreview.com/author/katherine-timpf
3. nymag.com/daily/intelligencer/2016/02/law-students-traumatized
   -by-anti-scalia-email.html
4. www.thecollegefix.com/post/23072/

5. thefederalist.com/2014/06/13/people-who-say-check-your-privilege-should-do-it/

6. dailycaller.com/2015/03/12/greg-gutfeld-forget-white-privilege-hilary-suffers-from-clinton-privilege-video/

7. www.weeklystandard.com/articles/house-stacked-deck-cards_946576.html#

8. www.thedailybeast.com/articles/2016/01/04/how-the-p-c-police-propelled-donald-trump.html

9. www.motherjones.com/kevin-drum/2016/01/are-liberals-responsible-rise-donald-trump

10. nymag.com/daily/intelligencer/2016/04/america-tyranny-donald-trump.html

11. www.wsj.com/articles/donald-trumps-america-1455290458

12. www.bloombergview.com/articles/2016-02-19/donald-trump-class-warrior

13. twitter.com/normative/status/701034801445343232

14. www.pbs.org/newshour/rundown/white-educated-and-wealthy-congratulations-you-live-in-a-bubble/

15. www.jacobinmag.com/2015/05/99-1-percent-income-inequality-class/

16. whatwouldphoebedo.blogspot.ca/2012/09/the-politics-of-ypis.html

17. www.americanthinker.com/articles/2015/04/its_past_time_to_acknowledge_black_privilege.html; www.nationalreview.com/article/431393/white-privilege-myth-reality

18. thoughtcatalog.com/mark-saunders/2014/04/18-things-females-seem-to-not-understand-because-female-privilege/

19. whatwouldphoebedo.blogspot.ca/2011/11/jewish-as-privilege.html

20. westandwiththe99percent.tumblr.com/post/12863423471/i-have-always-had-many-advantages-i-am-1-white

21. linkis.com/www.jta.org/2015/06/YcVjM

22. zeek.forward.com/articles/118273/; forward.com/opinion/198054/checking-your-jewish-privilege/; newrepublic.com/article/121474/holocaust-doesnt-discount-jewish-white-privilege; newrepublic.com/article/121498/jewish-privilege-doesnt-exist-jews-can-benefit-whiteness

23. zeek.forward.com/articles/118273/

24. www.tabletmag.com/jewish-life-and-religion/190070/being-jewish
-polite-society

25. forward.com/sisterhood/340322/sheryl-sandbergs-mea-culpa-and
-the-limitations-of-jewish-feminism

26. forward.com/opinion/340018/jews-of-color-get-personal-and
-political-at-first-ever-national-gathering/

27. www.youtube.com/watch?v=ylPUzxpIBe0

28. whatwouldphoebedo.blogspot.ca/2012/01/jews-were-slaves-too-you
-dont-hear-us.html

29. forward.com/sisterhood/149516/sh-jews-say-to-non-white-jews/

30. www.npr.org/2012/01/12/145101169/stuff-white-girls-say-offensive
-or-funny

31. whatwouldphoebedo.blogspot.ca/2011/07/anti-semitism-and-first
-world-problems.html

32. dish.andrewsullivan.com/2014/08/12/the-myth-of-pretext-free-anti
-semitism/

33. newrepublic.com/article/121372/david-brooks-nyt-column-anti
-semitism-wasnt-entirely-wrong

34. www.tabletmag.com/jewish-news-and-politics/189944/the-deboer
-tendency

35. observer.com/2015/06/the-pecking-disorder-social-justice-warriors
-gone-wild/

36. www.tabletmag.com/jewish-news-and-politics/189030/victimhood
-olympics

37. www.theatlantic.com/politics/archive/2015/04/why-garry-trudeau-is
-wrong-about-charlie-hebdo/390336/

38. www.theguardian.com/us-news/2016/apr/28/julia-ioffe-journalist
-melania-trump-antisemitic-abuse

39. forward.com/opinion/339243/two-campus-talesand-what-they-say
-about-american-vs-british-anti-semitism/

40. oberlinreview.org/9897/opinions/karega-masons-facebook-posts-anti
-semitic/

41. www.nytimes.com/2016/03/08/opinion/an-anti-semitism-of-the-left
.html

42. www.nytimes.com/2016/05/04/opinion/the-british-lefts-jewish
-problem.html

43. www.foxnews.com/us/2016/05/02/mizzou-silent-on-anti-semitism
    -even-as-racial-strife-engulfed-campus.html ; nypost.com/2016/04/02
    /anti-semitism-the-only-hate-allowed-in-campus-safe-spaces/

44. www.newstatesman.com/politics/2014/01/radicalism-fools-rise-new-anti
    -semitism; www.cambridge.org/gu/academic/subjects/history/european
    -history-after-1450/socialism-fools-leftist-origins-modern-anti-semitism

45. forward.com/news/327466/can-jews-back-black-lives-matter-and-be
    -pro-israel/

46. www.thedailybeast.com/articles/2015/12/02/the-student-activists
    -connecting-israel-to-campus-rape.html

47. www.slate.com/blogs/outward/2016/01/25/creating_change_protest
    _of_a_wider_bridge_was_anti_semitic.html

48. theprincetontory.com/main/checking-my-privilege-character-as-the
    -basis-of-privilege/; time.com/85933/why-ill-never-apologize-for-my
    -white-male-privilege/

49. www.tabletmag.com/jewish-news-and-politics/171960/check-your
    -privilege

50. www.tabletmag.com/scroll/172141/liel-liel-liel

51. forward.com/sisterhood/197705/tal-fortgangs-misguided-princeton
    -privilege-lament/

52. forward.com/opinion/318667/im-a-mizrahi-jew-do-i-count-as-a
    -person-of-color/

53. www.hebrewmamita.com/videos/viewvideo/27/performances
    /hebrew-mamita

54. whatwouldphoebedo.blogspot.ca/2008/07/gray-area.html

55. www.thedailybeast.com/articles/2015/12/10/the-most-horrific-cop
    -rape-case-you-ve-never-heard-of.html

56. www.nytimes.com/2015/07/17/opinion/listening-to-ta-nehisi-coates
    -while-white.html

57. www.jta.org/2016/02/19/news-opinion/politics/bernie-sanders-says
    -hes-lucky-to-be-white-but-what-about-jewish

58. www.rollingstone.com/politics/news/its-ok-to-care-about-gender-in
    -this-election-20160219; www.huffingtonpost.com/jennifer-gore
    /bernie-sanders-is-not-mag_b_9144488.html

59. newrepublic.com/article/129962/bernies-success-mean-jews-not
    -much

60. forward.com/opinion/317938/checking-my-privilege-as-a-korean-jew/

61. www.thedailybeast.com/articles/2015/12/11/cop-used-whiteness-as-his-weapon-to-rape-black-women.html

62. newrepublic.com/article/117922/elliot-rodger-race-isla-vista-shooter-was-not-just-white-guy-killer

63. www.nytimes.com/2016/02/13/nyregion/many-asians-express-dismay-and-frustration-after-liang-verdict.html

64. www.washingtonpost.com/posteverything/wp/2016/02/12/why-do-my-co-workers-keep-confusing-me-with-other-people-im-asian/

65. the-toast.net/2016/01/05/what-goes-through-your-mind-casual-racism/

66. www.nbcnews.com/news/asian-america/jason-wu-asian-privilege-freddie-gray-n356986; www.racefiles.com/2013/03/14/challenging-asian-privilege/

67. thisisasianprivilege.tumblr.com/about; thsppl.com/why-i-refuse-to-acknowledge-asianprivilege-51583f3610e6#.m3vzvajky; www.smh.com.au/national/is-there-such-a-thing-as-asian-privilege-20130217-2el1r.html

68. For an example of a satirical-but-bigoted use of the "Asian privilege" expression, see: takimag.com/article/tackling_asian_privilege_gavin_mcinnes/print#axzz3dXfaoqWf.

69. www.nytimes.com/2014/11/25/opinion/is-harvard-unfair-to-asian-americans.html

70. www.jacobinmag.com/2016/02/socialism-liberalism-social-justice-activism-tumblr-fandom/

71. www.nytimes.com/2015/03/06/nyregion/lack-of-diversity-persists-in-admissions-to-selective-new-york-city-high-schools.html; www.slate.com/articles/news_and_politics/politics/2014/07/the_case_for_shutting_down_stuyvesant_high_school_the_best_public_school.html; www.theatlantic.com/education/archive/2015/03/how-to-solve-the-diversity-problem-at-nycs-elite-public-schools/386944/

72. quickfacts.census.gov/qfd/states/36/3651000.html

73. www.nais.org/Statistics/Documents/NYSAISFactsAtAGlance201415.pdf

74. issuu.com/riverdalecountryschool/docs/riverdale_by_the_numbers_2015-2016, slide 23 of 62.

75. schools.nyc.gov/OA/SchoolReports/2014-15/School_Quality
    _Snapshot_2015_HS_M475.pdf
76. www.slate.com/articles/business/the_bills/2015/08/private_schools
    _getting_more_expensive_and_opulent_they_show_how_the
    _super.html
77. www.nytimes.com/2015/02/22/nyregion/at-new-york-private
    -schools-challenging-white-privilege-from-the-inside.html
78. www.salon.com/2015/03/08/the_1_percents_white_privilege_con
    _elites_hold_conversations_about_race_while_resegregating_our
    _schools/
79. whatwouldphoebedo.blogspot.ca/2015/02/today-in-ypis.html
80. www.theatlantic.com/politics/archive/2015/02/the-limits-of-talking
    -about-privilege/386021/
81. fredrikdeboer.com/2015/02/22/it-eats-everything/
82. www.academia.edu/4572341/McIntosh_as_Synecdoche_How
    _Teacher_Education_s_Focus_on_White_Privilege_Undermines
    _Antiracism

CONCLUSION: AFTER PRIVILEGE

1. www.theonion.com/article/white-male-privilege-squandered-on-job
   -at-best-buy-35835
2. jezebel.com/no-offense-1749221642
3. www.cjr.org/feature/womans_work.php
4. www.dailycal.org/2016/01/22/checking-privilege-serves-to-rein
   force-it/
5. www.rollingstone.com/politics/news/how-america-made-donald
   -trump-unstoppable-20160224
6. On Trump's use of Twitter: www.nytimes.com/2016/02/27/us
   /politics/donald-trump.html.
7. www.nytimes.com/2015/10/18/opinion/sunday/the-funny-thing
   -about-adversity.html
8. storify.com/JamilesLartey/on-fff (my initial response had been similar,
   but he came up with "tragedy hipsters": whatwouldphoebedo.blogspot
   .ca/2015/11/paris.html).
9. www.nytimes.com/2015/07/19/magazine/how-privilege-became-a
   -provocation.html (for a summary of Didion's YPIS, see: www.slate

.com/blogs/browbeat/2011/11/03/joan_didion_addresses_privilege _in_blue_nights.html).

10. www.washingtonpost.com/opinions/george-will-college-become-the -victims-of-progressivism/2014/06/06/e90e73b4-eb50-11e3-9f5c -9075d5508f0a_story.html

11. www.nytimes.com/2014/12/22/opinion/who-suffers-most-from-rape -and-sexual-assault-in-america.html

12. jezebel.com/5913942/how-to-feel-when-an-impossibly-promising-22 -year-old-passes-away; whatwouldphoebedo.blogspot.com/2012/05/end -of-ypis.html

13. www.nytimes.com/2014/04/27/books/review/inside-the-list.html

14. jezebel.com/5913942/how-to-feel-when-an-impossibly-promising-22 -year-old-passes-away#comments

15. jezebel.com/5913942/how-to-feel-when-an-impossibly-promising-22 -year-old-passes-away?comment=50130101#comments

16. jezebel.com/5913942/how-to-feel-when-an-impossibly-promising -22+year+old-passes-away?comment=50130298#comments

17. jezebel.com/5913942/how-to-feel-when-an-impossibly-promising-22 -year-old-passes-away#comments

18. www.poynter.org/how-tos/writing/92749/the-lure-and-peril-of -missing-white-girl-syndrome/; journalismcenter.org/when-a-child -dies/missing-white-girl.html

19. jezebel.com/5913942/how-to-feel-when-an-impossibly-promising -22+year+old-passes-away?comment=50135807#comments

20. jezebel.com/5913942/how-to-feel-when-an-impossibly-promising-22 -year-old-passes-away?comment=50131541#comments

21. jezebel.com/5913942/how-to-feel-when-an-impossibly-promising-22 -year-old-passes-away?comment=50136306#comments

22. whatwouldphoebedo.blogspot.ca/2012/05/end-of-ypis.html

23. blogs.scientificamerican.com/guest-blog/angelina-jolie-and-the-one -percent/

24. mic.com/articles/41725/angelina-jolie-double-mastectomy-support -her-health-and-recognize-her-privilege#.4aYoycxQZ

25. mattbruenig.com/2015/08/29/the-problems-of-identity-policing-and -invisible-identities-for-identitarian-deference/

26. Ibid.

27. medium.com/@johndevore/it-s-not-easy-being-a-white-heterosexual-male-3c4837497be9#.j4bwijnw6
28. fredrikdeboer.com/2015/08/31/how-much-smoke-before-youll-shout-fire/
29. www.nytimes.com/2007/10/24/dining/24appe.html
30. Caitlyn Jenner, of all people, revealed her privilege in December 2015 (www.upworthy.com/caitlyn-jenners-heartfelt-apology-after-her-offensive-man-in-a-dress-remark).
31. www.vulture.com/2016/02/why-white-privilege-is-everyones-burden.html
32. www.psmag.com/page/write-us Accessed 2/28/16
33. www.theatlantic.com/politics/archive/2015/04/why-garry-trudeau-is-wrong-about-charlie-hebdo/390336/
34. www.psmag.com/politics-and-law/sure-whites-are-privileged--but-not-me-personally
35. www.alternet.org/culture/why-white-people-freak-out-when-theyre-called-out-about-race
36. www.thedailybeast.com/articles/2016/02/13/meryl-streep-s-divisive-feminism-how-white-feminists-silence-people-of-color.html; www.latimes.com/entertainment/gossip/la-et-mg-meryl-streep-responds-berlin-film-festival-20160225-story.html

INDEX

Adams, Ryan, 129–30
admissions, college campus, 107, 238
    essays, 28, 99–100, 108–11, 119
    "holistic," 102–4, 116
    hypocrisy of, 100–101, 115–21
    rejection, 111–14
    voluntourism and, 33, 108–12
affirmative action, 19–20, 111, 112, 239
African Americans, 39, 59, 126, 215, 219,
    223
    as rape victims, 235–36
    slavery and, 138, 164, 225, 231, 296n34
    White Feminism and, 184–85
"Against Student Stories" (Bady), 97
Agness, Karin, 84–85, 93

Ahmad, Asam, 65, 66
AIDS, 19, 137
All in the Family (television show), 166–67
American Thinker (online magazine), 215
The American Prospect, 48
Anderson Robinson, Janine, 110–11
Angyal, Chloe, 181
Ansari, Aziz, 154–58, 167
anti-racism, 38–39, 137, 142, 185, 219,
    228
anti-Semitism, 183, 228, 229, 230, 232
    on college campuses, 222, 238
    with "Jewish privilege," 216–24
anti-YPIS essays, 62–66
Apatow, Judd, 148–49

Arceneaux, Michael, 53
Arquette, Patricia, 194, 202
arts, 129–33. *See also* cultural criticism; fashion; films
  cultural production and, 152–61
  origin story and, 145–48
  with outrage bait as marketing strategy, 135–37
  privilege theory with, 28–29, 148–52
  racism and, 137–43, 157
Asian Americans, 134–35, 161, 231
  in criminal justice system, 235–37
  as new Jews, 234–44
  with "privilege" imagined, 238, 246
"At New York Private Schools, Challenging White Privilege from the Inside" (Spencer), 241–42
The Atlantic, 79, 131–33
Atli, Efe, 249, 250
awareness
  disclaimer, 189–97, 202–5
  from have-it-all-ers, 197–202
  "privilege" and, 10, 96, 121, 267–72
  "woke," 137–38, 271, 296n32
The Awl, 86, 125, 195

Backlund, Mary, 118
Bady, Aaron, 97, 98
Bailey, J. Michael, 86
Baker, Katie J. M., 257–61
Baquet, Dean, 26
Barthwell, Ali, 157, 160
"Being Privileged Is Not a Choice, So Stop Hating Me for It" (Menendez), 34
Bellafante, Ginia, 188, 189
The Bell Curve (Murray and Herrnstein), 212
Bernie Bro phenomenon, 178. *See also* Sanders, Bernie
"Bernie Sanders or Bust? That's a Stance Based on Privilege" (Arceneaux), 53
Bernstein, Arielle, 131–33
Bernstein, Joseph, 86
Bérubé, Michael, 91
"The Best Part of *Broad City* Is How It Handles Class" (Schwedel), 153–54
Between the World and Me (Coates), 141

Beyerstein, Lindsay, 128
Bindel, Julie, 174
Biss, Eula, 37–39
Bitch (magazine), 42–43
Black Girl Dangerous (Web site), 49
"Black Lives Matter," 59, 223
"black privilege," 215
blackface, 134, 136, 137, 176–77
Bland, Sandra, 185
Bloomingdale's, 136
Blow, Charles, 54
Boko Haram, 94
bombing, of Syria, 184
Book Riot (blog), 43
Boston Museum of Fine Arts, 134–35, 161, 237
Bouie, Jamelle, 12–13, 25, 67
bourgeois feminism, 182, 200, 205, 254
Boylan, Jennifer Finney, 303n49
Brasunas, Tony, 52
Broad City (television show), 141, 153, 229
brochures, college campuses, 80–81
Brooks, David, 5, 6, 83–84, 231–32, 233
Brown, Amanda Christy, 109
Brown, Elizabeth Nolan, 184, 212
Brown, Kara, 157, 296n34
Brown, Michael, 12
Bruenig, Matt, 177–78, 262
Bruni, Frank, 104, 115–16
Buchanan, Matt, 195
bullying, 63, 64
Burgess, Tituss, 161

C. K., Louis, 34, 127, 146–47
cafeteria food, cultural appropriation and, 85, 237
call-out. *See* privilege call-out
Can't We Talk About Something More Pleasant? (Chast), 131
capital cultural, 46–47, 50, 92, 269
capital-capital, 47, 50, 269
Carlock, Ryan, 160
Carmon, Irin, 6
Carroll, Rebecca, 142–43
Carson, Ben, 101
celebrity, 4, 146–47
Chait, Jonathan, 28, 70, 71, 72–73
Charlie Hebdo massacre, 221

Chast, Roz, 131
"Checking My Privilege as a Korean Jew"
    (Yi), 234
"Checking My Privilege: Character as the
    Basis of Privilege" (Fortgang), 3–4,
    225
"Checking Whose Privilege" (Crawford),
    107
"Checking Your Privilege 101" document, 48
Chernikoff, Helen, 218
Cherry, Myisha, 140
The Chronicle of Higher Education, 87, 89, 91
Chung, Nicole, 237–38
Clark, Melissa, 102
ClickHole (humor Web site), 45, 123–24
Clinton, Bill, 177, 178
Clinton, Hillary, 5, 250, 273
    feminism and, 177–81, 201
    "privilege" and, 51–58, 209–10
Clooney, George, 123–24
Coalition for Access, Affordability, and
    Success, 115
Coates, Ta-Nehisi, 141, 230–31
"The Coddling of the American Mind"
    (Lukianoff and Haidt), 79
Coen, Jessica, 44
Cohen, Roger, 222
Colbert, Stephen, 143, 167
Cole, Jonathan, 102
Cole, Teju, 36
college campuses, 257
    admissions, 28, 99–104, 108–21, 238
    anti-Semitism on, 222, 238
    brochures, 80–81
    diversity on, 77–78, 96
    first-world problems on, 93–97
    ivory dildos and, 84–89
    memoirs, 104–6
    microaggression and, 85, 92, 96
    "privilege" and, 4, 82–84, 90–91, 208
    protests, 78–82, 84–86, 89, 94, 290n54,
        291n67
    racism and, 82, 83, 93, 113
    social media and, 92–93
    with student controversies in media,
        97–100
Collins, Greg, 209
Collins, Patricia Hill, 192

comedy, 126, 159, 219, 221
*Coming Apart: The State of White America,
    1960–2010* (Murray), 212, 213
comments, Internet, 258–61
confession
    confessional essay, 34–39
    YPIS online and privilege, 39–41
Cooke, Jim, 181
"Cop Used Whiteness as His Weapon to
    Rape Black Women" (Taylor), 235–36
Crawford, Lacy, 107
Crazy Ex-Girlfriend (television show), 237
criminal justice system, 6
    police, 37, 39, 231, 235–37
    "privilege" and, 253–54
criticism. *See* cultural criticism; political
    criticism, arts and
Crook, Clive, 212–13
Crosley-Corcoran, Gina, 40
Cross, Katherine, 172
cruelty, of "privilege," 253–63
cultural appropriation
    cafeteria food and, 85, 237
    fashion and, 125, 134–36, 161, 237
cultural capital, 46–47, 50, 92, 269
cultural criticism, 162, 164
    backfiring of, 165–67
    backlash, 126–30
    of Clooney, 123–24
    Dunham and, 149–52, 158, 163, 187
    privilege theory with, 28–29, 148–52
cultural production
    cultural criticism of, 158
    with think piece and sitcom, 152–61
"The Cultural Outrage Audit" (Paskin), 128
culture, of overshare, 16, 23–24

The Daily Beast, 37–38, 152, 231
Dallas Observer, 129–30
Dame Magazine, 184–85
Daum, Meghan, 94, 96, 97
"Day in the Life of a Feminist Writer/
    Activist" (Martin, C.), 169–70
deBoer, Freddie, 38, 52, 83, 84, 127
    on private schools, 243
    on Twitter, 132, 262–63
decency, 140, 261, 271
DeSteno, David, 251–52

INDEX

didactic novel (*roman à thèse*), 130
dildos, college campuses and ivory, 84–89
disclaimer. *See* awareness
Dish (blog), 211, 220
diversity
  on college campuses, 77–78, 96
  in education, 239–41
  ideological, 87, 245
  in television, 128, 153, 155–57, 160, 161,
    237, 239
Douthat, Ross, 213
Dowsett, Jeremy, 21
Drum, Kevin, 210–11
Dunham, Lena, 4, 177, 193
  cultural criticism and, 149–52, 158, 163,
    187
  privilege call-out and, 3, 298n54
Dzodan, Flavia, 61, 64–65

economic inequality, 181, 193–94, 197–98.
  See also finances
Edewi, Daysha, 20
education, 79, 87, 89, 91. *See also* college
  campuses
  affirmative action and, 19–20, 111, 112,
    239
  diversity in, 239–41
  imposter syndrome and, 202–3
  private schools, 240–43
  tutoring with, 110, 119, 240–41
Edwards, John, 4
Emery, Noemie, 209–10
Emmerich, Roland, 162–63
The End of Men (Rosin), 71
Epstein, Joseph, 85–86
Epstein Ojalvo, Holly, 109
"Explaining White Privilege to a Broke
  White Person" (Crosley-Corcoran), 40

fashion, 125, 134–36, 145, 161, 237
Fawlty Towers (television show), 31, 166
The Federalist (online magazine), 209
feminism, 169–70, 218. *See also* White
  Feminism
  awareness disclaimer and, 189–97,
    202–5
  bourgeois, 182, 200, 205, 254
  Clinton, H., and, 177–81, 201

  with misogyny, righteous, 205–6
  political left and right on, 29, 175
  "privilege" confronted by, 171–73
  race and, 172–73, 184–85, 192, 194
  second-wave, 196
  as toxic, 172, 174, 201
  "trickle-down," 200
  White Lady, 175–77, 206, 246
  YPIS and, 173–75
"Feminism's Toxic Twitter Wars"
  (Goldberg), 172
feminist bloggers, "privilege" of, 169–71
Feministing (blog), 169–71
fetishization, of powerlessness, 174–75
Fey, Tina, 160–61
Filipovic, Jill, 57
films, 86, 138, 148–49
  cultural criticism of, 162–65
  LGBT-themed, 162–63
finances, 8, 11, 16, 114
  economic inequality, 181, 193–94,
    197–98
  with far-left rejection of "privilege,"
    46–47
  tuition for private schools, 240–41
Finnegan, William, 146
Finnegan, William, Jr., 145–46, 147–48
Fiorina, Carly, 181
first-world problems, 93–97, 220
Fischer, Molly, 204
Fisher, Abigail, 112
Flanagan, Caitlin, 199–200
Fong, Melissa, 65–66
food. *See* cafeteria food, cultural
  appropriation and
Forbes, 84–85
Fortgang, Tal, 3, 5, 34, 208–9
  celebrity and, 4
  complaint of, 224–34
Forward (Jewish newspaper), 218, 234
Foundation for Individual Rights in
  Education, 79
Franzen, Jonathan, 165–66, 187–88
free speech, 79, 89, 95, 211
Freeman, Hadley, 14–15, 58
Friedersdorf, Conor, 66, 94–95, 96, 243,
  291n67
Friedman, Brandon, 60–61

Frum, David, 221, 264–65
Frye, Northrop, 126

Galanes, Philip, 138–39
Garber, Megan, 159
Garner, Eric, 12
Gavron, Sarah, 162
Gawker, 34, 152, 181, 186, 280*n*2, 281*n*8
  college campus admissions essays in,
    99–100
  privilege checking tournament and, 28,
    45
Gay, Roxane, 173
gay male misogyny, women and, 230
gender, 188, 199
  equality, 179–80, 200
  transgender, 40, 171–72
George Washington University, 116–17
Gern, Walter, 118–19
Gevinson, Tavi, 145
"Girl, You Don't Need Makeup" (parody
  music video), 154
Girls (television show), 3, 167
  cultural criticism and, 149–52
  influence of, 153
Goffman, Alice, 90
"Going Beyond Cliché: How to Write a
  Great College Essay" (Brown, A. C.,
  and Epstein Ojalvo), 109
Goldberg, Michelle, 54, 172–74, 201
Groetzinger, Kate, 117
Grose, Jessica, 197–99
Gu, Steven, 113
The Guardian, 38, 45, 53, 125
Gurley, Akai, 237

Haidt, Jonathan, 79, 84
Halloween costume protests, 81–82, 94
harassment, 172, 178, 222, 231
Harvard University, 82, 91, 95, 102, 111,
  147
Haskins, Sarah, 177
hate crimes, 217–18. *See also* Holocaust
have-it-all-ers, awareness from, 197–202
Hay, Carol, 192
Hayes, Chris, 53, 54
Hazlitt (magazine), 189
Herrnstein, Richard J., 212

Hess, Amanda, 60, 296*n*32
Hidary, Vanessa, 229
Hillman, Melissa, 53
"holistic" admissions, on college campuses,
  102–4, 116
Holmes, Anna, 151
Holocaust, 218, 219, 226, 228–29
Holtzclaw, Daniel, 235–36
"How 'Privilege' Became a Provocation"
  (Sehgal), 12
"How Serfdom Saved the Women's
  Movement" (Flanagan), 199
"How to Feel When an Impossibly
  Promising 22-Year-Old Passes Away"
  (Baker), 257–61
Hsu, Hua, 81, 97–98, 100, 139, 140, 236
humblebrag, 39, 69, 101, 203, 204
humor, "privilege" and, 44–46. *See also*
  comedy
Hunt, Tim, 70
"Hysterical Activism" (Newman), 74

"I Hope I Never Get Over My Imposter
  Syndrome" (Fischer), 204
"I Tried to Escape My Privilege with
  Low-Wage Work. Instead I Came Face
  to Face with It." (Phillips), 31–34
"identitarian deference" (ID), 262
ideological diversity, 87, 245
"I'm a Butch Woman. Do I Have Cis
  Privilege?" (Urquhart), 40
imposter syndrome, 202–5
Ingall, Marjorie, 227–28
Inside Amy Schumer (television show), 154
Internet, 248–49, 258–61. *See also* social
  media; "your privilege is showing"
  online
intersectionality, 14, 29, 40, 268–69
Into The Gloss (beauty blog), 145
Ioffe, Julia, 222
"Is Your Privilege Showing?" (Anderson
  Robinson), 110–11

Jacobin (socialist magazine), 50, 55, 214
Jacques, Elliot, 190
Jaffe, Sarah, 200
"jargon" case, 66–67
jealousy, YPIS, 143–45

Jerkins, Morgan, 113
Jewish Telegraphic Agency, 216, 232
Jews
    anti-Semitism and, 183, 216–24, 228,
      229, 230, 232, 238
    Asian Americans as new, 234–44
    college campus admissions and, 238
    feminism and, 218
    with first-world problems, 220
    Holocaust and, 218, 219, 226, 228–29
    oppression and, 216, 217, 219, 220, 222,
      223, 232
    "privilege" and, 215–34, 238, 246
    slavery and, 219
    White Jewish Ladies, 183
Jezebel (blog), 17, 24, 44, 89, 137, 296n34
    awareness disclaimer on, 192
    confessional essay and, 34–35
    cultural appropriation and, 134–35
    gender equality and, 180
    on "how to feel," 257–61
    on "offense" and online journalism,
      248–49
    with "privilege," inadvertent humor of, 45
Judd, David, 48
Jung, E. Alex, 158
justice. *See* criminal justice system; social
    justice

Kaling, Mindy, 158–59
Kaminer, Ariel, 118
Kampeas, Ron, 232
Kaplan, Sarah, 116–17
Keegan, Marina, 257–61
Kennedy, Jacqueline, 187
Kessler, Debra, 129
Kilpatrick, Connor, 50–51, 52, 214
Kimmel, Michael, 10
Kipnis, Laura, 87, 291n62
Kirchick, Jamie, 194, 202, 221
Kohner, Claire-Renee, 40–41
Kondo, Marie, 131–33
Krakowski, Jane, 160
Krems, Jaimie Arona, 112, 113

Lartey, Jamiles, 254–55
Latinos, 32, 153, 239, 240

Lawson, Richard, 162
Lean In (Sandberg), 176
left, political, 29, 175
    "privilege" rejected by far, 4, 46–51,
      208
    with YPIS online and liberals, 58–61
Leibovitz, Liel, 227–28
Lemieux, Jamilah, 185
"Let Them Eat Privilege" (Kilpatrick),
    50–51
Lewis, Aaron Z., 81, 96
LGBT-themed films, 162–63
Liang, Peter, 237
liberals, YPIS online and, 58–61. *See also*
    left, political
Lieberman, Joe, 233
Life at Yale (Web site), 77–78
Lopate, Leonard, 145–46
Lucky Louie (television show), 147
Lukianoff, Greg, 79, 84
"Lupita Nyong'o and Trevor Noah, and
    Their Meaningful Roles" (Galanes),
    138–39
Lyonne, Natasha, 146

males, 130
    privilege, 4, 9–10, 11, 156, 166, 171, 225,
      247–48
    women and misogyny with gay, 230
Malone, Noreen, 154
"mansplaining," 11, 130
Marche, Stephen, 141–42
Marcotte, Amanda, 139–40, 202
Marie Antoinette (Queen of France), 16,
    188
"Marie Kondo and the Privilege of Clutter"
    (Bernstein, A.), 131–33
marketing strategy, outrage bait as,
    135–37
Martin, Courtney, 48–49, 169–71, 172
Martin, Wednesday, 26, 188–89
The Mary Tyler Moore Show (television
    show), 120, 224
Massey, Alana, 195–96
Master of None (television show), 154–58,
    160, 237
McCarthy, Amy, 129–30

McIntosh, Peggy, 8, 9–10, 11, 18, 208
McKenzie, Mia, 49
McMillan Cottom, Tressie, 92–93
McWhorter, John, 37–38
media, 124, 129, 167. *See also* social media
  on "offense" and online journalism,
    248–49
  student controversies in, 97–100
Medley, Mike, 165
memes, 125, 150
memoirs, college campuses, 104–6
Menendez, Kate, 34
meritocracy, 5, 6, 103, 105, 112, 117
microaggression, 209, 213, 250, 271, 290
  college campuses and, 85, 92, 96
  racism and, 74, 113, 143, 218, 224
Midlane, Tom, 49, 59
"A Midlife Crisis, By Any Other Name"
  (Zimmerman, J.), 189–92
The Mindy Project (television show),
  158–59
minimalism, 131–33
misogyny, 55, 179, 182, 183, 187
  feminism with righteous, 205–6
  prevalence of, 188–89
  women and gay male, 230
model minority, 235, 237, 238–39
Monty Python's The Meaning of Life (film),
  86
Morris, Toby, 20–21
Mother Jones, 210–11
"Moving Past Acknowledging Privilege"
  (Martin, C.), 48–49
Murray, Charles, 5, 212, 213
The Muse (blog), 157
music industry, 129–30, 154

NASCAR, 5, 213
National Coalition Against Censorship
  survey, 88–89
Nayman, Adam, 126
Nazis, 131, 216, 217, 230
Neediest Cases Fund, 106
The Neurotic Parent (blog), 108
New APPS, 202
New Inquiry, 97
New Statesman, 59

New York City
  private schools in, 240–43
  race and demographics, 239
New York International Fringe Festival,
  257
The New York Times, 37, 138–39, 192
New York Times College Scholarship
  Program, 106
Newman, Sandra, 73–74
The New Inquiry (online magazine), 175
"The New Intolerance of Student Activism"
  (Friedersdorf), 94–95
"The New Privilege: Loudly Denouncing
  Your Privilege" (O'Connor), 68–69
The New Republic, 220
Nichols, Catherine, 192
Nichols, Tom, 210
Noah, Trevor, 138–39
Nolan, Hamilton, 45, 181, 281*n*8
Norton, Ben, 52
"A Note on Call-Out Culture" (Ahmad), 65
Novaes, Catarina Dutilh, 202–3
Nussbaum, Emily, 141, 151
Nyong'o, Lupita, 138–39

Obama, Barack, 4–5, 67–68
Oberlin College, 85, 222, 237
O'Brien, Soledad, 61
The Observer, 127–28, 221
Occupy Wall Street, 16, 48, 73, 257
O'Connor, Maureen, 68–69
"offense," and online journalism, 248–49
Olen, Helaine, 241
Oluo, Ijeoma, 164
"Online Bullying–A New and Ugly Sport for
  Liberal Commenters" (Stallings), 64
online journalism, "offense" and, 248–49
Oppenheimer, Mark, 233–34
oppression, 7, 24, 48, 74
  Jews and, 216, 217, 219, 220, 222, 223,
    232
  "tone policing" and, 25
  women and, 180
origin story, arts and, 145–48
O'Rourke, Meghan, 81–82
Osten Gerszberg, Caren, 104
outrage bait, as marketing strategy, 135–37

overexamination, of "privilege"
  examination of, 24–27, 36
  YPIS online and, 31–34
overshare, culture of, 16, 23–24

Pagano, John-Paul, 220–21
Palin, Sarah, 4, 181, 213
Paltrow, Gwyneth, 78, 177
Pape, Allie, 161
Paris, terrorism in, 254–55
Parton, Dolly, 111
Paskin, Willa, 128
"Pathetic Privilege" (Williamson), 187
Patton, Stacey, 129, 184–85
Penny, Laurie, 1–2, 13–14
"People who Say 'Check Your Privilege'
  Should Do It" (Collins, G.), 209
Petri, Alexandra, 101
Phillips, Noah, 31–34
Piketty, Thomas, 51
Planet Transgender (Web site), 40
police, 25, 37, 39, 237
  harassment, 231
  with rape, 235–36
political correctness, 127, 212, 270
political criticism, arts and, 130–33
Politico, 179
politics, 4–5, 15–16, 257. See also left,
  political; right, political
  Clinton, H.-Sanders privilege wars,
    51–58
  racism in, 273–74
  women and, 177–81
Poniewozik, James, 127
Popova, Maria, 143
Pound, Ezra, 119
powerlessness, fetishization of, 174–75
Primates of Park Avenue (Martin, W.), 26,
  188
private schools, 240–43
privelobliviousness, 11
"privilege." See also "your privilege is
  showing"
  beyond, 267–72
  Asian Americans with imagined, 238,
    246
  awareness, 10, 96, 121, 267–72
  case for using, 9–14

Clinton, H., and, 51–58, 209–10
on college campuses, 4, 82–84, 208
college campuses and studying of, 90–91
as content, 41–42
in context, 247–53
criminal justice system and, 253–54
cruelty of, 253–63
defined, 3, 7, 8, 18, 22, 67
downplaying, 4–6, 17, 68, 101, 285n97
feminism confronting, 171–73
of feminist bloggers, 169–71
gender and, 188
with humor, inadvertent, 44–46
Jews and, 215–34, 238, 246
male, 4, 9–10, 11, 156, 166, 171, 225,
  247–48
with mandatory-overshare culture, 16,
  23–24
from micro to macro, 269–70
new meaning of, 14–15
overexamination of, 24–27, 31–34, 36
political left with, 4, 46–51, 208
political right with, 29–30, 207–15
privilege critique of, 66–69
racism and, 7–8, 12–13, 67–68, 127
rape, 256
reach of, 27–30
from trend to zeitgeist, 263–67
Trump, D., and, 210–11, 212
why now?, 15–18
"Privilege, Among Rape Victims"
  (Rennison), 256
privilege call-out, 64, 65, 298n54
  feminism and, 173
  on social media, 1–3, 6–7, 61
  YPIS and, 21–22
privilege checking, 13–15, 18, 44, 64, 209
  in context, 3–4, 48, 107, 139–40, 225,
    234
  defined, 126
  tournament, 28, 45
privilege confession, YPIS online and,
  39–41
privilege theory, 239
  with arts and cultural criticism, 28–29,
    148–52
  awareness and, 10, 96, 121
"Privilege Tournament" (Nolan), 281n8

"The Privilege of Being Hillary Clinton" (Emery), 209–10
production. *See* cultural production
protests
  on college campuses, 78–82, 84–86, 89, 94, 290*n*54, 291*n*67
  Halloween costume, 81–82, 94
  Occupy Wall Street, 16, 48, 73, 257
public shaming, 1, 4, 19, 57, 85, 254
Pulliam-Moore, Charles, 137, 141, 296*n*32

race, 37. *See also* African Americans; Asian Americans; Jews; Latinos
  awareness disclaimer and, 192
  comedy and, 219, 221
  feminism and, 172–73, 184–85, 192, 194
  New York City with demographics and, 239
  White Feminism, 181–89, 194
  White Lady and, 175
racism, 129, 237. *See also* slavery
  anti-racism, 38–39, 137, 142, 185, 219, 228
  anti-Semitism, 183, 216–24, 228, 229, 230, 232, 238
  arts and, 137–43, 157
  blackface, 134, 136, 137, 176–77
  college campuses and, 82, 83, 93, 113
  microaggression and, 74, 113, 143, 218, 224
  in politics, 273–74
  prevalence of, 231
  "privilege" and, 7–8, 12–13, 67–68, 127
  reverse, 20, 181–82, 219
  social media and, 137
  white supremacy and, 220, 239
  "woke" and, 137–38, 271
Ramsey, Franchesca, 219
rape, 94, 136, 235–36
"rape privilege," 256
Read, Max, 151–52
"The Real Problem with 'Check Your Privilege': It's Too Generous" (Marcotte), 139–40
Reed, James, 130
refugees, 42, 54, 131–32, 210, 228, 246

rejection
  college admissions and, 111–14
  of "privilege" by far-left, 46–51
Rennison, Callie Marie, 256
"resilience," 96
Return of Kings (misogynist blog), 183
reverse racism, 20, 181–82, 219
Reynolds, Daniel, 162–63
Rice, Tamir, 12
Rifkind, Hugo, 42
right, political
  on feminism, 29, 175
  with "privilege," 29–30, 207–15
rights, 79, 171–72
Roberts, Molly, 179
Robin, Corey, 55–57, 58, 242, 243
Robinson, Kate, 50, 239
Roiphe, Katie, 144
roman à thèse (didactic novel), 130
Ronson, Jon, 19, 137
Roof, Dylann, 12
Rosen, Zack, 35
Rosenberg, Alyssa, 128–29
Rosin, Hanna, 71
Roth, Philip, 224
Rothman, J. D., 108
Rothman, Joshua, 10
Rothschild family, 217
RT≠endorsement, 124, 167
Rubio, Marco, 40
Rudnick, Paul, 110
Ruth, Jennifer, 91

Sacco, Justine, 19, 70, 137
Salaita, Steven, 181
Salam, Reihan, 213
Samuel, Sigal, 218
sanctibullying, 63
Sandberg, Sheryl, 176, 183, 184, 218
Sanders, Bernie, 5, 142
  Bernie Bro phenomenon and, 178
  Clinton, H., and privilege wars with, 51–58
  as Jew, 232–34
"Sandra Bland: A Black Woman's Life Finally Matters" (Lemieux), 185
Sarandon, Susan, 53–54
Saturday Night Live (television show), 126

Savage, Dan, 53–54
Scalia, Antonin, 6
Scalzi, John, 21
Schuman, Rebecca, 119–20
Schumer, Amy, 129, 154, 158, 177
Schwartz, Alexandra, 55–56, 57, 58
Schwedel, Heather, 153–54
Scott, A. O., 148–49
second-wave feminism, 196
Sehgal, Parul, 12, 13, 18–19, 96
Seinfeld (television show), 126, 167, 267
self-assessment essay, 41–42
self-effacement, with college campus
    admissions, 107
self-presentation, 131, 151, 266
Seltzer, Sarah, 228
Serial (podcast), 125, 128
Sevigny, Chloë, 146
Sex and the City (film), 148
Sex and the City (television show), 150–51
sex work, 171, 193
sexism, 12, 71, 179–80, 183, 188. *See also*
    misogyny
sexual assault
    Bloomingdale's and, 136
    college campuses and, 79, 82, 93, 94
    rape, 94, 136, 235–36, 256
shaming. *See* public shaming
Shechet, Ellie, 134
"Sheryl Sandberg's Mea Culpa and the
    Limitations of Jewish Feminism"
    (Chernikoff), 218
Shine, Jacqui, 27
"Shit White Girls Say . . . to Black Girls"
    (video), 219
"Shouts and Murmurs" (Rudnick), 110
Shulevitz, Judith, 70
Siddiqi, Ayesha, 175–76, 184
Silverman, Sarah, 229
sitcoms
    Broad City, 141, 153, 229
    cultural production with think piece and,
        152–61
    Inside Amy Schumer, 154
    Master of None, 154–58, 160, 237
    The Mindy Project, 158–59
    Seinfeld, 126, 167, 267
    Unbreakable Kimmy Schmidt, 160–61

Slate, 40, 128
Slaughter, Anne-Marie, 198, 199
slavery
    African Americans and, 138, 164, 225,
        231, 296n34
    Jews and, 219
Smith, Sharon, 66
social justice, 15, 152, 244–46, 271
social media, 16, 41, 73, 137. *See also* Twitter
    college campuses and, 92–93
    privilege call-out on, 1–3, 6–7, 61
Socialist Worker (news site), 48
Solnit, Rebecca, 11
South Park (television show), 90, 167
Spencer, Kyle, 241–42
Stallings, Ariel Meadow, 64
standardized tests, 116, 117–18
Stanley, Alessandra, 25, 26
Stern, Mark Joseph, 223
Stonewall (film), 162–63
The Stranger (blog), 53–54, 164
Streep, Meryl, 163, 270
students. *See* college campuses
Suffragette (film), 162, 163–64
Suk, Jeannie, 82
Sullivan, Andrew, 211
Sullivan, Margaret, 25–26
Supreme Court, 6, 112
surfing, 145–46
Swift, Taylor, 129–30, 177, 183
Syria, 131–32, 184

Tablet (magazine), 220–21, 227
Target: Women (Haskins), 177
Taylor, Goldie, 235–36
Tea Party, 15–16
television, 31, 90, 120, 147, 166, 224.
    See also sitcoms
    cultural criticism of, 126
    diversity in, 128, 153, 155–57, 160, 161,
        237, 239
    women on, 157, 161
terrorism, 221, 254–55
"There Are Only Two Issues" (Nolan),
    181
think piece. *See* cultural production
"38 Ways College Students Enjoy
    'Left-wing Privilege'" (Fortgang), 4, 208

This Is 40 (film), 148–49
Thought Catalog, 34
Thurm, Eric, 161
Time Out London, 164
"To (All) the Colleges That Rejected Me"
    (Weiss), 112–13
The Toast (humor Web site), 237–38
Tolentino, Jia, 17, 248–49, 296n34
"tone policing," 25
toxic, feminism as, 172, 174, 201
Traister, Rebecca, 178–79
transgender, 40, 171–72
transwomen, 172, 303n49
trend, "privilege" as, 263–67
"trickle-down feminism," 200
trolling, 64, 144, 217
Trudeau, Garry, 221, 264–65
Trump, Donald, 55, 137, 250
    microaggression and, 213
    "privilege" and, 210–11, 212
    Savage on, 53–54
    Trumpism, implications of, 273–74
Trump, Melania, 222
tuition, for private schools, 240–41
Tumblr, 73, 92–93
Turning the Tide, 116
tutoring, 110, 119, 240–41
12 Years a Slave (film), 138
Twitter, 12, 71, 172
    Clinton, H., on, 52, 53
    deBoer on, 132, 262–63
    privilege call-out on, 1–2, 6–7, 61
    racism and, 137
    RT≠endorsement and, 124, 167
    with white supremacy, 220
"2014: The Year of Outrage" (*Slate*), 128

Unbreakable Kimmy Schmidt (television
    show), 160–61
Upworthy (media site), 127
ur-privilege checklist, 9–10
Urquhart, Vanessa Vitiello, 40, 41, 67

Valenti, Jessica, 38, 39
Valenti, Vanessa, 172
violence, 63, 64, 184. *See also* sexual assault
    overuse of, 270–71
    terrorism, 221, 254–55

voluntourism, 33, 108–12
Vulture (blog), 157, 158

Waithe, Lena, 155
Walsh, Joan, 179
The Washington Post, 31, 33, 38, 99, 129,
    136
"We Built It," 4–5
The Weekly Standard, 85, 209–10
Weiner, Jonah, 146–47
Weiss, Suzy Lee, 112–13
Weissmann, Jordan, 119
"We're the Privileged Poor. Why Aren't
    We Talking About It?" (Wolfe),
    46–48
Wesleyan University, 89, 115, 117
Wharton, Edith, 68, 187–88, 209
"What Does It Mean to Be 'Privileged'?"
    (Bouie), 12–13
"What Is Privilege?" (video), 20, 23, 41
"What It Takes to Succeed in Academia"
    (Novaes), 202–3
"When Your Curriculum Has Been
    Tumblrized" (McMillan Cottom),
    92–93
White Feminism
    awareness disclaimer and, 194
    reactionary critique of, 186–89
    trademarked, 181–85
White Jewish Ladies, 183
White Lady, 175–77, 206, 246
"White Privilege and Male Privilege: A
    Personal Account of Coming to See
    Correspondences Through Work in
    Women's Studies" (McIntosh), 9–10,
    11
white supremacy, 220, 239
"White Women, Please Don't Expect Me to
    Wipe Away Your Tears" (Patton),
    184–85
"The White Man Pathology" (Marche),
    141
"Why I'll Never Apologize for My White
    Male Privilege" (Fortgang), 4, 225
"Why Women Still Can't Have It All"
    (Slaughter), 198
Will, George, 256
Williams, Mary Elizabeth, 19

Williams, Zoe, 174
Williamson, Kevin D., 187
Willick, Jason, 117
Willis Aronowitz, Nona, 192–93
"woke," 137–38, 271, 296n32
Wolf, Alison, 200
Wolfe, April, 46–48
women, 9–10, 11, 198, 199, 235–36.
    See also feminism
  with fashion and marketing strategies,
    136
  gay male misogyny and, 230
  oppression and, 180
  politics and, 177–81
  on television, 157, 161
  transwomen, 172, 303n49
  White Feminism, 181–89, 194
  White Jewish Ladies, 183
  White Lady, 175–77, 206, 246

xoJane (online magazine), 35, 189

Yale College Democrats, 257
Yale University, 77–78, 81–82, 94, 96
Yang, Wesley, 96
"The Year of the Imaginary College
    Student" (Hsu), 97
Yi, Samantha, 234–35
Yoffe, Emily, 70
Young, Cathy, 221

"your fave is problematic" meme, 125
"your privilege is showing" (YPIS), 14, 44
  in context, 18–20, 23, 208, 213, 215,
    252
  feminism and, 173–75
  jealousy, 143–45
  privilege call-out and, 21–22
"your privilege is showing" (YPIS) online
  in action, 42–44
  anti-YPIS essays, 62–66
  Clinton, H.-Sanders privilege wars,
    51–58
  confessional essay, 34–39
  in context, 27–28
  with far-left rejection, 46–51
  with humor, inadvertent, 44–46
  liberals and, 58–61
  moderation with, 69–75
  with overexamination of "privilege,"
    31–34
  privilege confession and, 39–41
  privilege critique of "privilege" and,
    66–69
  self-assessment essay, 41–42
Yuan, Jada, 153

Zack, Naomi, 7–8
zeitgeist, "privilege" as, 263–67
Zimmerman, George, 231
Zimmerman, Jess, 189–92